Access Your Online Resources

Trauma-Informed Practice in Education is accompanied by a number of printable online materials, designed to ensure this resource best supports your professional needs.

Go to https://resourcecentre.routledge.com/speechmark and click on the cover of this book.

Answer the question prompt using your copy of the book to gain access to the online content.

Trauma-Informed Practice in Education

Trauma-Informed Practice in Education enables educators to create safe, nurturing environments in the classroom for children and young people facing difficult circumstances.

The book accessibly outlines the principles of TIP before examining what trauma looks like in the classroom, focusing on learning, behaviour and concentration. Each chapter introduces a step in the journey to becoming a trauma-aware educator and explores key topics, from balancing curricular demands and vicarious trauma to the importance of boundaries and self-care. Top tips and easy-to-use activities that respect the voices of children and young people are included, and interviews with professionals and engaging vignettes further bring theory to life.

With approaches drawing directly from the author's frontline work and first-hand experience in diverse areas and settings, this book is essential reading for practising and student teachers, family support workers and youth workers.

Dr Norah Sweetman has been involved in education, training and development for 30 years, at primary and secondary level, adult education and specialised programmes. She is currently tutoring and lecturing on postgraduate programmes at Trinity College and Hibernia College, with a specialist interest in trauma-informed training and practice.

Trauma-Informed Practice in Education

Making it Work

Norah Sweetman

LONDON AND NEW YORK

Designed cover image: Ezra B of WriteHand Designs

First published 2026
by Routledge
4 Park Square, Milton Park, Abingdon, Oxon OX14 4RN

and by Routledge
605 Third Avenue, New York, NY 10158

Routledge is an imprint of the Taylor & Francis Group, an informa business

© 2026 Norah Sweetman

The right of Norah Sweetman to be identified as author of this work has been asserted in accordance with sections 77 and 78 of the Copyright, Designs and Patents Act 1988.

Illustrations by Ezra B of WriteHand Designs

All rights reserved. The purchase of this copyright material confers the right on the purchasing institution to photocopy or download pages which bear the support material icon and a copyright line at the bottom of the page. No other parts of this book may be reprinted or reproduced or utilised in any form or by any electronic, mechanical, or other means, now known or hereafter invented, including photocopying and recording, or in any information storage or retrieval system, without permission in writing from the publishers.

Trademark notice: Product or corporate names may be trademarks or registered trademarks, and are used only for identification and explanation without intent to infringe.

British Library Cataloguing-in-Publication Data
A catalogue record for this book is available from the British Library

ISBN: 978-1-032-63499-9 (hbk)
ISBN: 978-1-032-63498-2 (pbk)
ISBN: 978-1-032-66376-0 (ebk)

DOI: 10.4324/9781032663760

Typeset in Optima
by Apex CoVantage, LLC

Access the Support Material: https://resourcecentre.routledge.com/speechmark

For Lorcan and Caoimhe

Contents

Acknowledgements x
List of images xi

Introduction 1

1 **What is trauma-informed practice? What does it mean for me? It is always the children who suffer** 14

2 **What does trauma look like in the classroom?** 40

3 **A safe environment – what is it?** 72

4 **Building relationships that are positive and supportive** 92

5 **The three Rs: Reflection, resilience and relationships** 115

6 **Voice in the classroom** 138

7 **Trauma-informed practice in other disciplines: Equity in education** 158

8 **Boundaries and emotional first aid** 183

9 **Overwhelm, compassion fatigue, vicarious trauma and supervision** 203

10 **Working for change at different levels** 229

11 **Activities** 245

Conclusion 272

Index 274

Acknowledgements

Many thanks to Clare for her patient and helpful advice, and to Ezra for the beautiful illustrations.

Thanks are due to my tapping buddy and all those who encouraged me and believed I could do it.

List of images

0.1	The foundation of attachment – love	1
1.1	Secure, cared-for infant	25
1.2	Neglected, abused infant	26
2.1	Secure, confident child	42
2.2	Neglected, confused child	44
3.1	Word cloud response to questions around feelings of safety/unsafety	78
3.2	Trauma breaks trust and love	79
4.1	The interconnections in a child's development	96
4.2	Leave me alone – I don't care	98
5.1	It can be easy to bounce back!	119
5.2	Hard to bounce back if it's broken!	125
5.3	This is all your fault . . .	128
5.4	Working together – repairing relationships	135
6.1	Seesaw of feelings – finding balance	152
7.1	Equal resources	169
9.1	Feel like I'm drowning in problems and trauma stories	204
9.2	Flexible, adaptable, coherent, energised, stable	226
10.1	Working for healing	230
11.1	Heads	255
11.2	Sad head, Happy head and Aggro head	256
11.3	Spider's web diagram	263

Introduction

How I got myself into this

This book was born of a comment I made last year when I was reviewing an excellent book on trauma and working for healing with young people. I was asked if I thought teachers and youth workers working with traumatised and excluded young people would read the book.

I thought back for a minute on my working life with young people and their families in the underserved communities of Dublin. I could see myself coming in the door on a winter's evening, tired and cold, with a dinner to make for my own family. Even now, I am smiling at the idea of me reaching for a book that was full of technical terms and lots of bracketed references. A catch-up with friends and family, a phone call, a quick coffee with friends, energising music – something positive and easy to enjoy was what I needed.

Figure 0.1 The foundation of attachment – love

I did further training at night school, in teaching adults, conflict resolution and counselling skills. This was a hard slog and often irrelevant to my work. I remember one 90-minute lecture on concentration *in detail*. The key point of the talk: everyone loses concentration after *16 minutes* on average! I got most of my ideas from colleagues, from the young people and from adapting materials to meet their needs.

I expressed these reservations about readers for the book under review, and I was surprised when the editor contacted me and asked if I would be interested in writing a book on trauma that would be useful to educators working with traumatised people.

Oh yes, dear reader – as you see, I was taken with this idea and foolishly thought that making complicated topics easy to understand would be simple! It is actually much easier to make them very complex. . .

PhD on the effects of domestic violence on teenage social emotional development

I landed myself in studying for a PhD by the same faulty logic. I was working with individual pupils excluded from school, teaching up to 11 subjects, including three languages. The young people had different challenges – some were suffering from agoraphobia and anxiety difficulties; others had violent outbursts and were considered unteachable. I had some successes and some failures. One of my students emailed me ten years later to tell me she had recovered and was now at college. Days like that bring huge bursts of happiness for the bravery of this girl who was a talented writer. At the other end of the spectrum, I ran away from one student, as he was smashing furniture and throwing his TV out of the window. The most chilling aspect of this was that his siblings sat in the living room, unmoved, and when I asked if I should call someone, his sister answered, 'Ah, no, he'll be finished soon – everything is nearly broken now.' The underlying trauma involved in such a level of distress for the teenager and the passive acceptance of the family stayed with me for a long time.

A few weeks later, I got a call from the Department of Education to say I wasn't eligible to work as a tutor as I didn't have a second-level teaching qualification. I had a Montessori teacher's qualification, a Master's in Communication and Media, adult education tutor training, a counselling skills diploma and a Higher Diploma in Outdoor Education. I also mentioned my 20 years of teaching, working with the most difficult children, and the range of subjects I taught, including languages. The reply was: 'If you even had a qualification in P.E., I could give it to you.' I was so exasperated that I looked up the highest qualification, which is a PhD. There and then, I decided to do it. Ironically, that still doesn't qualify me to teach excluded 12-year-olds!

Previous work with young people and families

I worked for 25 years with young people who were excluded or were in class groups for challenging pupils. I worked with the Probation Service (diversion programmes), Youthreach (for early school leavers), School Completion Programme (in school, after school and holiday support for those at risk of dropout); my work included individual tuition, regular teaching hours in schools and special projects in schools.

I also ran personal development groups for men, women and young people in underserved areas. I wrote most of my own programmes and designed them to suit the individual or group I was working with. Literacy problems, challenging behaviour, cultural differences, drug feuds, homelessness, domestic violence, sexual and physical abuse, exclusion and low self-esteem were everyday issues.

I learnt about the resilience and hard work involved for families in keeping themselves cared for, keeping their children in school and paying their bills with a bit over for birthdays. I remember one mandatory course for community creche workers had a section called 'Financial planning and budgeting'. One woman said, 'Sure, I wouldn't have a clue about that stuff.' This from a woman raising a family on her own on a small, fixed income. I asked her, 'Did all your kids get fed today? Gone to school with all their school stuff and a lunch?' She looked offended and said, 'Of course they did!' and then laughed when I said, 'You should be the Minister for Finance. He has a lot more money than you and makes much worse decisions with it.'

The reality of research – computers and more computers

When I was researching a topic for my PhD, I wanted to do an active research project to understand some of the issues that had been dominant in my working life. I was drawn to exploring the effects of domestic violence on teenagers' social emotional development. I struggled with the computer and all the academic terms. I was used to making ideas and material as simple and accessible as possible. This was the complete opposite.

I completed my research study with five teenagers who had been affected by domestic violence and their parents. I met resistance to the active research approach of my PhD, as I was regularly told that the findings could be invalid as the teenagers might have been giving me the answers I wanted to hear. The ongoing review and feedback meant that their choice to engage in every activity was live each week. The assertiveness programme was referred to by the young people in interviews: 'I would tell you if your questions are too nosey – assertiveness and all that' (1 p.230).

The happy ending is that I did get it done with lots of help and support, and from that work I became very interested in **trauma-informed practice** (TIP). A big attraction for me in this work is sharing the hope and approaches to assist victims of trauma to recover and heal.

Some background to trauma-informed practice

Research into **Adverse Childhood Experiences** (ACEs) shows very clearly, in studies that followed individuals over decades (2), that traumatic experiences in childhood affect the life cycle in every way, including physical and mental health, academic success and employment opportunities. These effects were particularly negative when the resources for recovery were lacking in family and community circumstances. This research has shifted the responsibility away from the individual affected by ACEs, addressing the deep-rooted social injustice associated with ACEs, and looked to community services, including education, to support the person's access to recovery and a fulfilling life (3).

Trauma-informed practice has been appearing in discussion, theory and training, particularly in education and youth settings, over the last decade. What is it and what does it mean for the practitioner, especially teachers in mainstream education? These are the central questions of this book, with a focus on the areas of education and education support systems.

A body of research has dealt with approaches to supporting learners of all ages affected by trauma. Therapeutic tools and approaches have been well illustrated and explained. Many educators work with mainstream educational resources as their only resource within the school or institution, while others are working alone – for example, supplying evening classes in English or IT with no support structure at all. The ideal scenario, as recommended in all the trauma-informed literature, is that the whole organisation takes part in TIP training and works together to integrate TIP into every level of teaching, policy and discipline. The reality is very different, however, for the majority of teachers.

Trauma-informed practice for tutors and teachers

I currently teach at Trinity College Dublin on trauma-informed practice for teachers and tutors, and I have been inspired by the dedication and innovation of the educators. One thing I notice is that some of the research literature and the books can be very technical and written for specialists – therapists and teachers who have small groups or individual children to work with. They often seem to suggest that you are there, consistent and calm, in a well-resourced therapy room with one child and a care team on call. The typical situation of the mainstream teacher is that you have 20 kids in your class, four of whom have extra needs of different types, and you don't have many resources. This is even more pronounced if you are working in an underserved area or with a marginalised group who carry heavy trauma issues with them.

My idea was to write a book that somebody can pick up and go, 'That's great. I'll try that tomorrow.' And then from that, they might be encouraged to wonder, 'Why do the pupils like that so much? Oh, I see why. It calms their nerves when music and movement go together.' Basic activities that you can build on, with an enhanced understanding of why they are effective for the learners, are the main resource of this book. And any teacher who's committed and likes their job is doing a lot of that stuff anyway.

I wanted something that would reassure people and expand their knowledge. I also wanted to share loads of activities – art, drama, movement, games, projects that are easy to use. Twenty-five years of invention and adaptation available for use.

I planned to do interviews, to get ideas and feedback of what it's like for people working with traumatised individuals in different settings. I've interviewed teachers, school completion staff, psychologists and therapists, and I include quotes from their interviews (all fully anonymised).

I have included composite and altered vignettes of the lives of those children and families I worked with to illustrate the reality of the work. All the details have been mixed around, so no case study is an actual individual story, but they do all contain elements I have worked with every day.

The aims of this book

The main aim of the book is to provide an understanding of the roots and causes of trauma, how trauma affects development and how it may present in the learning situation. The use of trauma-informed practice will be related to the mainstream class, and I will demonstrate how the principles of TIP can be used in everyday class activities, which will benefit all students and especially help to support those affected by trauma. The contract between educator and student is to teach a particular skill or knowledge. The contract between an individual and a therapist is different, involving a willingness to address trauma and work for change and healing. The boundary is important and needs to be clear to both parties. In this educational space, the trauma-informed educator can minimise triggers for retraumatisation and include approaches and activities that build a safe environment and positive relationships. These have been identified as the key elements in building resilience and recovery from trauma. The building of trusting relationships allows the teacher to act as a bridge to referral for a therapeutic engagement with the appropriate person or centre for the student (4).

Staff meetings

The approaches to communications, group work and review suggested for adult education groups can also be useful for working with staff groups. The ***group poster review** is an easy way to gather up a range of views and experience on a topic like the use of TIP in the school. These approaches that enable a wide range of differing views to be heard in open discussion are very valuable in including everyone in the exploration of what can work for the particular group or school. I have used these materials with many different groups.

How the book is structured

Each chapter provides some background information and research on an aspect of TIP. There is an artificial separation in some chapters of themes and topics which are interlinked, but this is to clarify the approaches and activities of trauma-informed practice in action, in mainstream or small group classes.

The chapters will be divided into sections, one of which provides research and some theory about TIP.

Other sections present material about approaches to TIP, which is essentially a lens or view of working with students rather than a manualised programme. Useful activities, games and review methods, with notes on their purpose and tips for success (or salvaging failure!), are included.

The divisions for the age of activities follow the structure of the Irish education system below, but they can be adapted:

- Primary school age: 4–12 years old (junior infants to sixth class in the Irish system – eight years in total).
- Secondary school age: 12–18 years old (first year to sixth year in the Irish system – six years in total).
- Adult education: a wide range of learners from college students to evening classes, language classes and recovery from trauma and addiction groups.

Principles of TIP

A newly qualified teacher described the TIP training he received as follows: 'they [the trainers] freaked us out with a whole load of really scary stuff [about trauma] – at the end of the morning I didn't really have a clue what they were on about' (Pat).

After 20-plus years, I know the frustrations of those working in the field. The introduction of 'another initiative' is often greeted with the resentful feeling of another layer being added to an already heavy workload.

The principles of TIP are based on six elements: **Safety, Trustworthiness, Choice, Collaboration, Empowerment and Cultural Consideration**. These form the basis of the safe space and supportive relationships that are at the heart of TIP, and they provide an approach that can support your work, rather than increase your workload.

Many educators have been working with highly traumatised groups for years, often with little extra support or training being provided to them. I worked on Youthreach and School Completion Programmes where many of the students' problems were not educational or individual but directly rooted in their local environment and family situation. We were working with students who were affected by sexual abuse, family violence and personal and familial experiences of addiction. These were the causes of their school dropout and aggressive or disengaged behaviours towards education, and were not a result of their own behavioural choices. The staff were motivated and committed, and we offered a range of supports in the centres and linked with referral services as much as we could. However, this disconnect between the educator's remit as a tutor/teacher and the severe difficulties and traumas being experienced by their students hasn't changed very much since Youthreach 1990.

The gap between researchers and practitioners often appears too wide to cross and leads to many vital findings of research failing to reach the workers and clients who would benefit from them. In my work supervising trainee teachers and practitioners, and working with teachers and third-level tutors, trauma-informed practice, and how it works, is a concern for many of the learners.

Balance between students' needs and educator well-being

In my wide experience, I met so many young people and families struggling against the odds to achieve their dreams and keep their family together in very tough circumstances. In some cases, their teachers understood something of their struggles, but often the gap between the secure home and university education of the teacher and the traumatic experiences of the student remained.

This book aims to offer the TIP perspective of supportive environments and approaches to traumatised students while maintaining awareness of the toll this work takes on the practitioner by:

- Supporting educators in applying the principles of TIP as much as possible, looking at ways they can make small changes in their work and build on current practice.
- Highlighting the importance of having safe boundaries and self-care for educators in all situations, but particularly when working with traumatised and underserved communities.

This book will give some background research that has demonstrated the importance of ACEs and inspired the development of TIP. The implementation of aspects of TIP in the classroom or centre will be covered, with recommendations supported by theory and interviews with active practitioners. These interviews will include teachers, tutors, lecturers, youth workers and support staff in schools and centres. Experiences will be shared of those who already practise TIP and those who know very little about it. The approach will build on available resources and develop what many teachers and tutors are already doing in their work. The line between therapeutic supports/interventions and teaching becomes very blurred when educators are working in mainstream situations with highly traumatised student groups. Examples from tutors I have worked with include groups of refugees, people in recovery from addiction, homeless people and participants with extra learning needs such as autism and attention deficit hyperactivity disorder (ADHD). The mainstream tutor/teacher is following a syllabus or curriculum without any extra specialist learning or therapeutic supports.

The difference between being a supportive tutor and a therapist

This book builds some bridges for this gap with understanding and information about TIP that can be used in mainstream settings. The hope is to be supportive to all students while maintaining boundaries for students and educators. It is important to remember that the contract the students engage in with you is about a learning programme you are offering them. They have not signed up for therapy and you are not required – or qualified – to offer it! The difference between understanding the needs of traumatised or neglected students for supportive environments and approaches to teaching and the exploration of therapeutic interventions is very important to appreciate (4).

Other tutors have found that if students disclose traumatic events in the classroom, it can be difficult for the other students to cope with and can retraumatise others. It is so important to set out the limits of your ability to help and to clarify the purpose of the group and how you can support learners in making referrals or link with school/college services for this. Be very clear about what you can do. Another tutor found that they were being asked to find jobs and accommodation for students, and students felt let down when the tutor couldn't do this for them.

The essential difference between offering a supportive environment based on an understanding of the effects of trauma and the work of therapeutic interventions and programmes will be discussed. The emotional impact on the educator working with high incidences of trauma and distress will be addressed, and strategies to manage stress and avoid burnout will be included.

The fear of retraumatising students is something that concerns educators. There are principles and approaches to minimise the likelihood of this happening, but the most important of all is feedback from the learners. It is vital to develop easy communication, and this can be built up from day one. When students have many ways to give feedback, they develop confidence in the tutor's commitment to a supportive environment and can share their concerns and needs easily. Therefore, you will learn what is a trigger for some people in the group – and that it can be very unexpected.

I once did a team building workshop with a 'difficult class who had no interest in anything but making trouble', according to their teacher. It was Christmas, and I had brought some really fun art stuff (lots of gold glitter!) with me to start the session. I asked the class teacher before the group if there was anything I needed to know – special needs, disability, bereavements? 'Nothing at all, just bold behaviour' was the answer. I handed out all the materials and suggested making a Christmas card 'for someone you love', emphasising that it could be anyone close to them. Seconds later, a table was overturned and a young girl was screeching abuse while throwing all the equipment at me – 'you and your f---ing Christmas card' being the nicer end of it! There was a special needs assistant (SNA) in the room with me, and I asked her to take the girl somewhere quiet for a few minutes, and then she could rejoin the group if she felt better. The class immediately told me the girl had just been placed in foster care. There was no way I could have known that, but I should have been told. The girl came back and joined the games and activities for the rest of the day, but it was an experience she could have done without.

Making information accessible

In my experience, a formal academic style of writing can be very off-putting to the general reader and leads to a book being discarded as 'too difficult to follow' or 'too theoretical'. As the aim of this book is to reach the teacher, youth worker, volunteer and educator to provide useful, practical advice, each chapter will offer approaches and activities. I will supply some references to a wide range of information for any reader wishing to explore further.

Some details of the layout

Illustrations

Illustrations are used to show the effects of trauma on development in children.

Some drawings illustrate directly how activities are run; other materials will have samples and instructions for use.

Activities

The symbol * shows that an activity will be detailed in Chapter 11: Activities.

References

References are numbered in the order they appear in Vancouver style.

References to videos use current links, but if the link has been removed, you will find the video by searching the presenter's name and the video title as they are all well established in their field.

Terms

The word 'educator' is used to include teachers at all levels, from junior infants to adult education tutors, and support workers who work in educational institutions.

In Ireland, the term 'child' refers to 0–18 years old. The term 'young person' is also used to include under-18s, who are older teenagers. Some activities and approaches of the primary section could be used in early education/pre-school settings, but there is no special section for this age group.

I distinguish between **social emotional learning (SEL)** practices, which are developed for mainstream classes focused on social skills, and TIP approaches, which are designed to support pupils affected by trauma. In many activities and approaches, there is overlap that is positive and helpful.

The main difference is that the effects of trauma will produce physical and emotional responses and behaviours that operate at an unconscious level. Many of these responses originate in the body and are driven by the reptilian or 'old brain' survival responses. TIP approaches often include some activities to help self-regulation, some body movement and/or lots of visual information about the programme to calm anxiety about change.

SEL approaches are usually based on working with the conscious and logical brain. When using SEL materials, be aware that if some pupils are struggling, they may need help either to understand the task or to manage the feelings that the discussion is bringing up. If you need to slow or stop an activity, make it a group decision: 'I think it would be fun to take a break with a game of ***I spy**, or ***Count to 20** or a ***Quiz** – I'll start. . .'

Key points: Research, relate, respond, reach out and refer

- Information is referenced, and key references allow the interested reader to pursue the different topics at a deeper level. (These will be at the end of each chapter and in the final reference list.)
- The focus is on how these trauma effects show up in the classroom, and different methods and materials are explored for building a safe, supportive classroom for all students.
- Key learning points in reducing triggers for trauma and helping to restore balance identified in therapeutic work are related to SEL and TIP approaches suitable for mainstream educational settings.
- Visual exercises, movement, breathing, group games and activities, soft corners, toys, 'free passes' and many other tools are listed.
- Insights from interviews with teachers, educators and therapists are shared.
- The importance of safe boundaries for educators and pupils is addressed – the difference between friendly, reliable support and therapeutic interventions.
- Referrals and building supports for you and your students are covered.
- Self-care for the practitioner is an important issue, and practical steps are included.
- Relevant activities and approaches are included and photocopiable sheets supplied.
- Drawings and cartoons illustrate the work – some are professional and some are my own odd scribbles which make everyone of all ages laugh and feel confident in their own attempts!

References

1. Sweetman N. A culture of silence: A study of a social emotional learning (SEL) intervention for teenagers affected by domestic violence. PhD thesis. Trinity College Dublin; 2019. www.tara.tcd.ie/handle/2262/86088
2. Anda RF, Felitti VJ, Bremner JD, Walker JD, Whitfield C, Perry BD, et al. The enduring effects of abuse and related adverse experiences in childhood. European Archives of Psychiatry & Clinical Neuroscience. 2006;256(3):174–86.
3. O'Toole C. When trauma comes to school: Toward a socially just trauma informed praxis. International Journal of School Social Work. 2022;6(2):Art. 4.
4. Shevrin Venet A. Role-clarity and boundaries for trauma-informed teachers. Educational Considerations. 2019;44(2).

1
What is trauma-informed practice? What does it mean for me?
It is always the children who suffer

> This chapter provides some background information about how research into post-traumatic stress disorder (PTSD) in veterans in the 1970s led to uncovering the high levels of trauma that exist in the community. The Adverse Childhood Experiences (ACEs) research in the 1990s (1) demonstrated how these traumas have lifelong effects, and approaches to working with victims of trauma evolved. The understanding about how trauma affects all stages of development in children and young people grew from this research. The trauma-informed practice (TIP) approaches to working with victims of trauma developed in response to these findings and the earlier research into trauma.
>
> There are four sections in the chapter:
>
> - Section 1 gives some background to the research into PTSD, ACEs and TIP.
> - Section 2 looks at TIP research and important elements for the application of these principles.
> - Section 3 looks at a life story of a child affected by trauma, and some supports given to her, and asks the reader to look at some options and possibilities for supporting the child.
> - Section 4 explores the difference between understanding TIP, building a safe place and safe relationships in your classroom, and a therapeutic approach to pupils of any age.

My aim for this book is to give some useful information that will help people to make sense of the use of **trauma-informed practices (TIP)** in the educational setting. I am not a psychologist but write from my many years working and training in the underserved education centres, schools and communities of Ireland. I am writing for the teacher or tutor who has some understanding of TIP and wants to implement changes to support students affected by trauma. I have been working with young and old teachers and tutors, and there are big variations between schools and colleges in their approach to traumatised students. Some schools have full staff training, programmes and resources in place to support students impacted by trauma; others are still relying on exclusion and other punishments to manage challenging students.

This account of the research into **post-traumatic stress disorder (PTSD)** and **Adverse Childhood Experiences (ACEs)** gives some background and important learning points from the studies of trauma. There is a large body of specialised research into psychological, physical and emotional development and the effects of trauma. This is fascinating reading and can inform anybody's understanding of children's needs and how trauma affects them. Many of the books on TIP are written for therapists or special educators who have training and resources to provide interventions for individual and small groups of children.

The overall aim of this book is to encourage educators to make the small (or large!) changes in their practice that will help to support all their pupils in a safe environment, with an added understanding of the needs and behaviours of students suffering with trauma.

The references are to signpost further reading for anyone who is interested in learning more about the topic, and to provide a context for the development of TIP. I have also referenced videos by experts which are easy to listen to or watch when doing other things, such as making dinner!

Section 1: Early trauma research – PTSD
How the research informs practice today

Bessel van der Kolk and others were researching the effects of war on returning veterans in 1970 after the end of the Vietnam War. This was one of the early studies of PTSD. The researchers originally thought that the veterans' trauma resulted from having suffered awful events outside the realm of the ordinary human experience, discussed in the first chapter of van der Kolk's book *The Body Keeps the Score* (2).

Further study into trauma showed it was widespread at all levels of society and included those affected by domestic violence, sexual violence, severe emotional cruelty and neglect. The studies showed that victims carried the experience of their trauma in images, behaviours, responses and physical reactions to triggering situations. In his book *The Body Keeps the Score*, van der Kolk expands this theory (2).

Research into ACEs

Understanding the lifelong effects of trauma

This early research into PTSD was followed by the studies of ACEs. The ACE study of 17,000 adults, which asked them about abuse, neglect and family problems, was conducted by Anda and Felitti in 1997. The results showed how ACEs had a long-term negative effect on health and everything from employment to addiction for those affected (1).

In a video (3), van der Kolk explains the way trauma affects the body and our reactions to triggers that can be overwhelming and are not always conscious. He looks at the difference between trauma and stress. Van der Kolk clarifies that stress is caused by a one-off or time-limited difficulty in life. When it is over, it is done, and the person moves on. A trauma overwhelms the whole system and doesn't leave the person's body and mind. The memories are often stored in the body and the subconscious. This leaves the person affected by fears, anxiety, sudden triggers and other negative effects on daily life. He also discusses how understanding of trauma moved from a focus on the individual to the study of group and community-based trauma founded in racism, extreme poverty and unemployment.

The ACE studies and research, in the 1990s and beyond, such as the work of Bellis and colleagues in Wales (4), looked into how trauma affects all areas of development – mental, emotional and physical. One of the most important things we have learned about ACEs has been their long-term effects on all aspects of health, life choices and longevity.

ACEs recognised in research include:

- physical abuse and neglect
- emotional abuse
- sexual abuse

- loss of a parent/main carer by death, separation, abandonment or prison sentence
- a household where there is drug/alcohol abuse, mental illness or domestic violence.

The effects of ACEs on the child and into adult life

The immediate effects on the child's development and long-term effects on the adult's health and well-being include the following:

- The child's mental, physical and emotional development suffers ongoing damage.
- There is an increase in illnesses such as cancer and heart disease in adulthood.
- There is an increased risk of mental health difficulties, violence and becoming a victim of violence.
- There is a high risk of mental health problems such as anxiety, depression and post-traumatic stress. Many mental health conditions in adulthood are directly related to ACEs.
- The longer the ACE lasts and the more ACEs someone experiences, the bigger the impact on their development and their health.

Some other things exposure to ACEs can impact

Relationship skills and self-regulation are more difficult:

- Social interactions can often result in getting stuck in **fight, flight or freeze (FFF)** mode.
- Survival habits of 'high alert', causing aggressive or close-down responses, affect relationships negatively.
- Cognitive development is impaired by trauma, and concentration is damaged by the overwhelming emotions often triggered by seemingly innocuous events.
- The lack of ability to recognise and manage different emotions makes self-regulation hard.

- The capacity to make and keep healthy friendships and other relationships is reduced.
- There is difficulty in interpreting emotional signals and loss of trust in others, and in their intentions, even those who mean well.
- The ability to manage behaviour in school and other formal settings is reduced, especially with authority.
- Self-regulation is often very difficult because the person finds it hard to return to normal after an everyday excitement, challenge, fright or disagreement.
- There are difficulties coping with emotions safely without causing harm to self or others. Outbursts and arguments can upset and destabilise others in the group.

ACEs and underserved communities

The effects of ACEs on the individual are multiplied by living with endemic community problems.

These problems involving ACEs are often overrepresented in underserved communities that are burdened with severe poverty, crime and lack of access to services, so the impact on the individual child is increased. We all suffer traumatic loss and upset in our lives; it's how we make sense of it and continue living that will determine how much damage we carry into our future. In a family system that may be barely functioning, living in a community under pressure, a child's experience of trauma and loss in the family could be deep-seated and overwhelming. A child living a privileged life with a caring family, supportive home and school will be able to overcome a traumatic event or loss much more effectively. The intensity, duration and number of ACEs will intensify the negative effects for the unsupported child. In communities all over Dublin, I saw many grandmothers and other relatives raising children whose parents were unable to provide a stable home. In families affected by domestic violence or addiction, the grandmother was often the only safe haven for children to turn to. Her death was an earth-shattering event with no one to comfort the child. In contrast, in a stable family where a grandmother may be a beloved extra carer, the child can grieve with their parents, consoled by the happy memories they share. The central importance of the family and community situation for the child and how the original ACEs didn't address this is highlighted by the work of O'Toole (5).

[O]riginal ACE research treats the socioeconomic environment as a background factor, rather than an explicit object of interest. It fails to acknowledge a wide range of adversities associated with structural inequalities, such as being a member of a marginalized or oppressed social group, experiencing racism, poverty or homelessness, living in or having to escape conflict or war zones, experiencing or witnessing community or school violence, and being taken into care. (Art. 4)

Covid-19 effects

A clear example of this difference in circumstances was seen in Ireland during the Covid-19 pandemic. Affluent, well-resourced families with rooms to spread out in and access to PCs, books, crafts and art materials found it much easier to occupy and encourage their children. Families living in more crowded conditions without resources were also missing out on school meals and after-school clubs, and found it difficult to maintain their children's education and nutrition. Teachers in underserved areas report significant gaps developing in literacy and concentration. More important in the long term is the damage done to social emotional skills. The ability to cooperate and take direction was damaged by the long periods of isolation and loss of access to school and its various supports.

Anna, an experienced and dedicated primary teacher reported: 'I've never seen anything like it. The younger kids are so wild and don't seem to know how to play. They are all behind on their schoolwork, but the worst effects seem to be on their social skills.' Similarly, Zoe, a frontline support worker in an underserved area, found that 'the level of aggression is through the roof. I have eight-year-olds in the clubs telling me to go f --- myself on a daily basis. It used to be stuff kicking off, now it's continual – every day.'

Reflective questions

- Did you see effects of the Covid-19 lockdowns when the children returned to school?

- What did you notice? Were there any extra supports available to you to support the children?
- Are there other community difficulties that affect your students' learning?

Section 2: Why learn about trauma? TIP research and application of the principles

I have enough to worry about with a big class and packed curriculum.

In 2001, the U.S. Substance Abuse and Mental Health Services Administration (SAMHSA) established national initiatives to research trauma effects, with a focus on children. Their report published in 2014 outlined the TIP approaches arising from the research (6).

The report identified six vital elements to TIP: **Safety, Trustworthiness, Choice, Collaboration, Empowerment** and **Cultural consideration**.

The work of TIP has developed in the fields of education, social science, childcare and legal approaches to punishment of offenders, mostly in the last 20 years.

An increased understanding of the effects of trauma and the effective supports that help children to settle and learn is the aim here. I know from many colleagues and friends working in the community and in education that what they would like is a broad understanding of how trauma affects young people's learning and behaviour, and then some workable approaches and activities to support young people/children who are suffering from trauma.

It is important to remember that most of us experience trauma in our lives at some stage; children are no different, so a supportive environment based on sound principles of social emotional learning (SEL) and TIP will benefit everyone in the room. For many of us working with people at all levels, this type of training gives lots of 'Aha! Of course!' moments – but if we have no practical suggestions to follow up on our understanding, it can get swamped in the daily rush.

I will share some of my lived experience before ACEs and TIP were widely studied and discussed, when I was working with groups with high trauma levels located in underserved communities.

My current work on programmes with tutors and teachers who are teaching in various situations, including traumatised groups, suggests that small changes that increase a feeling of belonging and some social contact and ongoing review have great positive impact on the students.

The foundation of learning and the importance of attached relationships

Attachment in early childhood is vital to positive development

Scientists and psychologists are learning more about how the brain system builds neural pathways for responding to life's experiences and challenges (7). The foundation of these social and cognitive skills are secure relationships that allow the child to learn and explore their environment and the people in it while feeling safe. Attachment theory is the basis of this understanding of the need for secure relationships. If you look at a secure young child 'running away' – a favourite game in a shopping area or restaurant – they are sure of being followed and caught. The adventure is a safe one and ends with their 'rescue' by their carer.

Neurobiology showed how these essential skills are stunted by childhood and ongoing trauma as the brain pathways that connect new experiences to old and encourage learning are damaged. All childhood traumas will involve the lack or breakdown of important nurturing relationships for the child. The child loses confidence in the world as a safe place and in the love and protection of their carers.

There are the seemingly individual factors of alcoholism, addiction, mental health issues and consistent neglect, which are often compounded by poor living conditions and multiple community disadvantages (5). These are not the result of individual choices, but that of ACEs experienced in youth, by the parents themselves, and then by their children. The good news is that these effects can be reduced, and the resilience of the children increased by TIP and therapeutic supports.

TIP research and important elements for application of these principles

The research into TIP grew from the ACEs research and expanded our understanding of how trauma affects development over the whole life of a person.

Trauma is always an individual experience and is measured by the impact on the person, not the event itself.

A key part is the serious breakdown of trust. If the trauma is caused by a person, especially a trusted person or family member, the 'safe place' is destroyed for the victim, and this can have ripple effects into every relationship interaction. If the trauma comes from the universe itself – for example, war, flood or fire – the sense of safe belonging in the world is ripped apart, and high levels of anxiety or hyper-vigilance can drain the energy needed for other functions, such as learning, thinking, relating to others or relaxing.

Attachment

The essential need for loving attachments for a baby was highlighted by John Bowlby (8) in the 1930s. Attachment theory has become established in psychology and sociology, and has looked at the human need for secure, loving relationships from childhood into adult life. For the dependent baby and child, this means their survival (9). When this safe, loving relationship is not there, or is not sustained due to illness, absence or the inability of parents, the child's physical, social, cognitive and emotional development is negatively affected. Attachment is the foundation stone of a child's development in all areas. Feeling safe and secure allows a child space to explore, to interact with others, to play, to learn social emotional skills with a safe pair of arms to return to. Eimear, a family therapist working in an underserved area with children and teens, noted that despite their difficult lives with traumatic experiences of addiction and abandonment:

> *Well, if I look at all of them, they all have one person they trust, yeah, bar one actually, the guy who lost [two carers recently] . . . Even the one who's [in a tough situation with Mum not coping and who is caring for young siblings] adores her, and would do anything for her. Actually, the granny is so . . . important. So, they all have one person, one adult in their lives that is important.*

If a child lacks this security, their development may be damaged by their survival mechanisms being on high alert, blocking access to cognitive development. Neural pathways that link up new learning are damaged. Other traumatised children retreat from engagement with the world, disassociate and zone out. Many children and young people swing between both extremes, with a limited ability to self-regulate; this will be significantly pronounced in those affected by trauma.

A young person always scanning for danger and anxious about ongoing traumas lacks energy for concentration and learning. The work of Schore (7) and others highlighted the effects on learning of early trauma:

> [T]hese early dysregulating experiences lead to more than an insecure attachment, they trigger a chaotic alteration of the emotion processing limbic system that is in a critical period of growth in infancy. The limbic system has been suggested to be the site of developmental changes associated with the rise of attachment behaviors (Anders & Zeanah, 1984) and to be centrally involved in the capacity 'to adapt to a rapidly changing environment' and in 'the organization of new learning' (Mesulam, 1998, p. 1028). These limbic circuits are particularly expressed in the right hemisphere (Joseph, 1996; Tucker, 1992), which is in a growth spurt in the first two years of life. (p. 209)

Early studies of resilience focused on the individual's ability to manage change and difficulties including traumatic events. Later research recognised the importance of the networks a person lives in (10), the first being the immediate family, then the extended family, neighbourhood, community, school, health service, leisure facilities and the systems of government, culture and religion that operate, as shown by Bronfenbrenner (11).

Studies of TIP have highlighted the lack of equity in education, and how endemic poverty, racism, non-living wage work and living with community violence and addiction all provide a high risk for traumatic effects. Dr Nadine Bourke gave an inspirational TED talk (12) on the physical symptoms of traumatic stress she found in her care of primary school children in California. The support systems she suggested were welcoming, thoughtful approaches that build relationships with children and also reach out to their families. Supports can be put in place to increase resilience and build relationships within the school and class systems. The research into trauma and reviews of TIP in education settings all share a focus on *relationships, resilience* and *reflection* which are essential tools, noted by Dr Dan Siegel (13), for reducing trauma-based responses and fostering a space for trust and learning.

Examples of trauma

- Sexual emotional or physical abuse.
- Neglect or abandonment by carers.
- Domestic violence – observed and/or experienced.
- Natural disasters.
- Car accidents.
- Suicide/sudden death of a close loved one.
- War or political/racial violence.
- Living with a terminal illness.

Effects of trauma

- Cognitive development affected as energy for brain growth goes to survival.
- Anger issues-easily triggered by a seemingly trivial event.
- Attention problems – difficulty in focus and completion, frustration at any setback.
- Changes in appetite.
- Development of new fears.
- Increased concerns about death or safety.
- Irritability.
- Loss of interest in normal activities.
- Problems sleeping.
- Sadness.
- School refusal.
- Physical stress-related effects like headaches and stomach aches.
- Risk-taking behaviours.

Examples of behaviours associated with traumatic distress

- Lack of motivation – no interest in getting involved.
- Panic attacks.
- Fear of new challenges or changes.
- Aggressive reactions to everyday interactions.
- Misreading social cues – seeing threat or insult in well-meaning comments.

- Finger is always on the panic button, not relaxed or present.
- Difficulty in joining group activities or taking direction from authority figures.

Trauma and how it affects development at each stage of childhood

What does a cared-for, happy child experience in their world?

Figure 1.1 Secure, cared-for infant

The happy child with good enough (not perfect!) parent/guardians

In the cared-for child's development, there is steady progress from the overwhelming needs of food and comfort (which cause a hungry baby to shriek as though an attack by wolves was underway) – those functions of the reptilian or 'old' brain which is all about survival. The ability to regulate immediate needs develops with the understanding that carers are constant. Baby talk, laughing and smiling exchanges help baby to engage and connect with the carers and the wider world. This paves the way for developing other relationships, getting to know more people and, later, making friends and interacting with peers. This social emotional development is dependent on secure attachment, leading to interest and confidence in exploring the world. These developments are also cognitive and develop neural pathways in the brain for learning patterns, habits and new skills. Cognition or abstract thought is believed to be the last part of the brain to develop and uses a lot of energy in development and working things out. Children as young as four are asking complicated questions and pondering what death is and other big questions. The period from ages two to six is thought to be a time of massive brain development, leading to cognitive front-brain engagement. The years from birth to three years old are especially significant in forming the relationship skills and a confident attitude to the world. These are general guidelines, of course, with children showing a wide variety of achievements on their own timeline.

What does a neglected, abused child experience in their world?

Figure 1.2 Neglected, abused infant

Baby's basic needs for care and safety are not being met. This means that a lot of energy may be going towards survival, and the making of connections to the world may be very limited or fearful, which will slow down development. The child will be very anxious or distressed and may scream a lot or appear very detached. A lack of interaction and mirroring from carers means that regulation will be affected as the child has no secure base. As each stage builds on the previous one, the child's experience of people may not be loving or happy, so their curiosity and exploration of the environment can be very limited. Relationships are the most important way the child learns new skills and develops confidence in the world around them.

The energy needed to expand the neural pathways and learn all the new skills of the thinking or abstract brain is diverted into survival. The need to scan for danger keeps the child on constant alert, and the reptilian brain is very active in survival mode. This is how the child's academic and cognitive abilities are negatively affected by trauma at each stage.

Each chapter in the book will have details of some approaches and activities that help build safety, supportive relationships and self-regulation, which in turn will increase resilience and build confidence.

Section 3: My experience of trauma and young people

How trauma affected learning, concentration and people skills

Youthreach was set up in Ireland in 1988 to offer an alternative education to early school leavers aged 15–18. The rationale behind it was research that showed a huge negative impact on life chances by early school leaving. I taught catering, life skills, literacy and outdoor activities for over a decade. The staff were compassionate and highly motivated to find ways of engaging what was often an unwilling group in learning new skills and building on previous ones. At that time, there wasn't a range of counselling supports for trainees or staff in Youthreach.

Trauma as a normal event

Every day, young people aged 15–19 arrived at the centre in the midst of some crisis. The focus of our work was a skills-based training, which included what were called 'life skills' sessions. It became obvious to all of us that many trainees were living with high numbers of what are now called ACEs, and as staff developed relationships with the trainees, we learned of addiction, family violence, extreme poverty, crime, incarceration and sexual abuse.

I look back now and have all kinds of memories of just dealing with each crisis as it happened. I remember finding one trainee eating heels of bread out of the bin as there was no food at home and they couldn't wait for breakfast. Many of the girls became pregnant or already had children, and for some of them it was because of one sexual experience, often believing 'you can't get pregnant the first time you do it'. Trainees arrived looking exhausted, saying they had slept in a shed or a porch as they couldn't go home. As we received more training and awareness grew in society of abuse, I asked myself: Why would a young person sleep in a shed rather than go home? Sexual abuse and family violence made home a dangerous place for some of our trainees. Many of the young people went into jobs, apprenticeships and training, but for some the odds were too stacked against them. There were tragic cases of suicide and addiction among the young people.

Mary Gordon from the National Education Psychology Service (NEPS) conducted a study of Youthreach participants in 2017 (14) and found that two-thirds of the trainees had suffered four or more ACEs, showing a much higher level of ACEs than in the general population. The reasons behind their early school leaving and behavioural difficulties were found in trauma, not in 'bold or challenging behaviour' by the individual which had led to school dropout. Frequent instances of depression, challenging and risky behaviour and mental health difficulties were associated significantly with those young people who suffered sexual and physical abuse in the family home.

The principles of trauma-informed practice

The good news for those who work and live with children is that the right supports can help to repair this damage. We are learning more about the plasticity of the brain and how new neural pathways can be developed that enable learning and help to build trusting relationships (15). This is the rationale for TIP in schools, which have been identified as an ideal place to provide supports. With attendance mandatory, the school is a constant in the child's life, offering a chance to build relationships and security – the essentials in recovery from trauma and ACEs.

What does TIP mean to me as an educator?

Application in everyday classroom situation

The approach of TIP can be adapted to each situation. There is a lot of research on TIP that is specifically aimed at therapists or those working mainly with traumatised groups with resources to do this work. The work of Karen Treisman (16) gives clear explanations of trauma, its effects and healing approaches. Her work provides many inspirational studies and ways of working with trauma.

Julie Nicholson and colleagues (17) explain the difference between SEL curricula that need the pupil to use cognitive conscious thinking and TIP which focuses on providing a safe place and safe relationships.

> [A] child's brain will heal when we intentionally and actively plan to create a sense of safety relationally and in the environment. When children feel safe and their activated stress response system has been rewired to be more regulated, *then and only then* will they be able to access the executive parts of their brain where they can think, focus, follow instructions, remember things, learn expectation and recall the schedule of the day. (p.131)

A young child living with trauma, coming into school

Adele was eight years old. Her mother and father were both involved with drugs. She was a very pretty child, and her mother kept her very well dressed as her day usually didn't fall apart until after lunch when she took drugs.

Adele had been returned to her mother's care under supervision, but she and her mother were experts in colluding against the social worker.

Her mother frequently warned her that *'they* would take her (Adele) away if she told them stuff'. She often came to school with no lunch and had the most elaborate stories to explain why – 'Mam was baking bread, and it wasn't ready'.

Adele used many strategies for joining after-school activities because not getting collected was a common thing for her. She would turn up with a big smile at the older children's club with another tale about why Mam would be late, and she would beg to sit quietly and do her homework. Her determinedly bouncy approach, with panic showing through, was distressing to watch and difficult to resist.

The combination of her confident manner and well-cared-for appearance led to her being seen by some as spoilt and cheeky. Her learning in class was not in line with her ability, as so much of her brain power went into keeping up a front and planning ahead to avoid the emergency social work services being called. The class teacher reported that Adele was 'well cared for and bright, so she wasn't achieving due to being spoilt, never doing her homework and often forgetting books and other things she needed'. It was awkward to access extra supports for Adele as her circumstances were confidential, and she showed no learning needs that could be assessed by tests. Her difficulties were trauma-related.

Reflective questions

Have you seen this type of mismatch before? A child seems well cared for and talks a lot about the lovely times at home, but you may have noticed some inconsistencies – perhaps the child always seems hungry, and when they took their shoes off for an activity, their socks literally fell apart in your hand?

- What steps could you take to get more information without labelling the child?
- What supports are available in your school or your local area?

Steps taken for Adele

A short meeting was held with the class teacher, special needs teacher and the support worker who had raised some concerns. The support worker shared that Adele was rarely collected on time and was always asking for food from the various after-school clubs. The class teacher and special needs teacher had a look at her work and agreed she was behind in her literacy and numeracy, and her work was jumbled and unfinished. The support worker shared that there were many challenges in Adele's home life and asked for activities, extra snacks and reading help for Adele. It is important to note that this was done without breaking confidentiality. A plan was agreed, and a copy given to the assistant principal who was the chair of the pastoral care committee.

Supports given to Adele

- Adele was invited to join the breakfast club to get a healthy start. As she was frequently late, her teacher agreed that the support worker could give her breakfast and bring her into class.
- Adele joined a small group of readers doing an extra withdrawal class. The teacher held her books for her, and she collected them each morning.
- Adele joined the homework club, and her concentration improved with a calm place to do her homework.
- Adele joined a group run by a specialist service to support children living with addiction. The approach was gentle and child-led, and she discovered that other children were living in the same situation. One evening she asked, 'Does it mean your mam doesn't love you anymore if she takes drugs and forgets about you?'

Eventually, there was a crisis, and Adele was removed to the care of her grandmother. She continually asked to go home and maintained the fantasy of the caring home she had shared with her mother. The support group helped her to understand something of addiction and its effects.

This study illustrates many of the complicated aspects of working with children in crisis.

Challenges in giving support to traumatised children

Difficulties in engaging with families and gaining insight into the problems

- I often found the ability of children to cover up for their parents was inventive and convincing, so serious issues remained hidden.
- The deep-seated fear of removal was often well founded, as children going into the foster system were placed wherever a place could be found, often far away from their own school, friends and wider family. This fear leads to lack of engagement with services by parent and child.
- The pressure of many clients meant social workers lacked time for ongoing contact with teachers and other services.
- Confidentiality made it difficult to involve the school personnel in support if they didn't know about the problems in the child's family.

Section 4: The difference between TIP methods and a therapeutic approach to pupils' social emotional learning

Working on building a safe place and safe relationships

Many educators without therapeutic training are not comfortable using approaches that would seem to encourage disclosures or emotional responses in pupils. The majority of teachers and tutors work alone, often with highly traumatised groups of all ages.

The aim of this book is to explore the aspects of TIP that will work in conjunction with SEL principles for mainstream classes or specialised groups. SEL principles are given on the website of the Collaborative for Academic, Social, and Emotional Learning (CASEL) (www.casel.org):

> Social and emotional learning (SEL) is the process through which children and adults acquire and effectively apply the knowledge, attitudes, and skills necessary to understand and manage emotions, set and achieve positive goals, feel and show empathy for others,

establish and maintain positive relationships, and make responsible decisions.

TIP principles include aspects which focus on supporting traumatised individuals, such as:

- having structured sessions and days – routines enhance feelings of safety
- building strong supportive relationships
- empowering students through choice
- supporting self-regulation
- exploring individual and community identities
- being aware of support services in house and locally for those affected by trauma.

The development of that safe space in the classroom with the students will be an important part of this work.

The SEL principles are the basis of the well-being and Social Personal Health Education (SPHE) curriculum in Ireland. The TIP approach looks for compassion, understanding and positive relationships in the classroom with the students. Challenging behaviour or emotional outbursts are viewed as a form of communication, and a working outcome rather than a punishment is sought. An example was given by a teacher working with students living in unstable accommodation who were getting shut out of school for late arrival after long bus journeys across town. This language teacher organised theirs to be the first class and encouraged the students for having made the effort to come in.

In a group with flexible timetables and an emphasis on SEL, there are lots of possibilities for providing one-to-one supports and spaces for calm and rest. In single-teacher classrooms, physical resources are limited, but one adult education tutor said, 'I realised I am the main resource in the classroom.' The UK programme of SEL in schools has similar roots in CASEL principles, and shows ongoing research into the efficacy of programmes in creating and maintaining change in students' attitudes and SEL ability. The study by Durlak and colleagues (18) of 270,034 kindergarten to secondary school students in the United States highlighted the benefits of SEL programmes and acknowledged the difficulty in assessing these results as materials and programmes varied so much. This was noted in Irish and UK review of SEL programmes. The UK research shows an emphasis on measuring effectiveness and grading programmes by certain standards (19). More recent research by the Education Endowment Fund (UK) is focused on which programmes appear effective rather than trying to measure results (20). The Irish approach appears to be more a review of the curriculum materials and approaches with an emphasis on teacher training and whole school involvement (21). The policies in both countries recognise the value and necessity for SEL programmes in schools. The extra need for such programmes for disadvantaged pupils and the worsening mental health of students following Covid-19 form part of both countries' education policies.

A change in attitude and the growth of positive relationships will spread in the classroom, and more peer support will become available as a result of using effective SEL and TIP methods.

As Alex Shevrin Venet (22) says:

> In my community college courses, I start each day with a quick 'rose/thorn' check-in, in which students can share one thing that's going well for them that week (a 'rose') and one thing that's not going so well (a 'thorn'). This five-minute investment in checking in helps to establish a tone of mutual care in the classroom. If a student shares a particularly meaningful rose or thorn, it's common for her classmates to follow up and offer their support. (p.7)

Application of the key principles developed by SAMHSA

As mentioned above, the research done by SAMHSA (6) in the United States identified six elements vital for TIP in action:

- **Safety** – feeling welcome, accepted and free to ask questions, to make mistakes and to ask for needs to be met.
- **Trust** – receiving consistent care from the educator and transparency around timing, tasks and their purpose.
- **Choice** – selecting tasks and learning methods, setting own pace, as appropriate and possible.
- **Collaboration** – teacher working with students to achieve outcomes, students working together, links with local agencies where feasible.

- **Empowerment** – students' decision-making developing as skills and confidence grow. Exploring the outside world and its possibilities.
- **Cultural considerations** – being aware of cultural beliefs and preferences as an ongoing process and responding to needs.

These guiding principles overlap and develop as they become part of daily practice. They will be explored in depth in the following chapters. How these principles can translate into the daily work of the educator will be discussed in practical terms throughout the book.

Benefits

- A friendly atmosphere reduces anxiety and promotes learning.
- Ongoing review allows for asking questions easily – even difficult ones.
- Learner feedback helps in modifying/delivering material effectively.
- The use of reflection and review builds confidence and engagement for students.
- Respect spreads in the peer group, and support in shared learning and social skills grows.

Challenges

- Uncertainty for staff about how to begin this approach.
- Concern about pressures of curriculum/ lack of time.
- Boundary issues – inappropriate disclosures that educators are unable to deal with.
- Overwhelming expectations of students that teachers can solve all their problems.
- Other staff seeing this method as giving in to bad behaviour/time wasting.

The key thing is communication. Start with small steps. TIP awareness teaches us that some people in any group will have suffered separation, bereavement, violence or neglect. In some groups, we are aware, by their nature, that trauma incidence is very high. For example, groups affected by addiction, homelessness, refugee experiences and marginalisation. For many adult learners, returning to education is a frightening experience due to negative and humiliating experiences in early school years.

It is impossible to be aware of every trigger to trauma for your group. You can reduce the level in the physical and social environment and then rely on your group feedback to inform you.

Environment

- Label your door with the name of the class, adding a symbol like a flower or butterfly, or any symbol agreeable to the group. This lets students know they are in the right place – if you change rooms, you can put up the sign.
- Warm welcome – tutors of primary, second level and third level reported big improvements in the atmosphere and attention of their groups from taking the first few minutes to greet pupils by name and have a general chat about the day and the work in hand.
- Only have the furniture you need. I went to work with a 'special class' in a mainstream school, and five students were scattered between 30 desks. Our first task was for each student to select a desk and chair and bring it to the front while we pushed the rest back. Each student created an A4 sheet design of their name which I laminated and brought with me each week to put on their desk.
- Choose where you sit. If you are at the top of the room because of a projector or whiteboard, create some other sitting spaces among the group for short periods. One tutor teaching an IT computer course for adults changed from central information giving with slides to a short presentation at the start. Then she went around the group, supporting learners with their questions. On review, the students reported a big reduction in stress, the fear of not keeping up was gone, and peer support developed among the group. A flexible break of 20 minutes to be taken at will was also very effective. Students said it was great to be able to take a short break when feeling overwhelmed and return to work relaxed.
- Avoid loud noises – if there are timed bells that sound or fire alarms, give a warning.

Approach

- Create a welcoming atmosphere.
- Use visuals such as posters and charts to show transparency about what will happen in the classroom and why. This is helpful for students of all ages.

- **Soft space** – if possible, have an area for a couple of soft cushions, toys, fidgets in the classroom.
- Quiet chair – for young adult students, in a corridor, corner of the room, repurposed storeroom.
- **Free flow** in the class – have a free pass to leave the room for ten minutes, especially for senior students and adults.

With younger groups, you can adapt and build up to these privileges gradually.

Maintaining effective boundaries

For the majority of mainstream teachers and tutors, their employment contract and training are about the skills or subjects that they teach the pupils of any age. There may be some extra supports and small group work available, where pupils can be referred, but the educator is not a therapist. A TIP approach asks the teacher to be aware, informed, flexible and accepting of different experiences, which may include trauma. Pupils may exhibit challenging or withdrawn behaviours that require extra support from the educator in terms of the six principles of SAMHSA. The exploration or unpacking of the trauma itself is the work of a therapist or therapeutic team. The educator acts as a kind supporter offering the most conducive environment for learning, but diagnosis and treatment is not their work or responsibility. Each school or college should have a referral system to professional support.

Key points of Chapter 1

- Background to PTSD, ACEs and TIP research – how trauma-informed practice developed.
- Principles of TIP in the education space.
- The effects on body, mind and social development of trauma – developmental damage.
- Attachment and how it is so vital for the child's development.
- Safety, trusting relationships and improving self-regulation – vital elements of TIP.

- Some benefits and challenges of using TIP, especially in mainstream education.
- The difference between a TIP supportive approach and a therapeutic intervention – the importance of safe boundaries for the educator and pupil.

References

1. Felitti VJ, Anda RF, Nordenberg D, Williamson DF, Spitz AM, Edwards V, et al. Relationship of childhood abuse and household dysfunction to many of the leading causes of death in adults: The Adverse Childhood Experiences (ACE) Study. American Journal of Preventive Medicine. 1998;14(4):245–58.
2. van der Kolk BA. The body keeps the score. USA: Viking Penguin; 2015.
3. van der Kolk BA. 7 surprising ways to heal trauma without medication. Dr Rangan Chatterjee. www.youtube.com/watch?v=lrOBHyDRS-c&t=1719s
4. Bellis MA, Ashton K, Hughes K, Ford K, Bishop J, Paranjothy S. Welsh Adverse Childhood Experiences (ACE). Liverpool: Public Health Wales, Centre for Public Health; 2016.
5. O'Toole C. When trauma comes to school: Toward a socially just trauma informed praxis. International Journal of School Social Work. 2022;6(2):Art. 4.
6. Substance Abuse and Mental Health Services Administration. SAMHSA's Concept of Trauma and Guidance for a Trauma-Informed Approach. Rockville, MD: Substance Abuse and Mental Health Services Administration; 2014.
7. Schore AN. The effects of early relational trauma on right brain development, affect regulation, and infant mental health. Infant Mental Health Journal. 2001;22(1–2):201–69.
8. Bowlby J. A secure base: Clinical applications of attachment theory. London: Routledge; 1988.
9. Sroufe A, Siegel D. The verdict is in: The case for attachment theory. Psychotherapy Networker. 2011 (March).
10. Committee on Integrating the Science of Early Childhood Development – Board on Children Youth and Families. From neurons to neighborhoods: The science of early child development. Shonkoff JP, Phillips D, editors. Washington, DC: National Academy Press; 2000.
11. Bronfenbrenner U, Ceci SJ. Nature-nuture reconceptualized in developmental perspective: A bioecological model. Psychological Review. 1994;101(4):568–86.
12. Burke Harris N. How childhood trauma affects health across a lifetime. USA; 2014, www.youtube.com/watch?v=95ovIJ3dsNk.
13. Solomon MF, Siegel DJ, editors. Healing Trauma: Attachment, mind, body, and brain. London: Norton; 2003.

14. Gordon M. A profile of learners in Youthreach: Research study report. Dublin: National Educational Psychological Service; 2017.
15. Steele W, Malchiodi CA. Trauma-informed practices with children and adolescents. New York: Taylor and Francis; 2012.
16. Treisman K. Working with relational and developmental trauma in children and adolescents. London: Routledge; 2017.
17. Nicholson J, Perez L, Kurtz J, Bryant S, Giles D. Trauma-informed practices for early childhood educators. London: Routledge; 2019.
18. Durlak JA, Weissberg RP, Dymnicki AB, Taylor RD, Schellinger KB. The impact of enhancing students' social and emotional learning: A meta-analysis of school based universal interventions. Child Development. 2011;82(1):405–32.
19. Baker CN, Augenstern JM, Moberg SA, Robey N, Saybe MC, Rossen E. Developing school staff buy-in for trauma-informed schools. In: Rossen E, editor. Supporting and educating traumatized students: A guide for school-based professionals, 2nd ed. Oxford: Oxford University Press; 2020.
20. Education Endowment Foundation, UK; 2025. https://educationendowmentfoundation.org.uk
21. O'Sullivan C, Moynihan S, Collins B, Hayes G, Titley A, editors. The future of SPHE: problems and possibilities. Proceedings from SPHE network conference 29th September 2012. Dublin: SPHE Network, DICE; 2014.
22. Shevrin Venet A. Role-clarity and boundaries for trauma-informed teachers. Educational Considerations. 2019;44(2).

2
What does trauma look like in the classroom?

> This chapter provides more detailed information on the different effects of trauma and how these may appear in students' behaviours and responses in education at three levels – primary school, secondary school and adult education.
>
> The worst result of trauma shows as damage to relationships and the ability to trust and relax in relation to others. That's why the vital ingredients in TIP are a safe space to be and supportive and understanding relationships in that space.
>
> My focus is on offering resources that help create safe learning spaces for pupils and educators. The supports suggested are intended to reduce retraumatisation and help self-regulation, and build positive relationships with the educator and among the group using the principles of SAMHSA (1) and the Scottish trauma handbook (2).
>
> The six principles of TIP are detailed and related to the common challenging situations in the classroom.
>
> There are three sections in this chapter:
>
> - Section 1 looks at the effects and behaviours related to trauma.
> - Section 2 looks at the principles of TIP.
> - Section 3 gives examples of reactive and challenging behaviour in the classroom.

Everybody shows individual reactions or symptoms of trauma. The behaviours will be very different from primary-aged children to adolescents to adult learners. Traumatic stress is a very complex psychological condition, with many approaches to therapy and recovery. The detailed study of trauma is not the work of this book, however; here, the aim is to enhance understanding for educators of how trauma impacts children and young people. This will expand readers' knowledge of how these effects of developmental trauma show up in the classroom, and explore approaches, activities and materials that encourage a calm and supportive learning environment. Many people affected by trauma, of all ages, have difficulties with building relationships and maintaining concentration, so these approaches will be of benefit to everyone in the group, following the 'good for one, good for all' approach – the supportive environment and TIP approach will be good for the individual who needs it and good for all the pupils as it is a positive element in the classroom.

Section 1: Trauma examples and effects

These were detailed in Section 2 in Chapter 1.

Examples of trauma

These include all kinds of violence, abuse, neglect, natural disasters, and war. The event can be a single horrific experience of violent attack, a serious accident or a prolonged trauma such as long-term neglect and violence to children or adults in their home or institution.

Effects of trauma

Cognitive development is slowed down as energy is diverted for survival and attention span is lessened. Social and relationship skills are damaged – reactions can be extreme and misread social cues. Worries about death, safety and health can become pervasive and ill-health and depression can develop.

The effects of trauma on developing life and learning skills

The interlinked phases of child development

Shonkoff and colleagues (3) stress the importance of loving care and responsive caregivers as essential to the baby's need for connection. The baby is born wired with this need for love and human response. This is the basis of all the stages of development that reach towards the stage of cognitive/

abstract thinking and problem solving. If this attachment has been absent for the baby, child and adolescent, the foundations and confidence for learning about people, places and things are rocky and easily unbalanced.

> [C]hildren get off to a promising or a worrisome start in life. These scientific gains have generated a much deeper appreciation of: (1) the importance of early life experiences, as well as the inseparable and highly interactive influences of genetics and environment, on the development of the brain and the unfolding of human behavior; (2) the central role of early relationships as a source of either support and adaptation or risk and dysfunction; (3) the powerful capabilities, complex emotions, and essential social skills that develop during the earliest years of life, and (4) the capacity to increase the odds of favourable developmental outcomes through planned interventions. (pp. 1–2)

The different developmental experiences of the secure child and the abused child

The happy child with good enough (not perfect!) parent/guardians

The child moves through the stages of development at their own pace with some forward and backward stages – a typical one is when a new baby arrives, the toddler may revert to a bottle or other baby things.

Figure 2.1 Secure, confident child

What does trauma look like in the classroom?

- **Early survival mode:** Overwhelming reactions to physical and emotional needs – hungry baby cries to get a response, frightened baby cries for comfort or soothing. As their needs are met, baby starts to know that loving hands are coming and develops a feeling of safety.
- **Self-regulation:** Coping with change, while sure of support – routines vary, other minders come, and adjustment is needed to different people. The baby of a few months knows the voice of the carer and will be soothed when crying by hearing 'OK, Baba, I'm coming.' Then weaning brings a change of diet, which is not always welcomed! The environment continues to be adapted by the adults as baby is still helpless and needs others to respond to their needs. The ability to manage emotions and behaviours is already being modelled by the carer, and baby is learning to recover from shocks like the fright of a sudden noise or unexpected event.
- **Social emotional skills – relationships:** This begins at the infant stage, as the baby of some weeks old starts to smile and respond to voices and movements and hugs. Each little achievement is noted and welcomed by carers – first teeth, first sit-up. Baby starts to reach for toys and makes sounds, and develops preferences for foods, locations and toys. The young child explores the environment, physically and socially. For toddlers, meeting other children is not always a success at first, but then the benefits of having buddies gradually become obvious as games become more social and involved. The happy child has a safe haven they can return to – that is, their carer.
- **Cognition:** All this time, the child aged 0–3 is learning and expanding their understanding at a huge rate. They are making connections and learning new things every day. The foundations for abstract thinking, which is the basis of academic learning, are being gradually created by the child's experiences of life. The confidence and curiosity to learn about the world are absolutely grounded in their secure attachment to carers. The cognitive, front-brain function for abstract thinking is developing all the time and is typically important in the years 5–7. Each stage of development depends on the other as the neural pathways expand according to the range of behaviours and new understanding of the child.

The traumatised child who is neglected/abused/living with addiction or violence

The child is lacking the attachment and consistent care that builds trust and interest in the world. This can damage the development of new skills; an example is an excessive fear of or aggressive response to strangers.

Trauma-Informed Practice in Education

Figure 2.2 Neglected, confused child

- **Survival mode:** This is an ongoing state for the traumatised child. The baby may have learnt to demand attention with high-level screaming or become passive due to lack of response. Eventually, if no one comes, baby moves into withdrawal and apathy. The child can become desensitised to feelings of pain, hunger and discomfort like a nappy that needed changing hours ago.

  I worked in an orphanage many moons ago, and there was an eight-month-old baby who never sat up. When the doctor came to do check-ups, he asked, 'Who plays with this baby?' There was silence, and the doctor said, 'This child has no incentive to sit up.' I thought it was one of the saddest things I had ever heard.

  As the child grows up with abuse/neglect, they learn to scan for danger, to be alert to changes or any opportunity for care or food. This high alert will continue to increase if no intervention is made, and uses up essential energy that is needed for development of new skills and experiences.

- **Self-regulation:** This is a solo endeavour for the neglected child. Their fears and tantrums are unheard, so without help to manage emotions and changes, they are at the mercy of their immediate feelings. The adults who live with them may be very dysregulated and suffer from mood swings and temper fits, especially if substance abuse is involved, so modelling of self-regulation is not there. The responses of carers to baby/child needs are unreliable or absent. As the child grows, they are often stuck in survival, old 'reptilian' brain states, overwhelmed by feelings or in freeze apathy mode. This slows down their learning about themselves and others and has detrimental effects on their social development.

- **Social emotional skills:** The issues connected with serious life problems block the baby/child's development of relationships. Family isolation is common in domestic violence households as there are secrets to protect. Addiction brings poverty, the rage of withdrawals or a zoned-out state for the addicts and their family. Substance abuse brings criminal activity to the house, buyers, sellers or very nasty debt collectors. Exploring the environment and building relationships are scary activities for the child in this scenario. The endemic problems that go with extreme poverty may affect the carer's availability to play with and enjoy their child, as their own survival struggles to keep the home going are exhausting. The ability to make friends is based on secure attachment as major research by Sroufe and Siegel found (4):

Those with secure histories are liked best. This finding can be best understood by recognizing that early attachments create social expectations in children, and may incline them to see the present in terms of negative past experiences. For such children, their attachment history can become a self-fulfilling prophecy as they behave toward new people in their lives – like peers or teachers – in ways that reproduce old, negative relationships. Teachers, too, with no knowledge of the child's history, treat children in the different categories of attachment differently. (pp.5–6)

- **Cognition:** The traumatised child is using their energy for survival and has adapted neural pathways in the brain to maximise alertness and escape patterns. The solid base to build knowledge and understanding of the world in stages is not available, and so the child's development can be slowed down as energy for new growth and learning is diverted to the old/reptilian brain concerned with survival. The stress chemicals that flood the system are designed for response to a crisis, not for continual use. Cortisol, for example, is harmful to the organs such as the liver, and the child's health can be damaged by toxic stress. That is defined as overwhelming and ongoing experiences that the system cannot cope with (2).

The abused pupil brings their trauma and resulting behaviours to school or centre with them as shown in the following story of a teenage girl, a victim of sexual abuse.

What does trauma look like in the classroom?

It often looks very angry.

The first time I met Lee, aged 16, was the first day of 'Life Skills' sessions in Youthreach. My reflexes are fast from years of dodging spit balls and other missiles, so when I had to turn my back for a second, I dodged the heavy book she flung at me. This was followed by a stream of abuse – 'What would you know, f---ng stuck up b---? Some nerve coming in here to tell us what to do. You can go and f--- off.'

She stormed off to the office to complain about whatever had triggered her in my introduction to the work.

We had a meeting the next day, where she explained that something I said about communications gave her the idea that I would be asking loads of 'nosey questions'. I explained that it was a skills-based session, not a counselling approach, and she agreed to give it a try.

As I got to know Lee, her story unfolded. She had been sexually abused for several years by a trusted family member. Her mother was disgusted and angry with Lee when she disclosed to her – she told Lee it was shameful to make up stories about such things.

This second betrayal pushed her over the edge, and she went wild, taking drugs, dropping out of school and having tantrums at home. Then she was referred to psychiatric services who diagnosed her with borderline personality disorder and started a drug regime to control her behaviour. This led to 12 months in a psychiatric ward as she fought, sometimes violently, against the system.

By the time she came to Youthreach, she was very angry and suspicious of everyone, and had only come to us as an alternative to a hospital stay. Lee had received no real education since she was 13 years old, so was very self-conscious about her low literacy and maths levels. This led to more raging outbursts. It took weeks for her to become accustomed to the individual approach we took to the work, which let each person go at their own pace.

What does trauma look like in the classroom?

> The group got used to the Life Skills class and gave me the name of 'the headwrecker', which I decided to take as a compliment! We discussed lots of issues and ideas, always generally or in the third person. The understanding was that if you wanted some personal referral, you waited behind to tidy up. Lee settled into the centre, made friends and gradually began, grudgingly, to trust the staff.
>
> Sadly, she couldn't sustain this when she left our centre, and her life was very unhappy and problem-saturated.
>
> I often thought of her years later and what her life could have been if she had been heard and supported at her first disclosure.

Note: I want to emphasise that these cases I present are extreme situations with consistent and dangerous levels of neglect. Parents of all types and backgrounds have bad days and feel like a failure and a bad parent. As my tutor on a family support training programme said to me a long time ago: 'No one sets out to be a bad parent and wreck their children's lives – most people want to be good parents and have a happy family.'

Equally, nobody declares that their life ambition is to become an addict and have their children taken into care. I struggled in my work to be empathic to parents who neglected and ill-treated their children because of addiction, and I often repeated these words like a mantra when dealing with hungry, dirty, angry children. I realised that so many addicts were traumatised themselves and were unable to care for their children. One grandmother raising a family for her daughter said in one of the family groups: 'Sure, God help them, they are all lost – the whole lot of them. Can't help themselves.' Her kindness and understanding were healing for me. The psychiatrist Gabor Maté, who has worked with addicts for decades, maintains that every addict he has worked with has suffered trauma and uses drugs to self-medicate the pain. His video (5) explains this very clearly.

Eimear, a family therapist working in an underserved area, finds these extremes of behaviour in the young people she works with. From apathy in one pupil:

> *Parent is in prison. She is being cared for by a sibling. She presents as feeling very depressed, not very interested and not very motivated to get out of bed in the morning, to come to school. All she wants to do is to go home, to go back to bed . . .*

To anger and challenging behaviour in school for another:

> Trust and attachment issues would be very prevalent with him, and he has awkward behaviour in school. Yeah, in his own words, he holds [grudges] so if the teacher asks him to take out his book, he will retort with something, and then he gets in a fight, and he will hate that teacher for the rest of his life and make a point of not behaving for that teacher, because he finds it hard to do that rupture, repair, yeah. And so yeah, we're working with him. On the whole concept of forgiveness, on who suffers the most in a situation and conflict resolution and anger management.

Section 2: The six principles of trauma-informed practice (TIP)

These principles are designed to guide educators and other support staff in learning about trauma effects, signs and triggers and are based on the approach of SAMHSA (1). The aim is to reduce triggers for retraumatisation and enable healing and recovery for those affected by trauma. In Chapter 3, where the focus is on building a safe environment, there will be strategies and activities for primary school through to adult education.

Safety

What is safety or a safe environment? It is different for each person, but there are common essential elements in the educational space.

1. Physically: Is the place warm/cool enough and fit for purpose? Are the other learners safe to be around?
2. Psychologically: Am I treated with kindness, accepted as I am? Is the educator consistent and welcoming?
3. Learning approaches: Do I know what is happening and in what sequence?

It is important to remember that in every group some people, and in many groups the majority, will have experienced trauma which damages safety at a deep conscious and unconscious level. Every person and every group is different, so the important thing is to be aware of participants' needs, both seen and unseen.

'You can only know if people tell you.' I worked on a personal development programme for a homeless charity, and on the final day, the group voted for a trip to the bowling alley for their outing. Mostly middle-aged men, some were now settled in hostels, some were still homeless. After an hour, a little group approached me: 'We need help.' 'What's happened? Has someone fallen?' 'No. Can you bring us to the toilet; they won't let us in.' The badge of homelessness was visible even though we were paying customers. I felt saddened and touched that they could share it with me.

Trust

This is another concept we use without examining it. How is trust built up? How do we know we trust another person?

1. Physically: Is my personal space respected? Is it clear what I need to bring and where I am to be seated or standing?
2. Psychologically: Is there a clear contract as to our purpose here and how we will approach it?
3. Learning approaches: Are my needs met? When I am struggling, am I supported without judgement? When I get upset and frustrated, am I met with understanding and given the space I need?

Trauma breaks trust, so rebuilding it in the group is vital and needs to be done at the individual's and group's pace, with small steps and lots of feedback from the learners about how they experience the group process and their learning.

'All the teachers were looking weird at me or being extra nice.' A teenager told me how he had shared about alcoholism in his home affecting his work and happiness with his class teacher. The next day, the other teachers were either embarrassed or over-nice, so he felt they all knew his business, and his trust was violated.

Choice

By its nature, trauma removes choice from the person affected, whether it is globally by war or individually by abuse. How am I experiencing choice in this class group?

1. Physically: Can I select my own seat and leave the room without comment if I need to?
2. Psychologically: Is it easy for me to choose my level of engagement and decline some aspects of the group work?
3. Learning approaches: Am I offered choices in methods of presenting and completing tasks?

> *I realised this is ridiculous – an assigned 'toilet break' for adults. So, I suggested everybody take a 20-minute break during the class when it suited them. Stress was massively reduced, and interaction increased as people shared information and chatted in smaller groups.* (Adult tutor of computers)

Collaboration

Collaboration builds peer support in the group.

1. Physically: Does the room layout encourage mixing? Is it possible to move around?
2. Psychologically: Are there efforts or activities to help the group to integrate? Are there cooperative or team projects or tasks?
3. Learning approaches: Are we encouraged to support each other and share our learning? Are individual contributions that reach beyond the classroom respected and utilised?

I often made *wall friezes of a word chosen by the group, with each person selecting a letter to decorate. The frieze was then laminated and put on the wall. This simple task led to lots of sharing of materials and ideas, and those who could do curly or bubble writing were in high demand. Small steps start to build a safe, trusting atmosphere in the group.

Empowerment

Trauma and abuse can leave the person very withdrawn or aggressive and suspicious of others' motives. Empowerment tries to restore choice at all levels, both in the class itself and reaching beyond to leisure, further education, community organisations and other adult groups. The aim is to increase

What does trauma look like in the classroom?

participation in the wider society and grow understanding of rights, responsibilities and possibilities.

1. Physically: Does the environment encourage my engagement and opinion about layout and interaction?
2. Psychologically: Do I feel a valued equal member of this group, even though my academic standard may be low? Is there sharing of resources and engagement with appropriate activities and opportunities beyond this room?
3. Learning approaches: Are my life skills and experience valued and utilised in formulating tasks? Is my review taken after activities?

The visual and interactive***assertiveness programme 'Happy head, aggro head and sad head'** that I used with all my groups showed great results with all ages.

Once, when I was with a group of older lads, we were asked to leave the National Museum for no reason other than they were obviously 'townies' as inner-city locals were called. As we left, one of the lads said to me, 'How do you think we felt getting chucked out like that? It was very embarrassing.' They wrote an excellent letter, which resulted in an apology and a private tour of the Museum, with books gifted to our library.

Cultural consideration

What does this mean in this classroom? How do I as a tutor know about the needs and sensitivities of others? How do I find out what these issues are? How can a student safely share cultural customs or religious observances?

1. Physically: Is the area receptive to the needs of others concerning placement of genders and gender equality? Is the student system facilitating identification choices around gender and ethnicity?
2. Psychologically: Do others understand my cultural issues with things like asking questions or critical analysis of the tutor's work?
3. Learning approaches: Do they make space for my standard of English, my struggles to read slides that are too fast, or my difficulties with sitting still for long periods because of anxiety?

A young student in my group didn't want to attend an event as it was Ramadan and they were fasting. When this arose, I made a general comment about it being Ramadan in reference to a newspaper article. Later, at the event, it was easy for the student to refuse refreshment with an occasional reminder to classmates that they were fasting.

Effects of trauma – how they appear

Physical

Trauma can stunt physical growth and damage cognitive development as energy is diverted to surviving rather than thriving. The alarm button is on all the time. Physical effects of trauma include digestive problems caused by anxiety, disturbed sleep, headaches, somatic effects like aches, pains and skin problems, and delayed growth in the frontal lobes, the thinking areas of the brain. The trigger reactions to traumatic memories lodged in the body can appear as panic attacks. Trauma is lodged in the body and shows a range of physical and psychological effects; many of these are unconscious reactions beyond the control of the person affected (6).

Psychosocial

The learning of trusting relationships and the attachment to a safe adult that lets the child explore the world with all its senses are the basis of social emotional growth (4). When this is lacking, the ability to form intimate connections can be harmed into adulthood. Emotional literacy in recognising one's own feelings and reading those of others can be limited. This causes difficulty in engaging with peers and joining group activities or taking direction from authority.

This social interaction is where we all learn about life and ourselves in the world, and it is ongoing through the life span. If trauma has occurred, this ability to reach out to others and return to a safe base is damaged into adult life (as seen in ACEs research). According to Dr Gabor Maté (7), caring relationships are necessary for a healthy life.

Neurological

The brain forms neural pathways, which are the way a child learns and forms connections and understanding of the world. The most used will be the most developed; new pathways are formed by building on new and known

What does trauma look like in the classroom?

experiences. The child who is traumatised has narrower scope for expanding learning and understanding. They develop over-reliance on the survival or reptilian brain, which operates the fight, flight or freeze (FFF) response. Neurological development is the wiring aspect of the brain and is closely related to emotional development and security (3). If the old or reptilian brain systems are humming on high alert, the cognitive part, the thinking brain, is switched off, and reflection is limited as behaviour is dictated by primitive emotional responses. These are called survival mechanisms for a reason! If two inhabited caves were attacked by wild animals, which clan survived? The ones having a meeting to plan strategy or the ones hurling brands from the fire and any weapons to hand while roaring and screeching?

Developmental

Research finds that the most damage is done by trauma that happens during the intensive growth period of infancy (0–3 years), as this is a period of tremendous growth and physical and psychological learning for the child. Developmental trauma occurs over a period of time and is believed to be the worst when it happens during infancy or adolescence. However, as each stage of the child's life has important skills and experiences for them to learn, it seems clear that the damage continues through childhood. The effects in all the areas will be intensified by the repetitive nature of the trauma, giving no time to recover or process the horrible experiences. The nature of development is that it is interwoven and builds one stage on another. As Figure 2.2 showed, if the baby's needs for comfort, food and love are not met, secure attachment to a carer is missing. The young child is then affected at the next stage of responding to others' sounds and movements, starting to laugh and smile and enjoy relationships with family and friends. If these first stages are not happening for the traumatised or abused child, their development of social skills and learning about the world continues to be restricted. The later stages of the development of the frontal cortex will be limited and damaged by trauma. The traumatised child is working from the fear and survival brain level.

The environment magnifies the effects, or they are embedded in the life story of the family

The traumatised child suffers all these effects, intensified by the family and community they live in. Studies of resilience have shown that living in areas that are underserved and seriously affected by drugs, poverty, crime and unemployment make individual effects of trauma much worse (8):

> In a body of emerging research with human caregivers, studies have shown that when families are faced with stressful psychosocial and physical conditions within the home, parents are at greater risk for becoming less sensitive and warm in their patterns of early caregiving. In turn, lower level of maternal sensitivity increases the likelihood that children will demonstrate elevated cortisol levels and lower executive function ability, with commensurate difficulty regulating emotion and behavior. Notably, however, just as early caregiving functions in a mediating role as a conduit for stressors in the environment, it also functions as a moderator, or a buffer of stress. To be sure, many families provide high levels of sensitive and nurturing caregiving despite the struggle to make ends meet. (p.5)

The early adolescent period is another time of significant development, physical and psychological, so it is another time where interventions and supports can be very effective in healing some of the negative effects of early life trauma (9). Whereas puberty and cognitive development are largely biologically determined, the greater part of psychological and social development will depend on environmental and sociocultural influences. In non-Western cultures, the social and psychological domains may be markedly truncated (p.302).

Some patterns of behaviours that are trauma-based

The range of behaviours commonly goes from hyper-alert, easily triggered to panic, aggression or flight, to withdrawal, low energy, lack of engagement, social isolation and self-blame. Trauma has caused a major breakdown in trust and relationships for the victims, whether in a one-to-one situation, a family, an ethnic group or a population subjected to exclusion, attack, natural disaster or war.

These experiences can result in major outbursts over something that appears trivial, a heightened sense of threat so a casual remark is met with aggression, and violent responses to personal comments made by others (10).

The lack of confidence and security leads to a reluctance to take part in the group and the person's use of confrontation to avoid exposure. Lower standards in literacy, due to disrupted schooling, could make reading-based activities embarrassing and lead to challenging behaviour in class that is intended to avoid shame at exposing a lack of academic skills. Low self-esteem and self-blame for the violence in the family may be part of the pupil's makeup. A young person on a support programme for domestic violence victims that was the subject of my PhD thesis (11), said: 'I used to think maybe it [the domestic violence] was my fault for getting born or something.'

Trauma effects in the classroom/ training situation

What does it mean for my work?

The most important thing is that children and young people affected by trauma can be supported and enabled to recover and heal. The plasticity of the brain means that positive relationships and experiences can help build new neural pathways that enable learning and happier living. In the midst of rather depressing statistics and research on trauma, TIP is a light in the dark.

Steele and Malchiodi (12) emphasise that working with trauma victims to develop their personal strengths and the ability to resolve challenges and find equilibrium is an individual process. There are essential stages of recovery, but each person will have different needs and experiences. The type of supports that are effective and the pace of development are all unique to the person.

The approach of TIP can be adapted to each situation. There is a lot of research on TIP that is specifically aimed at therapists or those working mainly with traumatised groups. This book explores the aspects of TIP that will work in conjunction with social emotional learning (SEL) principles for mainstream classes or specialised groups. CASEL is the original organisation that promoted SEL in the USA. Their website has a huge amount of useful material. There are videos, publications, class sessions, tips and reviews (13). SEL principles are compatible with the well-being and Social Personal Health Education (SPHE) curriculum in Ireland (14). The approach in the UK shows a lot of research into SEL and its effectiveness by foundations such as the Education Endowment Foundation (EEF). The connection between socioeconomic disadvantage and less effective SEL skills is highlighted in the report of the EEF (15). SEL principles are the foundation of programmes in Ireland and the UK:

SEL interventions seek to improve pupils' decision-making skills, interaction with others and their self-management of emotions, rather than focusing directly on the academic or cognitive elements of learning (16).

The TIP approach also aligns with this approach as it also looks for compassion, and supportive relationships with students in the classroom. Some trauma-informed educators suggest that SEL is not useful for those affected by trauma as SEL requires conscious engagement, and the traumatised person may be offline to this and stuck in emotional states or holding trauma in the body. However, there are many useful activities and ideas on CASEL's site, and they offer seminars that have developed more awareness about trauma, so SEL is a good place to start.

In the TIP approach to discipline, a working outcome is sought, rather than the application of an exclusion-type sanction. Behaviour is communication, according to Treisman (10).

All the examples are from my own work with tutors, pupil groups, individuals and out-of-school pupils, and trainees on alternative education schemes. All the details are changed.

In this section looking at trauma in the classroom, the divisions are a guide for easy reading as all the different effects and behaviours vary for each person and often overlap. Physical challenges for the pupils include issues with kit and school equipment, which are often a trigger for disruption and the path to suspension and early school leaving as a common outcome.

Section 3: Trauma in the classroom through the ages

Issues emerging in the classroom

The preschool child may have formed strong carer-type attachment to the preschool staff, which is a loss to them on moving to primary school. This may affect their integration into primary school where they may be acting out, due to feeling unsafe, or remain very guarded and withdrawn. Either way, traumatised children start primary school with major disadvantages. Their social and friendship skills may be patchy, with aggression as defense, or a lack of interest in joining with others. Their cognitive development will have suffered setbacks at the physical level, and their range of life experiences may be more limited than those of other children. Very young children are already aware of their lack of quality school equipment, clothes and outings as they hear others talking about weekend trips and see their new outfits.

Primary school

Trauma effects appear in the classroom

Physical

The neglected child will appear untidy, sometimes dirty, often hungry and lacking basic equipment or payments for school trips. Their ability to focus and remember things using short-term memory is very often damaged (12). This makes it difficult to retain and follow instructions and can appear as deliberate defiance or disruption. Refusal to be seated or remove a coat or change into sportswear can be a combination of the actual lack of appropriate gear and fear of losing items in frequent moves and changes. It can also be related to experiences of physical or sexual abuse. Trauma triggers and flashbacks are part of body memory; these can produce sudden uncontrollable responses for the victim to random triggers that are not in their conscious memory or control (6).

Example: Challenging behaviour

Mary, aged five, and her six-year-old brother John join the class a few weeks late. The teacher is under pressure to get 27 five- and six-year-olds into some semblance of group order, listening, cooperating and learning from a packed curriculum. The teacher offers the children a welcome, shows them their seats and asks them to hang up their coats. Both children refuse point-blank to hang up their coats. When the teacher tries to coax them and help them to open their coats, they become very distressed, and Mary kicks her teacher. John uses abusive language and refuses to sit down; the whole class is upset, and the teacher is at a loss.

> **Reflective questions**
> - What might be the cause of their refusal?
> - How could it be handled differently?

A current support worker shared that:

Mary is always in trouble in the yard and last week was wrongly blamed. She was very agitated and sat on the floor beside the blackboard and refused to sit in her seat. Everybody became focused on making her sit down, which she refused. The class teacher, the special needs assistant (SNA) and another teacher got involved. There was 40 minutes of chaos, and she still wouldn't budge. I thought it would be better to just leave her sitting on the floor and start class, or using the TIP approach just ask her 'What happened?'

Psychological

The confidence that permits the child to explore the environment and make new discoveries needs a secure base of attachment to reach from and return to. Development is built on stage by stage, and the stages are all interlinked. If this early essential attachment and care has been lacking for the child, their view of the world and other people tends to be suspicious, fearful, withdrawn or aggressive. Their survival in the places that should be safe – home and family –may depend on endless alertness to threat or aggression (12). Their ability to trust and interact with other pupils can be limited.

Example: Withdrawn behaviour

Kylie is very withdrawn and responds to questions about things she likes or invitations to play with sullen refusals or mean comments. The senior infants have stopped asking her to play and she is becoming

What does trauma look like in the classroom?

more isolated and aggressive. The teacher tried a few inclusive strategies like the 'I want to play' bench and also a group skipping game. Kylie tripped over the rope and got very angry with the others and refused to play anymore.

Reflective questions

- What might be behind this behaviour?
- What might the teacher try as a way of getting her involved with the others?

Psychosocial

The ability to read body language and respond to other children's games and conversations is lessened by trauma, so that simple interactions or comments are often read as aggressive. The traumatised child may find it hard to understand simple social signals from peers and adults. This emotional literacy is very damaged by being ill-treated or neglected by adult carers. As it is through relationships that we are programmed to learn skills and grow in confidence, this lack affects all aspects of development, including academic progress.

Example: Challenging behaviour

The teacher turns around to find Jack and Trish rolling on the floor. Trish is scratching and kicking, and Jack seems shocked. The teacher tries to reason with them, to no avail, Trish is hysterically crying by now. The teacher eventually uses the agreed signal for everyone to stop activities, and they stop long enough to extricate the two of them. He sends Jack to the nurse for his scratches and asks the SNA to take Trish to the sensory room till lunchtime. She is led away sobbing uncontrollably. Trish's mother is sent for; her granny comes to school, and Trish is suspended for four days.

> **Reflective questions**
>
> - What might have been the trigger for Trish?
> - What other approaches might have been helpful (while acknowledging that the class must remain a safe place for all the pupils)?

Neurological

The development of the brain, for both cognitive and social skills, depends on the building of neural pathways. The system is designed to explore new experiences and expand the range of knowledge and responses by means of new connections and pathways in the brain. If this development is restricted by the child being stuck in primitive, reptilian brain survival, their cognitive ability and memory will be negatively affected. The combination of the high-adrenalin fear response and the lesser ability to focus has a detrimental effect on academic ability.

> **Example: Difficulty with focus**
>
> Luke gets very angry when asked to complete any mathematics task. Even when the teacher sets him something he is capable of, he gets very upset if he can't do it straight away, and he throws equipment around the room in a tantrum. The teacher has tried small-group work and using materials such as blocks or beads for his calculations, but she is very discouraged. In consultation with the special needs teacher (SNT), they agree to drop the maths for a fortnight and let him join her 'settling into school group' for two hours each day. In this group, the SNT focuses on creating a safe atmosphere in a small group of four to six children. They play games that help with self-regulation and learning about feelings and emotions. A number of active games and movements from brain gym (17) help the pupils to concentrate. After two weeks, the pupils rejoin their class on a phased system and go to the SNT for occasional extra support.

> **Reflective questions**
>
> - Do you think this will be helpful? What else could the class teacher do?
> - Why might this work for Luke?

Secondary school

Trauma effects appear in the classroom

Secondary school hits young people who are unsupported like a train wreck. The demands of changing class, having so much more equipment, dealing with so many teachers who are strangers can see school drop-out starting in the first year and ending with leaving in the second year before Christmas. I have had so many meetings with parents, class teachers and the principal where the teachers are recounting impossible behaviours and the parent is saying, 'But . . . I never had this trouble before; s/he was fine in primary school.' Adolescence is a time of significant change according to a study by the National Academies of Sciences in Washington (18):

> Adolescence is a particularly dynamic period of brain development, second only to infancy in the extent and significance of the neural changes that occur. The nature of these changes – in brain structures, functions, and connectivity – allows for a remarkable amount of developmental plasticity unique to this period of life, making adolescents amenable to change. (Introduction)

These changes – physical, emotional, and social, with the addition of hormonal changes – find many young people who managed in primary school struggle in secondary. Primary school – with the structured day and a teacher who often filled in gaps for equipment and extras – offered more support. Young children tend to enjoy going to withdrawal for extra reading or social skills groups, while teenagers find it embarrassing and feel 'stupid' going out for individual classes. This can make offering support very tricky at secondary level.

Physical

The pupil may be small for their age and often without lunch or equipment, including sports clothes. Hygiene can be of a low standard. Attendance, particularly in the second year, could be very poor, interspersed with suspension. The pupil already has a foot out the door. A teacher said to me once: 'We don't like you because you keep on bringing back the pupils we want to be rid of.' One of my club members had a very late night as her mother had returned from prison. She came into school as she had promised to take part in a group presentation. She was sent home for having the wrong shoes on.

Traumatised pupils may often say they are very tired and put their head down on the desk and disengage from the class. They could be lacking all equipment, and even when equipment is supplied, it doesn't come back to school. Living conditions can be unstable, with nights spent at different family members' or friends' homes. Literacy and numeracy could be well below class standard. The student could be very dreamy, seemingly in their own world, or acting as a bully disrupting class and jeering at others.

Example: Challenging behaviour

Leo was very quick-witted but often cruelly, at the expense of others. It was a class with many pupils affected by trauma and difficult living situations, and a lot of time was being lost on rows or near fights in the classroom, many instigated by Leo. His academic ability was much lower than his class, and he often started trouble during any activity that was challenging for him. The teacher decided to run a team-building programme using a double class period for six weeks. The mix of active games and small group tasks enabled the group to let off steam and get to know each other.

Reflective questions

- How might this programme help to address Leo's problems?
- What else could the teacher have done?
- What activities and what boundaries might you need with a difficult class?

Psychological

The abused or traumatised pupil will see the world as a dangerous place he or she faces alone. This is the root of the aggressive behaviour and the lack of trust in others. Particularly if addiction, mental health or domestic violence are involved, home life will be chaotic, unpredictable and violent. The teenager is acutely image-conscious and struggles with shame and secrecy about their family life. The student may be in the role of carer to younger siblings or their parent, leaving little energy for schoolwork or leisure. Risk-taking behaviours are also an issue. ACEs research showed higher rates of addiction and challenging behaviours in young people affected by trauma. Eggleston and colleagues (19) found many more pupils from disadvantaged backgrounds were getting regular suspensions, leading in many cases to dropout and getting mixed up in minor criminality, which then led to jail.

Example: Withdrawn from class

Shannon is often late, looks exhausted and rarely has her homework done even though she is very capable. She never hangs out after school or goes to any of the after-school clubs. She resists all offers of help, saying that everything is fine at home; her mum has just had the flu, so she has to bring the kids to school. The teacher asks the support worker to check out facilities for after-school clubs for the younger ones in the primary school. Then she invites Shannon to join a science and art club that meets after school. The other day that the younger ones are busy, Shannon does her homework in the school library.

Reflective questions

- How was this supportive for Shannon? Was there anything else the teacher could do?

Psychosocial

The difficulty in making relationships is compounded by teenage self-consciousness. The student who lacks a sense of identity and self-worth is vulnerable to all kinds of peer pressure and is at higher risk for risky behaviour of all types according to ACEs research (20). The need to be heard can show up as class clown or class bully. The young person can gain a bad reputation that is very hard to shift.

Example: Labelled as troublemakers

These second-year students were called the 'worst class in the school' and were banned from every league and club in the school, so, of course, they were my class. It was a small class but very difficult to work with due to constant 'messing' and damage to the equipment. One day, a video I showed of the damage done by a huge hurricane sparked their interest. They asked if they could have a cake sale to raise money. Dire warnings were issued by all staff as to the chaos that would ensue and the risk of having money in the room. In the end, the cake sale was a huge success. In the review of the event, five of the wildest lads told me how they had come across a lad getting 'hammered' and kicked in the hallway and had chased off the bullies earlier in the year. However, they were standing there when the teacher came and they got the blame. Due to the seriousness of the assault, they were assigned to my class and banned from contact sports; following the local code on 'rats', they never spoke up. After this, I explained the injustice, without naming the actual bullies (a condition insisted on by the five lads), to the principal. They rejoined the football league, which was followed by a huge improvement in effort and attention in class.

Reflective questions

- Why was this so important for the five lads? Was there more the teacher could have done?
- How could you challenge this culture of taking blame for others and not being a 'rat'?

Neurological

Short-term memory and the ability to focus and follow sequences are badly affected by trauma. This can lead to frustration for those who engage or work with the young person who often seems inattentive and keeps asking the same question or making the same mistake. Attempts to help or fix the mistake can be met with indifference or aggression. This is the age for trying so hard to be different that you are the same as everybody else! Adolescence is also a period of all types of development. Neural pathways can be extended or reduced in intensity as a form of 'pruning' of these neural pathways takes place. This is why adolescence is often seen as a useful time to make supportive interventions for young people affected by trauma.

Example: Difficulty in focus and recall

In an exam class, one pupil, Terry, aged 17, keeps interrupting and holding up the class with repeat questions. He is a loner and doesn't mix with the rest of them. The others are getting impatient and annoyed as deadlines are not met. One student, Jenny, pointed out to the teacher, 'In my last school, there was one guy with all sorts of stuff he couldn't cope with – like bangs, balloons, fluttery curtains – loads of stuff; but we all knew about it, so we could look out for him. What's the story with Terry?'

The teacher thanked the student for her thoughtfulness and tried a few new approaches for Terry. He provided visual charts of the sections of the work that would be covered and started a revolving buddy system, working in pairs to review the work.

Reflective questions

- Would this be useful for Terry? What else could the teacher do?
- How can you know when to share information about a student's needs?

Adult education

Trauma effects appear in the classroom

Physical

Community-based adult education can be a very different group from the students who return to postgraduate courses to pursue an interest or promotion at work as adults. For most adults returning to education, managing technology will be a challenge. Community-based adult education includes many marginalised groups such as people without a home, those in recovery from addiction, and refugees and asylum seekers, among others. Family responsibilities, physical care, nutritional needs and the effects of addiction can make attendance and participation challenging for many adult learners. High anxiety and ongoing worry about other family members are part of the life of the refugee or asylum seeker. Somatic complaints such as stomach ache and headaches can be an expression of these issues. One tutor established links with local support services and provided information about services such as counselling and homeless supports to the group.

> **Reflective questions**
>
> - What can the teacher/tutor do to encourage attendance?
> - Have you had these challenges?
> - How can you support pupils in foster care or homeless accommodation?

Psychological

Among adult learners, tutors find that anxiety is the greatest challenge. Very difficult life situations cause ongoing high stress and anxiety, and previous trauma can cause fear and panic reactions for many adult learners. Confidence in trying new things and learning new skills can be very low, and asking for help may not be easy, as adults are attempting to learn new and sometimes complex skills. One tutor teaching IT changed the format of his class: he set some tasks and then, after a brief explanation, he moved round the class and worked with groups of two and three students, rather than delivering the information from the front of the room.

> **Reflective questions**
>
> - What other ways can we reduce learner anxiety? Why was this useful?
> - How can the tutor know if a student's difficulty is academic or anxiety-based?

Psychosocial

Adapting to a new culture with all the social mores and educational styles is challenging for all adult learners. Whatever their background, the return to education can be frightening. Many adults returning have had very negative experiences of education, left school early and have not been in a classroom since they were children. Learning new skills can be frustrating, and resilience to try again may be low, leading to dropout from the class. The social interaction may be hard for those lacking confidence and with low self-esteem. One tutor of English changed his approach to let language groups sit together, contrary to popular belief that they should be separated to increase immersion in English. Anxiety was instantly reduced, and there was laughter as the groups compared the meanings of words in their language and small groups supported each other in trying out English phrases.

> **Reflective questions**
>
> - Why was this approach effective? What else can be done?

Neurological

Adults affected by any kind of trauma will have suffered effects on their ability to focus and remember things. So previous educational experiences, such as being labelled stupid, may have added to their trauma. For those who have sought refuge from war, triggers such as loud noises or yelling can lead to flashbacks, and the urge to seek cover is instinctive. A Ukrainian refugee was woken terrified by the sound of the planes flying over Dublin, en route to an airshow. A text reassured him that it was not a bombing raid. Open communication from the learners and review of ongoing work and logistics in the classroom will help the tutor to be aware of possible triggers.

> **Reflective questions**
>
> - What action can a tutor take to reduce possible trauma triggers in the classroom?
> - There are physical noises and activities and also social anxiety. How can you reduce these?

Regular reviews of the group process and the pace of the work are the way to find out what is important for your learners and to become aware of different issues. The practice of being available to greet students individually allows time for a student to inform you of a particular need or worry that they have. As the students become familiar with the ongoing feedback loop, they will gain confidence in your commitment to the process. It is important to be open and consistent about what can and can't be changed, either in the physical environment or the course work.

Important factors are creating calm, reducing stress, supporting emotional regulation to increase concentration and involvement in the class group and the work, and aiming for balance to reduce fight, flight or freeze (FFF) response.

Application of the key principles developed by SAMHSA for all ages

These guiding principles overlap and develop as they become part of daily practice.

Benefits

- A friendly atmosphere reduces anxiety and promotes learning.
- Ongoing review allows for asking questions easily – even difficult ones.
- Learner feedback helps in modifying/delivering material effectively.
- The use of reflection and review builds confidence and engagement for students.
- Respect spreads in the peer group, and support in shared learning and social skills grows.

Challenges

- Uncertainty for staff about how to begin this approach.
- Concern about pressures of curriculum/lack of time.
- Boundary issues – inappropriate disclosures that educators are unable to deal with.
- Overwhelming expectations of students that teachers can solve all their problems.
- Other staff seeing this method as giving in to bad behaviour/time wasting.

Start with small steps. TIP awareness teaches us that some people in any group will have suffered separation, bereavement, violence or neglect. In some groups we are aware by their nature that trauma incidence is very high. For example, groups affected by addiction, homelessness, refugee experiences and marginalised groups. For many adult learners returning to education is frightening due to negative and humiliating experiences in early school years. It is impossible to be aware of every trigger to trauma for your group. You can reduce the level in the physical and social environment and then depend on your group feedback to inform you.

Environment

- **Warm welcome.** Tutors of primary, second level and third level reported big improvements in the atmosphere of their groups from taking the first few minutes to greet students by name and have a general chat about the day and the work in hand.
- **Arrange the furniture to reflect the atmosphere.** The students of all ages can select the arrangement of furniture in small groups, or circle as appropriate to the work.

- **Mix with the group and sit down with them when possible.** If you are at the top of the room because of the projector or white board sit among the group for short periods. One tutor suggested the students draw out a room plan for the furniture, and they tried it out to gain greater engagement and social interaction.
- **Avoid loud noises.** If there are timed bells that sound or fire alarms or local events such as building or drilling warn the students.

Key points of Chapter 2

- Case studies of how trauma-linked behaviour can show itself in the classroom.
- The six principles of TIP, and what they can mean for the students in the classroom.
- Child's stages of development – how trauma affects each stage and impacts learning.
- Trauma effects on development – examples of different age groups and how they may act.
- Trauma in the classroom – some case study examples from primary, secondary and adult education.

References

1. Substance Abuse and Mental Health Services Administration. SAMHSA's Concept of Trauma and Guidance for a Trauma-Informed Approach. Rockville, MD: Substance Abuse and Mental Health Services Administration; 2014.
2. NHS Education for Sctoland. Transforming psychological trauma: A knowledge and skills framework for the Scottish workforce. Scotland: NHS Education for Scotland, Government of Scotland; 2017.
3. Committee on Integrating the Science of Early Childhood Development – Board on Children Youth and Families. From neurons to neighborhoods: The science of early child development. Shonkoff JP, Phillips D, editors. Washington: National Academy Press; 2000.
4. Sroufe A, Siegel D. The verdict is in: The case for attachment theory. Psychotherapy Networker. 2011 (March).
5. Maté G. Addiction is not a choice – it is a response to human suffering; 2020. www.youtube.com/watch?v=ys6TCO_olOc
6. van der Kolk BA. The body keeps the score. USA: Viking Penguin; 2015.

7. Maté G. The Power of Saying NO; 2022. www.youtube.com/watch?v=x6l-eJNvqAY
8. Blair C, Raver CC. Poverty, Stress, and Brain Development: New Directions for Prevention and Intervention. Acad Pediatr. 2016;16(3 Suppl):S30–6.
9. Christie D, Viner R. Adolescent development. British Medical Journal. 2005;330(7486):301–4.
10. Treisman K. Working with relational and developmental trauma in children and adolescents. London: Routledge; 2017.
11. Sweetman N. A Culture of Silence: A study of a social emotional learning (SEL) intervention for teenagers affected by domestic violence. [PhD]. Trinity College Dublin; 2019. www.tara.tcd.ie/handle/2262/86088
12. Steele W, Malchiodi CA. Trauma-informed practices with children and adolescents. New York: Taylor and Francis; 2012.
13. CASEL. CASEL – implementation of SEL in the classroom USA; 2024. https://casel.org/systemic-implementation/sel-in-the-classroom
14. Department of Education & Science, NCCA. Social, Personal & Health Education: Junior Cycle syllabus. Dublin: Stationery Office; 2000.
15. Education Endowment Foundation, UK; https://educationendowmentfoundation.org.uk/2025
16. Education Endowment Foundation. Social and emotional learning UK; 2021. https://educationendowmentfoundation.org.uk/education-evidence/teaching-learning-toolkit/social-and-emotional-learning
17. Little People's Montessori Pre-School. Fun Brain Gym exercises and routines for children: Little People's Montessori Pre-School; 2022. www.youtube.com/watch?v=q-e0E1V5Ls4
18. National Academies of Sciences E, and Medicine; Health and Medicine Division; Division of Behavioral and Social Sciences and Education; Board on Children, Youth, and Families; Committee on the Neurobiological and Socio-behavioral Science of Adolescent Development and Its Applications. 2. Adolescent Development. In: Bonnie R, editor. The Promise of Adolescence: Realizing Opportunity for All Youth. Washington, DC: National Academies Press; 2019.
19. Eggleston K, Green E, Abel S, Poe S, Shakeshaft C. Developing trauma-responsive approaches to student discipline. London: Routledge; 2021.
20. Hughes K, Bellis MA, Sethi D, Andrew R, Yon Y, Wood S, et al. Adverse childhood experiences, childhood relationships and associated substance use and mental health in young Europeans. Eur J Public Health. 2019;29(4):741–7.

Video

van der Kolk BA. How the body keeps the score on trauma. www.youtube.com/watch?v=iTefkqYQz8g

3
A safe environment – what is it?

This chapter begins the more hopeful task of looking at ways to support all students, reduce retraumatisation and strengthen our skills and understanding for working with those damaged by trauma. This work needs a safe space to build trust and positive relationships. If we become aware of the important factors that lead to inner balance and calm confidence, we can seek to genuinely model them and also build a physical and social environment that supports this experience.

There are three sections in this chapter:

- Section 1 looks at some background to the meaning of the *safe space* and the principles of SAMHSA (1).
- Section 2 looks at the understanding different people have of 'safe space, feeling safe, and feeling unsafe' by means of a short online questionnaire.
- Section 3 looks at building a safe environment for all three education levels: (i) primary school, (ii) secondary school and (iii) adult education.

What is a safe learning environment? How can I begin to build this in my classroom?

Key elements in developing your classroom as a safe place are:

- Self-regulation – managing upset and emotional highs and lows. Educator modelling is an important tool in this learning.
- Open communication with ongoing review and discussion of process and materials.

- Acceptance and consistent respect in the relationships in the classroom.
- Transparency about the work and the approaches used. This can be visual in charts and plans, oral explanations and physical rituals that mark transitions in the day.

Section 1: What is a safe space?

The idea of a 'safe space' was originally part of activism. The aim of creating 'safe spaces' was part of building protest- and rights-based forums for marginalised groups – a space where issues that involved repression could be addressed without the victims having to explain and justify their histories. This included historical injustices such as racism, sexism and homophobia. It became controversial as individuals and groups were banned and prevented from speaking or sharing their ideas if they were judged to be unsafe or threatening to others. The need to maintain a safe environment where individuals feel supported and free from harm can come into conflict with what others demand as the right to free speech.

Currently, there is disagreement about the nature, meaning and value of safe space. Critics maintain that this approach can lead to a stifling of discussion and avoidance of important but difficult topics – when, for example, events, talks and lectures are cancelled, particularly in universities. Believers in the safe space are convinced that it offers specialist supports for marginalised groups and individuals and lessens their burden of having to repeatedly explain their negative experiences of institutionalised racism, disablism and other discrimination to their peers.

In 2016, University of Chicago Dean of Students, John Ellison, commented on what he and many others in higher education felt was a disconcerting trend toward intellectual isolationism on college campuses. He published a letter to incoming students, stating that the university would no longer tolerate the use of trigger warnings or safe spaces: 'We [at the University of Chicago] do not condone the creation of intellectual "safe spaces" where individuals can retreat from ideas and perspectives at odds with their own' (2). In contrast, earlier that year, Morton Schapiro, President of Northwestern University, affirmed the value of safe spaces, stating, 'I'm an economist, not a sociologist or psychologist, but those experts tell me that students don't fully embrace uncomfortable learning unless they are themselves comfortable. Safe spaces provide that comfort' (3).

These are political and philosophical arguments that may seem removed from the school classroom, but it is important to allow difficult topics to be explored, and the safe environment can be maintained using the five points listed below in the work on 'brave spaces'.

The term 'brave space' was popularised by Brian Arao and Kristi Clemens in 2013 in their book *From Safe Spaces to Brave Spaces* (4). A brave space within an educational environment is seen to have five main elements:

- 'Controversy with civility' – where varying opinions are accepted.
- 'Owning intentions and impacts' – in which students acknowledge and discuss instances where a dialogue has affected the emotional well-being of another person.
- 'Challenge by choice' – where students have an option to step in and out of challenging conversations.
- 'Respect' – where students show respect for one another's basic personhood.
- 'No attacks' – where students agree not to intentionally inflict harm on one another.

According to SAMHSA (1), the physical, psychological and emotional safety of service users and staff is prioritised by:

- people knowing they are safe or asking for what they need to feel safe
- there being reasonable freedom from threat or harm
- attempting to prevent retraumatisation
- putting policies, practices and safeguarding arrangements in place.

People knowing they are safe or asking what they need to feel safe

> A young man I worked with was in a recovery programme from addiction which included a maths class. There were eight students of all ages and an enthusiastic young teacher. The basic problem was that only one person could follow and understand the maths. So, everybody was 'copying the homework' frantically during tea break. 'Sure, she was

A safe environment – what is it?

> like, delighted we were all doing so well and then it got ridiculous where we couldn't disappoint her by telling her we hadn't a clue except for the one lad.' The way he told it was very funny, and we were both laughing, but it is also an example of kindness from the students and a sad story of lost opportunity. Individual or small group review would have picked up the problem.

In Eggleston and colleagues' book (5) about alternative discipline, there is an example of a child who can't grasp a maths concept and a teacher who is praised for her efforts to help the pupil grasp this skill. However, the pupil, whose challenge lies in maintaining positive engagement, due to trauma, and who lacks the skills to concentrate and learn, moves quickly towards sanctions and exclusion, while the teacher is commiserated with for having a pupil who is 'unmanageable or impossible'. The open communication of needs and experiences is the bedrock of inclusive environments.

There being reasonable freedom from threat or harm

If the threat to safety is in the community such as problems with gangs, addiction and the crimes it brings, or within the family structure itself, it is even more important to create a safe space in the classroom.

This includes safety from being bullied, called names and threatened. This is difficult to achieve if your group contains angry individuals who can lash out physically and verbally at others. The adult educator has a duty to maintain safety for all the group while working with the needs of the traumatised child. Chapter 8 on boundaries explores this in some detail with suggestions for maintaining order and safety while working with all pupils to foster safety and inclusion.

The first thing is setting expectations and modelling them yourself. This seems to cause less resistance to working towards positive aspirations than negative detailed rules which invite breaking!

I regularly took club groups out. The official term for pupils needing our support was 'targeted pupils', but I felt this would be labelling and an upsetting term for parents and children to hear, so all our supports were *clubs*.

There was a chant repeated by all ages before the bus left: 'Kind hands, kind feet, stay in your seat.' We always did it, even with some stomping and jeering from older groups!

I took the feedback of the bus driver who worked with groups all over Dublin when he said:

> *You charge for everything, and you have rules and apply them and all the outings are full – it's odd because other groups have expensive trips like rock climbing that the lads ask for, but they don't come on the day, or they are so wild the trip ends up a disaster or is cancelled.*

My experience of many years has been that groups and individuals need to be invested in the learning or activity, and to feel safe due to a structure that is agreed and maintained. A parent or young person who has paid something towards an outing will turn up, and all participants feel safer knowing that violence of any sort will not be tolerated. The same is needed in the classroom.

Attempting to prevent retraumatisation

Getting to know the pupils and, if possible, their parents is a key to this work. A pupil could have had a bereavement, an eviction, a beating or an individual trauma. A family or community trauma of natural disaster or refugee experience should also be considered.

All the elements of a welcoming environment and consistent approach by the educator are part of avoiding retraumatisation. If a student must be sanctioned or removed from the group, use a gentle approach, explain what is happening and why, and state that your hope is that they will rejoin the group as soon as possible. The ideal is that the teacher will have the time and resources to work with the needs of the student to regain calm so that they can remain in the group, but this isn't always possible. Triggers caused by being removed can be made worse by being left alone in a small space or large open space. An abused or ill-treated child may fear a beating is coming, so a handover to another calm adult is very important in crisis situations.

Transitions can be scary for pupils of all ages who have suffered sudden upheavals, fights, evictions and unwelcome strangers in their space. The use of timetables helps to reduce this, and if a change is about to happen, advance warning can be given to help reduce anxiety. For younger pupils, or those with less fluency in the language, visual timetables are very helpful.

The structure of the day needs to offer consistency and a repeated pattern, that can be illustrated with these *visual charts for the group's daily schedule. *Individual ones for pupils who need more detailed timetables and more support with any change or transition are helpful.

Options to withdraw for a time, where there is a support worker or special needs teacher, and to take a soothing break can forestall a storm. A *cosy corner can offer a break within the classroom.

Putting policies, practices and safeguarding arrangements in place

All staff need to be trained in the protocols for managing disclosures by pupils and in handling crisis situations, whether it is in a school or other institution. These policies should be shared with all pupils and available publicly. Boundaries should be clear to all participants in terms of what the work entails and how much disclosure is appropriate in the group. One adult tutor shared that in a group with many refugees, one participant disclosed more than one horrific story and upset many in the group. The tutor wanted to be supportive but felt helpless to stop the conversations. It is important to set out these boundaries in advance, so that it is understood why you are doing it when you intervene and suggest a referral to a private conversation with the counsellor or another person.

Section 2: What does 'safety' or 'feeling safe' mean to individuals?

I wanted to learn more about how people understand this concept of safety. So, I asked 30 people of all ages and backgrounds, male and female, 16–80 years old, these questions:

- What does a 'safe place' mean to you?
- How do you know it's a safe place?
- What makes you feel safe?
- What makes you feel unsafe?

Figure 3.1 Word cloud response to questions around feelings of safety/unsafety

A safe environment – what is it?

Twenty-five people replied. The most common responses were about 'feeling accepted, not judged, able to express all sides of myself, being with loved ones'. Nature was mentioned by several as supporting feeling peaceful. It was noticeable that there was not much difference among ages and backgrounds – being loved, able to be yourself and feeling secure were the top choices in safety. One definite difference was in women and girls mentioning night-time, being out alone and encountering groups of young men as causing fear or feeling a lack of safety. Another important point for educators is that 90 per cent of answers concerned 'feelings'. One or two mentioned low crime areas, effective locks, financial security and the responses of emergency services as adding to feelings of safety. The vast majority spoke of 'feelings and vibes' – this reverts to the original difficulty for educators in trying to provide this safe space and feeling of safety. It seems to be an individual emotional experience without many concrete elements that would be easier to supply. Some people focused on concrete examples of physical safety, which included crime rates, fears around burglary and secure boat moorings.

I also asked a group of trainee teachers this question: What is a safe place for students? How does the tutor know they feel safe? Answers included: 'if they turn up; if they participate; if they are asking questions; if they disagree with you; if they ask you to justify or explain something.'

Figure 3.2 Trauma breaks trust and love

> **Reflective questions**
>
> - What is your understanding of safety and a 'safe space'?
> - What steps can you take to develop this in your classroom?

Asking questions – it is not always that easy!

I remember taking a primary school group to the animal shelter on an outing. The young assistant spoke passionately at length about how animals were her whole life, and she loved them so much. The pupils were getting restless till one of the group raised her hand for a question and it was: 'Hiya, do you eat meat?' There was silence, and then the young woman answered, all flustered, 'Well, yeah, I do but . . .' The young pupil cut in: 'That's OK, just wondering.'

Another time, there was a workshop on refugees in second year, and the presenter gave a moving presentation about the plight of those who fled their country and came to Ireland to build a new life. There were some questions about rights and supports offered to refugees, which let the presenter clear up some false negative ideas. Then one pupil said, 'There is a family from XX country on our road and they have two BMWs at their house.' Silence fell as everyone local knew they were notorious as suspected drug dealers in the area. The presenter wasn't prepared to discuss the rumour mill and how it affects people, how criminals come in all shapes and sizes, but that there is no evidence to suggest migrants are involved in more crime than locals, so it was left like that, undoing all the good work of the presentation.

Elements of any 'safe space' – a place where we feel accepted, valued, heard, equal and safe from interpersonal violence or bullying – include the physical environment, the tutor or facilitator, the materials used, the relationships and the approach taken. These are the constant elements needed at all ages.

Section 3: Creating a safe space in the classroom
(i) A safe space at preschool and primary school

The key factor is that the traumatised child is very unlikely to have words to describe their experience and their panic responses. Karen Treisman (6) has written extensively and given international training on trauma and TIP. A powerful concept of hers is that behaviour is a form of communication.

We know from the previous research and readings that 'the body holds the score' and that children carrying the weight of trauma are often held back in their emotional and learning skills and may be out of touch with their physical experience or disassociated from their body. They may be stuck in fight, flight or freeze (FFF) mode, and this makes it very difficult for them to learn and participate.

For young children, this means trust has been desperately broken for them with carers and/or their basic needs for food, shelter, comfort and love have been very neglected over time. So, for children who have suffered greatly, their alarm system is always scanning for danger or they have withdrawn physically and mentally to curl up in a corner.

The building of a nurturing relationship with the pupils and among the pupils is a process that takes time and small steps, especially for the traumatised pupil.

The principle in building a safe, supportive classroom can be 'what's good for one is good for all'.

Self-regulation

All of us need to self-regulate and calm ourselves for both trivia and tragedy during our lives, so it starts with yourself. It is vital to become aware of your own triggers and work to release them safely. For example, is it the child who acts the bully, lies or takes others' food or toys that gets under your skin? Or is it a sad memory or experience of your own that is upsetting you?

This type of check-in with yourself becomes habitual and fast when you practise regularly.

I often cringe when I remember approaches I took to difficult, disruptive children and young people that did not respond to their needs; really, I sought to contain them and silence them.

Modelling the positive behaviours and skills

This can be done overtly with commentary, especially for young pupils.
The educator is *modelling the steps of self-regulation when they:

- identify a feeling/emotion or sensation ('I'm feeling very let down; we can't go out today')
- mention its impact and location in the body ('I feel GRRRR . . . a bit like a cross cat' or 'I feel sad in my chest or wobbly in my tummy')
- share how they will release or express it ('I think I am going to draw my cross cat and make some growling noises as I do it' or 'I'm going to breathe or move or take a break in the soft corner')
- reset and show how the storm has passed ('Now that I feel relaxed again, let's think of a good game for the hall today').

The group chooses something with big body movements to begin with, winds down with something soothing (7). Pupils of all ages can help to design and modify games, whether class quiz games or active games for the hall or yard.

Setting the scene – the environment

The safety principles of SAMHSA and the evidence from research view the trusting relationship with the adult educators as the basis of a safe environment. The classroom layout needs to be part of this:

- Consider the pupils' needs when arranging the furniture and provide a cosy corner where comfort objects like soft cushions, soft toys, fidget toys, paper and drawing materials are available. Puzzles, especially big floor types, are very calming. One teacher stuck Velcro under the table for a child who needed to move their fingers up and down on a tactile surface.
- Offer choices of engagement and activities for the pupils. The Montessori principle of the 'exercises of practical life' is very useful for maintaining order and helps the growth of self-esteem. These exercises include tidying and cleaning the room, caring for plants and pets, looking after their own work and belongings. This builds a foundation for independent work and application.
- Provide lots of 'big body movement' in class time, break times and physical education time – such as running, jumping, rolling, marching, chasing,

throwing, skipping, stretching. Some of these need to be outside, but others can be adapted to the classroom or hall.
- Provide a visible timetable of each day that is understood and kept to. If changes are necessary, ensure that they are announced in advance.

The use of the trauma-informed principles

- The educator is committed to hearing the pupils and working to see behaviour as communication rather than defiant or destructive without reason.
- The teacher is consistent in their approach to learning as an ongoing activity, with success and challenge a part of it.
- The class takes part in whole-group and small-group activities that help them to get to know and support each other.
- The teacher encourages regular conversation and feedback about the things they do in class and the learning approaches used. The focus is always on how these methods could be improved and made more helpful. The pupils are often working together on small projects or sections of the curriculum that are proving difficult.
- There are lots of small but important responsibilities in the room, which are rotated, from watering plants to checking the lights are off before home time. Group selections and chore allocations are done by a drawing of names in front of everyone. The list of jobs should include as many as possible. For example, the 'Sellotape keeper' is responsible for returning the tape with a small tag on it at the end of every day. This is a vital role in a busy room!
- There are lots of celebrations as different things are completed or difficulties overcome. Parents and guardians are regularly involved, and the invitations are always individually designed and produced by the pupils. This increases attendance enormously as the pupil will take the invitation home and present it, and then personally pressure their adult to attend!

Review and feedback

When I worked in schools, I always found the youngest children knew all about the next half day or a change that was coming because they are expert eavesdroppers on a daily basis! Students from young primary to adult are very capable of giving precise feedback if offered appropriate methods.

For younger children, this can be using coloured stickers, emoji or physical thumbs up or down to small changes in routine or approach. This can be included in circle time.

(ii) A safe space at secondary school or education centre

Teenagers may be harder to engage, especially if struggling in school and lacking support.

Adolescence is a time of major change and is challenging for the majority of teenagers – and for their carers and teachers! The struggle for independence and identity is combined with insecurity and the need to belong to the group. Parents and guardians may find their authority and beliefs are questioned in a negative way that puts strain on the relationship. The traumatised and neglected child is now an adolescent and still lacks the emotional loving support to negotiate these years. The lack of support and boundaries leaves the young person at further risk for anti-social or unhealthy behaviours. A study of young people affected by ACEs (8) found that:

> [I]t is important to note that exposure to adversity is not deterministic in terms of cause and effect. In other words, it is not inevitable that individuals experiencing high numbers of adversities go on to experience poor outcomes, either later in childhood or as an adult. There is strong evidence, however, that there is a graded increase in the probability of experiencing poor outcomes associated with the number of adversities experienced in childhood. (p.25)

As adolescence is a period of intense growth, it is an opportunity to develop supports to enable young people to make positive life choices and heal trauma effects that limit their engagement in school and society.

The gaps in academic ability, lack of support in home life and restricted resources to join peers socially are all magnified in secondary education for the neglected young person. The extra equipment and other help often supplied by the primary teacher who knew their class individually are not available. Supports at secondary school often involve 'being eligible' or some kind of 'application for assistance' which will be embarrassing for a teenager (9). Sometimes these gaps are unknown to the teacher. One school had a 'no-uniform day' to raise money for the local hospital. Several mothers told me their teenager wouldn't go to school as they didn't have the right tracksuit. Another took a loan to buy new clothes for her daughter.

My experience of working with adolescents is that the most effective interventions and supports are those chosen and developed by the group. The use of third-party debate and discussion is essential to develop open communication. The nature of the shifting alliances and friend groups typical of adolescence make 'group confidentiality' an unlikely achievement. The use of 'what if' scenarios and questions about a fictional teenager give a safe space to share.

The safe environment and supportive relationship are more challenging to achieve as classes are short and always changing, and the curriculum is teaching towards exams at secondary level.

The environment

Building that comfortable safe space

The environment in your classes can still be welcoming even if you have to keep changing for each class period. You could have a couple of small mascots or quotes you hang up when you come in. If these are funny or quirky, they will make the students laugh, which is always a good start. The initial greeting you give is also vital and lets the students know you are there for them.

If you can agree with the other people who use the room to include some nature posters and to clear out unused or broken furniture or equipment, this will go a long way to making a more pleasant space to be in. The contrast between primary school, which is usually a riot of colour, posters, artwork and projects, and secondary school, which can look like a detention centre with no personal work on view, and very little colour or personality in the room, can be improved.

The use of trauma-informed principles

Concentration

- *Breathing exercises or simple movements and stretches can help with concentration and transitions from active to quiet work.
- Short breaks to check in with progress, or listen to music while colouring for five minutes can reset the brain. (You choose the music!)

Communications

- Getting to know each other means both the pupils getting to know each other and the teacher getting to know the pupils. ***The question game** is very effective in starting conversations. Always begin with the easiest level which asks about favourite foods, pets and other easy topics.
- Debates and discussion can lay the foundation for essays, comprehension exercises and analysis of text. They can be fun if done in the language being learned! I remember one lad trying to chat to a French girl and pestering me for phrases – he wished he had 'listened to my Ma and worked in school at my French'!
- Using the third person for discussion with teenagers works very well. Always begin with impersonal topics such as curfews, chores, wages in part-time work and age limits for different activities and rights. As discussion skills improve, you can introduce more contentious issues. ***The walking debate** is useful here for topics like 'Would a 16-year-old feel angry about being called thick for being dyslexic?'
- Inbuilt motivation to complete sections of the work grows as celebrations and games are timetabled after completion of stages of the curriculum.

Working together

- Peer support means working on tasks together, sharing skills and information. Start with short group tasks with a definite objective. This can be completing lettering for a poster or making a ***wall frieze**. As students become accustomed to group work, you can extend the length and difficulty of the tasks.
- All subjects have an oral requirement, so you can use games, quizzes and assertiveness in these slots. Even mathematics can benefit as learning occurs for both when one student explains a theory to another.
- Work towards events that celebrate their achievements. Some events can support others such as fundraising, volunteering or being part of a project that, for example, engages with the local senior care home or coaches younger children with the PE teacher's support.
- The cartoon and activity-based ***assertiveness programme** is effective in developing interpersonal skills and personal confidence.

Review and feedback

Ongoing feedback about the process and the learning targets. This needs to be a regular part of the class where the process of the group and the learning and teaching of each section of the work is discussed. Games, quizzes and the review can be very short – five minutes is enough for some valuable feedback. This will help the educator to stay aware of the students' hopes, dreams and difficulties that are part of their lives and education.

(iii) A safe space at the third level – further education centre

Many adult learners are living with complex trauma and challenging life situations

There can be a lot of anxiety among those who are returning to education, especially in groups already marginalised, such as those in recovery from addiction, travellers or people displaced for any reason. Learners returning as adults may have had humiliating and physically hurtful treatment in primary school. This ill-treatment may have been as a result of undiagnosed difficulties in learning, or bullying by teachers due to pupil poverty or other vulnerabilities. This means that there will be triggers for trauma in the classroom itself. It is essential to build effective communication channels, so you are in touch with students' needs, as it is impossible to be aware of all possible triggers or anxieties in your group at the outset.

Another thing to remember is that your contract with your students is to deliver a skill or complete a syllabus to an agreed level. You are not a therapist or a counsellor and should not take on that role. Safe boundaries will be discussed in detail in Chapter 8. Your aim as a tutor is to create a safe, supportive learning environment. You need to be aware of students' needs and difficulties, which may include sensitivities and trauma triggers, so that they can be supported to focus on their learning.

A tutor told me of high anxiety in an IT class when learners couldn't understand parts of the work. After review with the learners, the tutor provided a flexible 20-minute break and let the students work together as the tutor moved around answering queries. Anxiety levels dropped, and student interaction and support rose each week.

The environment

The environment is important as the arrangement and the amount of furniture gives the first impression. You can have some plants or posters of beautiful plants or greenery. Hang an attractive picture with the class name on the door – this will also help if you have to move. Avoid trite signs like 'Bee happy' – they are not always helpful. A welcome and friendly smile as students enter is a positive start.

Communications

Getting to know each other

- Ask the students to make a ***name plate** and take them with you, laminate them and return them. Gather them up each week so they don't get lost.
- Have a short introduction chat in pairs, and then each person introduces their partner by name and says one thing they hope to get from the class.
- A discussion of the boundaries of the group regarding personal disclosures and the overall aim of the programme or class is very important to have at the start.

Layout of the work in stages

Divide the work into sections and allot time to each section

- Include a clear explanation of the timetable in both written and visual form. A timeline of the learning outcomes and targets should be regularly updated with review.
- Include regular review of progress with the group, with space for a student to say if they are totally lost and panicking. This can be tricky with a large group, so start with the ***group poster review**, to identify general needs.
- Have students work in small groups on issues as you go round and check out who needs more help.
- The curriculum and the exam deadline are probably outside your remit, but you can alter your approach to maximise support and build

confidence in your learners. Students in Youthreach had negative experiences of school, so, at first, we avoided all forms of assessment. I found out that completing sections of the work in special sessions on customised sheets was very satisfying for the students. They called it 'the exam' and it ran for 30 minutes each Wednesday in silent individual work. All the targets were very achievable, and you could do them as many times as you needed. The presentations of certificates for completed folders were happy occasions which celebrated work done and reduced fear of assessment, which is part of all training and apprenticeships.

- Try different methods for review and feedback.
- Frequent celebration of steps to success is important. For example, if a section of the work has been completed, take ten minutes, have a round of applause for the whole group and ask a couple of learners to speak about their high and low points. If you have a colleague who has five minutes to come and view the work, all the better.

Ongoing review and feedback

Older students may need small groups or anonymous methods such as Padlet online or comment boxes as they become more self-conscious about possible disagreement with others. Posters which ask for a *star* and *wish* (something going well and something I am needing support with) can be anonymous and give the same information as a Padlet. Movement review such as the ***walking debate** is great with older pupils and adults. This ongoing review habit, starting with small things and always keeping to what you can deliver, is the foundation of two-way communication and building trust. As Laura Lundy (10) says, the effective use of voice for anyone needs communication skills, a platform, a focus and someone to listen to you who has power and influence to effect change.

A participant in my workshop for young people affected by domestic violence looked up from his art project and said, 'I think I need more of this kinda stuff, talking about what happened. Where could I get more?' Noone raised their head or commented as I suggested he hang back after group for a chat. The group shared a trust that meant there were no smart remarks or particular interest in this request.

Key points of Chapter 3

- Looking at the definitions of a safe place from major research, such as SAMHSA. Communication and positive regard are the basis for building safe spaces – it's an ongoing process, not a word!
- Feedback from a live survey of what this 'safe place' means to 25 people of all ages and backgrounds – it's all about feelings and relationships.
- Approaches and activities to create a safe place at all levels of education. These take time and groups have different and developing needs and abilities.
- Review as an ongoing effort that informs the teaching style and process of the class.
- Your students of all ages will inform you of their needs, successes and challenges if you find a way to communicate well with them.

References

1. Substance Abuse and Mental Health Services Administration. SAMHSA's Concept of Trauma and Guidance for a Trauma-Informed Approach. Rockville, MD: Substance Abuse and Mental Health Services Administration; 2014.
2. The College: The University of Chicago [press release]. Chicago; 2020.
3. Shapiro M. I'm Northwestern's president. Here's why safe spaces for students are important. Washington Post. 2016 15-01-2016.
4. Arao B, Clemens K. From Safe Spaces to Brave Spaces. In: The Art of Facilitation: Reflections from Social Justice Educators. London: Routledge; 2013.
5. Eggleston K, Green E, Abel S, Poe S, Shakeshaft C. Developing trauma-responsive approaches to student discipline. London: Routledge; 2021.
6. Treisman K. Working with relational and developmental trauma in children and adolescents. London: Routledge; 2017.
7. Nicholson J, Perez L, Kurtz J, Bryant S, Giles D. Trauma-informed practices for early childhood educators. London: Routledge; 2019.
8. Devaney J, Bunting L, Davidson G, Hayes D, Lazenbatt A, Spratt T. Still vulnerable: The impact of early childhood experiences on adolescent suicide and accidental death. Northern Ireland Commissioner for Children and Young People; 2012.

9. Hickey G, Smith S, O'Sullivan L, McGill L, Kenny M, MacIntyre D, et al. Adverse childhood experiences and trauma informed practices in second chance education settings in the Republic of Ireland: An inquiry-based study. Children and Youth Services Review. 2020;118.
10. Lundy L, McEvoy L, Byrne B. Working with young children as co-researchers: An approach informed by the United Nations Convention on the Rights of the Child. Early Education and Development. 2011;22(5):714–36.

4
Building relationships that are positive and supportive

This chapter develops the theme of relationship building in the education setting. The activities and approaches to building relationships following the 'good for one, good for all' approach will be detailed with explanations, instructions and links to sites as needed to make the material accessible.
There are two sections in this chapter:

- Section 1 explores some background to the nature and variety of relationships. The positive aspects usually found in all types of relationships and what helps them to grow will be discussed, with particular focus on educational relationships. The reason the damage to trusting relationships in trauma is very severe for the victim and why the classroom is a place you can take some small steps to repairing this fracture will be looked at.
- Section 2 considers in detail aspects of relationship building at each level of the education system: (i) primary school, (ii) secondary school and (iii) adult education/third level.

Section 1: Some background on relationships and essential elements that make them work well

The Oxford Dictionary defines relationship as 'the way in which two or more people or things are connected, or the state of being connected' and as 'the way in which two or more people or groups regard and behave towards each other'; 'the landlord–tenant relationship'.

Important elements in all relationships

There is less written about relationships with family, colleagues, students, friends and acquaintances, even though these relationships take up a lot of time and energy for most of us. The focus in many forums is on parenting and couple relationships.

So, leaving the romance to the expert dating coaches, what are the important things in any positive relationship?

Everyone has different aspects of themselves where it is vital to have needs met. Some people are very picky and critical, and others are more tolerant and accept more varied behaviour from friends and family. Most people will list trust, acceptance, respect, communication, truth, loyalty, equality, support, shared interests and humour as basic requirements for a successful relationship. The people we interact with intermittently or formally will require different types of relationships from those we have with family, couples or close friends where there is high emotional investment.

Damage done by trauma

In the previous chapters, research showed us very clearly that trauma occurring in the family, at a young age and repeatedly, causes untold damage to the child's development. This includes damage to children's health physically, socially, psychologically and mentally. It also affects brain development. All the child's developmental needs must be first met and built on within close carer relationships (1). If these carers don't offer a safe place to grow and learn, all areas of the child's growth are badly affected. Close supportive relationships are vital to a child and to all of us throughout our lives (2, 3).

A study of adult attachment by Picardi and colleagues (4) found that adults with secure attachment:

> tend to see themselves as valued and worthy of affection and to see their partner as trustworthy, dependable, and available for support when needed. Individuals with high attachment-related anxiety display a tendency to be preoccupied with their romantic relationships, to feel unappreciated, and to worry about insufficient love or abandonment. Adults with high attachment-related avoidance find it difficult to trust or depend on others. (p.967)

These issues with relationships, whether they were anxious or avoidant, were in line with the findings of the original 'stranger situation' research with babies completed first by Ainsworth (5) and recreated and analysed many times since. The basic theory was that how the baby reacted to the mother leaving the room, a stranger entering and then leaving, and the mother returning showed a lot about the nature of the bond, or attachment, between mother and child. The seriously neglected and traumatised child is predisposed to carry these attachment losses into adult relationships.

The word 'relationships' often implies romantic ones, but actually the communication skills and emotional intelligence needed for positive relationships are common to all interactions.

I remember teaching my first 'relationships and sex education' group in Youthreach years ago. I started off by asking, 'What is a relationship?' As usual, they were initially slow to answer, so I told them, 'You have a relationship with me!' Shock and stunned silence all round, they looked at each other to see who I was talking to, and then the discussion began in earnest. We got to the topic of feelings, and after a few girls shared, the lads were asked about important feelings in different relationships. Just a few laughs and then a girl said, 'Fellas don't have feelings.' That got the chat going as the lads were out to prove they did have feelings.

Way back then, before I learned much about SEL, I knew from experience that these relationship skills have to be learned – if not informally through family and society, then in a structured environment such as school. I used to say to the young people, 'You train for football, don't you? You can't just turn up to the match on the day. You practise music to get it right. Well, this stuff we do here is the same, except more important.'

The US foundation CASEL (the Collaborative for Academic, Social, and Emotional Learning) has developed the theory and practice of SEL internationally, and conducted extensive reviews to show how teaching these skills in a structured way has a positive long-lasting effect on students' personal and academic confidence and ability (6). Relationship skills are included in the whole package of SEL for schools. The CASEL website has a lot of material for all student levels and research to support the reasons for and success of the work of teaching SEL (https://casel.org).

The CASEL list of relationship skills prioritises effective communication and the ability to work in teams to collaborate and problem-solve. This forms the base for a lot of important relationship skills including being empathic and supportive, showing leadership in groups and knowing how to seek support.

One thing to be aware of is that SEL does require some conscious engagement and effective communication skills. If the young people don't have the basic skills, this can become another failure for them or lead to anger or disruption. For children living with trauma, there are risks involved when we give the child tools for stress management, if their living situation is overwhelming and frightening. As Gerry, an experienced teacher, principal, and counsellor, pointed out in an interview with me:

There is a problem with the teaching of 'well-being' in schools. We are teaching children how to breathe or do yoga and then we send them back to a domestic violence situation. We are making the child responsible for their own healing.

A study (7) completed in 2025 in the US noted the foundational work done by SEL in schools, while stressing the need for educators to use a trauma-informed approach. This means an awareness and a responsiveness to the individual and community-based traumas of the students that will inform the content and interaction around the SEL materials.

The six principles of trauma-informed practice, according to the SAMHSA research (8), are:

- Safety
- Trust
- Choice
- Collaboration
- Empowerment
- Cultural consideration.

The five core SEL competencies according to CASEL are:

- Self-awareness
- Self-management
- Social awareness
- Relationship skills
- Responsible decision-making.

Stacey Bailey (9) responded to trainee teachers asking how to use social emotional skills when a pupil is about to hurl a desk at you by devising the

Figure 4.1 The interconnections in a child's development (10)

*CHILL strategy. She noted it is important to practise when students are *not* upset, so the skill is available when they are dysregulated:

> [T]eachers can use self-regulation strategies such as the one I call 'CHILL'. CHILL is an easy-to-implement five-step process designed to reduce tension in moments of crisis and create the conditions whereby students are prepared to reengage with instruction, both with the teacher and with the class. C is for Calm down, H is for Hear yourself breathe, I is for Investigate your condition, L is for Let yourself know what you need, and the second L is for Let others know what you need. (Abstract)

Using trauma-informed principles in the classroom

Enabling trusting positive relationships

The practice of 'good for one, good for all' tries to bridge the gap between the teacher with a class of 20 and a curriculum to follow and the therapeutic space where there are small numbers and specialist services available for the traumatised child. The ongoing work of making a physical and emotional safe space in the classroom will benefit all the pupils and the teacher. Modelling and teaching positive relationship skills, from the friendly morning greeting to the ongoing reviews of work and group process, will build trust and allow pupils to express their needs. The teacher needs an effective referral system within the school and to other services and to have clear boundaries as to what they can and can't do. This needs to be clear to pupils of all ages. It is always better to say no with a reason than to promise what can't be done.

Setting clear boundaries

Hearing it from 12-year-olds!

When I was doing my PhD thesis on the effects of domestic violence on teenage SEL, I did some pilot workshops. One was with a group of 12-year-old boys. I did a presentation on feelings and behaviour using a rainbow arc to show the breadth of feelings and how they can change, and how it can be frightening if there is bad fighting in your home. I asked for questions and got these three:

1. 'Hiya. Who are you to come in and talk to us about this stuff?'
   Interesting question. I explained that I was a teacher, and I did extra programmes about feelings and learning to get along with others, the way the class teacher taught their lessons, and the school psychologist helped with worries.
2. 'My brothers kill each other at home and even roll down the stairs kicking the legs off each other. My Ma says they're driving her crazy. Is that domestic violence?'
   Another precise question. I asked, 'Has anyone broken anything or is there blood?'
   'Oh, not like that – just yelling and cursing.'
   'I think that's OK – if it got worse, it could be a worry.'
3. 'There is a lot of bad fighting in my house and sometimes there is . . .'
   I saw the teacher signalling to stop, so I said, 'That sounds very frightening. Have you talked to anyone about it?'
   'Yeah, Ms Brown [teacher] and the youth worker.'
   'So, I'm glad you have some help.'

Afterwards, the teacher shared with me that a multi-agency referral was in place for that lad, and he was getting support in school as well. This was a good example of the ability of young people to speak up and their awareness of life situations. The teacher was modelling a safe place by stopping an overly public disclosure while enabling an open conversation.

I often thought of that class when I was struggling to get my research taken seriously and was regularly told, 'But you could be influencing their responses . . . they might not be engaging with your programme freely . . . their feedback could be to please you.' If I had a massive incentive available, like a trip to Disney or a sports car, maybe this fake cooperation would be a reality. Participants in my programme 'up2talk' (10) received a lunch and some lively group activities with a safe place to explore the impact of domestic violence on their teenage development – not much for attending 12 Wednesday afternoons! Which incidentally was their half-day from school.

The ability to build relationships

If we have a quick look back at the neglected and abused child in Chapter 1, we can ask where could they learn or experience these skills and ways of relating?

Figure 4.2 Leave me alone – I don't care

One thing jumps out regarding these relationship skills, and that is that victims of serious trauma will not have experienced these positive skills in early relationships, and if they are stuck in fight, flight or freeze (FFF), they will not have the ability or willingness to share a relationship with you. Just a reminder that we are not all Michelle Pfeiffer in *Dangerous Minds*, the impossibly gorgeous teacher whose pupils are all eating from her hand in a week! In many cases, the work we do and the efforts we make will be received by traumatised students with anger, resentment or indifference.

Difficulties in building relationships and learning

The following snapshots of how children's lives are affected by trauma represent many young people I have worked with. The common threads of misdiagnosis of trauma symptoms as intellectual or behaviour problems, and the difficulty for the tutor in building a relationship with a young person who has lost trust and motivation appear in these vignettes and many other life stories.

Jenny aged 15

Jenny was very smart and very angry. The first day I arrived to offer home tuition lessons, she ignored me for 20 minutes and then yelled at me: 'Where's your newspaper? I don't do any work for anyone.' I explained that I was there to work and that I couldn't claim my salary if we didn't do anything. She stormed around the room for a while, kicking things and cursing at me, and then told me to wait in the hall while she had a think. I agreed to wait in the hall for ten minutes. After that, I went back in, to some more yelling and my stuff all over the floor. She had found some magazines, and I could see she wanted to look at one. So I suggested we each read for five minutes and then say what we had read. Jenny didn't answer me, but I could see she was reading, so I continued to read myself. After a few minutes, she threw hers down, saying, 'That is a load of crap. No girls I know act like that, and the fellas round here would laugh at you.'

We had a short discussion about that, and I was to share mine. 'Don't bother, it's just more shite.'

I asked her for a cup of tea, which was often an ice breaker with home tuition students, but Jenny just opened the door and screeched at her mother: 'Hey, she wants tea, and I want my chicken roll.' I tried to say something, but Jenny said, 'She has to go to the shop for my roll and then make tea anyway.'

This was the pattern of our days for the remaining months, with some days worse than others and some small progress at other times. I found out that Jenny had a quick mind and was well able to write and analyse what interested her, so I tried a lot of different approaches and topics. She liked to cook, and we tried out and wrote up a few recipes. The 'Junior Cert' – state exams for 14–16-year-olds – were coming up, and she agreed to register for a couple of subjects at the local school. Preparation was torturous, but we made it to the first exam, and as she got out of the car, I said, 'Well done getting here – you can do this.' She gave me a withering look and yelled, 'You're always the f---ing same!' She slammed the door and stormed off. I know she did a couple of subjects as I brought her in, but I never heard how she got on or any more news about her after her hours were completed.

Tom aged 14

Tom was another homeschool tuition student who told me politely on day one that he didn't want to learn to read, he didn't need to, and he was staying at home on the dole (welfare) with his computer games for the rest of his life. In this case, an offer of tea led to toast and chats about his interests, which included jigsaws and the world map. A detailed psychologist's assessment of his needs had suggested he was unable to sequence and had little feeling for others, and these were key factors in his inability to read and in his isolation. I asked him what colour folder he would like and apologised for forgetting the folders that day. He chose blue and said, 'You know what you wanna do? Put the folder in your bag tonight when you get home so you don't forget it.' Sequencing, anyone?

We worked on puzzles, jigsaws and different activities. We looked at picture books of the world and went to the library together. We had some laughs, such as our attempts to measure rainfall after discovering there were places in the world that had no rain for years! So we cut a plastic bottle, marked it in millilitres and put it in the garden. There was no rain that week, but I came back to record rainfall – the bottle was half full! Tom got a bit upset when I asked him, so I just let it drop. His father came in and saw the bottle and said, 'That f---ing bottle – he knocked it over and was freaking out, so I just filled it.' We all had a good laugh about the Dublin monsoon. A few days later, we were making pancakes, and I asked him to lift down the flour. He jumped up, opened the cupboard and stopped: he couldn't read the labels on the flour, oats, etc. The next day, he suggested looking at the recipe for pancakes. We made a few recipe sheets and then tried a few of the words and sentences in the library books. I knew he had previously memorised class readers, so we used a Montessori moveable alphabet to start making words. Tom learned to read and decided he would go back to a school locally that had small classes and plenty of different supports. The last I heard, he was still attending and enjoying all the activities. It is great to have a happy outcome and it gives you hope to keep trying in difficult circumstances.

Reflective questions

- What do you think might be the reason for Jenny's rage and refusal to engage?
- What could you do the build a relationship with limited time and resources?
- How did Tom end up with such a diagnosis and in such isolation?
- Is it necessary to know their trauma story to work positively with these young people?

The school is a place where we can work to build relationships and repair emotional damage for young people first because they are there, hopefully on a regular basis, and in a group. Second, the opportunity is there to model and teach positive relationship skills over a period of time. The school also has the remit to teach subjects and competencies to the pupils attending, and TIP should be built into this work, which is what the students have signed up for.

Section 2: Aspects and activities – building relationships in the classroom

(i) Primary school relationship building

Building positive relationships and a supportive happy learning environment is a process, and the methods and ideas in the previous chapters, especially on the safe space, will be included in the framework.

Aim

To reduce triggers for trauma such as angry corrections, exclusion, public criticism, loud noises, strangers in the environment or unexpected changes to the daily programme.

To build kindness, confidence and curiosity in the classroom, leading to positive relationships and joy in learning (11).

Approaches

- Transparency. Explain what is happening and why. Flag changes clearly and in advance – visual timetables are great for this.
- Modelling kindness and self-regulation. Taking a breath: 'Oh, that's a pity it's all broken. Let me think a minute how we can fix it.'
- Fun and laughter. Making cartoons together, sharing jokes and rhymes, singing.
- Making games inclusive and avoiding games that leave a pupil 'on the spot' or being chased down. ***Musical statues, *Musical chairs, *Build-up chasing**. Many traumatised pupils can't tolerate any type of exclusion, even when it is very short. Many games can be altered to make them more inclusive.
- Developing active listening and attunement to the pupils, on an everyday basis and especially when they are overwhelmed, as explained by Anna, a teacher in a very underserved area:

OK, so to hear what form she's in, and where to push where not to push, you know. And sometimes she just needs to go into a little cosy corner made up of beanbags and dark curtains off the sensory area, that she just needs to go, and she takes off her shoes as we go down there. Yeah.

And she'll emerge then in a little while. Yeah, that's obviously what she needs to do, because that's what she's bringing to the classroom. There's some days more than others. Yeah, because she could come in and you can tell nearly by her eyes or, you know, the way she looks. Those tiny things you notice after working with a child all year.

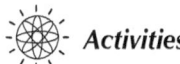 **Activities**

For concentration

- **Listening to the gong**, identifying sounds with eyes closed (can be paper rustling, tinfoil, water poured into a cup, pencil falls on the floor . . .).
- Brain gym exercises.
- Marching on the spot with arms swinging and then with crossover elbow to knee. This is very effective in settling and focusing. There are many videos, this one is easy to follow (12): www.youtube.com/watch?v=q-e0E1V5Ls4

Making art, stories and games together

- The *tree of helping hands is a fun art group activity.
- Inclusive games such as *Who has the ball?

Self-regulation

- *Cosy corner – safe place.
- **Understanding how the brain works:** It is essential to attune yourself to the child's emotional (right) brain and help them to regain balance before attempting logical left-brain approaches. If the reaction is trauma-based, it is vital to encourage them to be part of the plan to resolve the situation in a better way. This means boundaries of discipline and consequences are maintained but with some input from the child/person involved. '[W]hen a child is upset, logic often won't work until we have responded to the right brain's emotional needs' (13 p.33). When the child has calmed down and feels heard and connected, the left brain can be involved in working out what happened and helping the child organise their feelings, integrating both sides of the brain's experience. Movement and exercises

that swing the arms across the body help integration. Shevrin Venet's book *Equity-Centred Trauma-Informed Education* (14) contains cartoon drawings of the brain which are very useful.
- Teacher *__modelling self-regulation__ as s/he talks through an annoying or upsetting situation in class aloud, to share with the children. Example: 'I feel really let down that the drums group never came today like they promised. I feel cross and boiling up in my head, I feel like yelling. I am going to take five deep breaths; I am going to swing my arms forward and swish all that temper out onto the floor three times.' After all the actions, the teacher smiles and says, 'OK, I feel better now. Let's make up a new game, and we will take a longer hall time to play and maybe sing some songs as well.'

Physical movement

- Even short moments of movement within the classroom can relieve intense sensations or emotions. Regular movement breaks help all pupils to stay balanced and keep energy flowing.
- *__Breathing__ – keep it short and focused, count the breaths and have a simple grounded intention. A young person, affected by abuse, told me, 'I hate meditation when it's too long. I can drift into panic or dissociation.'

Building bonds

- Comforting, familiar rituals.
- Fun ways to talk and listen, such as *__'Can't say no or yes'__, swapping games such as *__'What's changed?'__, *__Hunting an object in the room__ using 'hot and cold' for how near they are to the object.
- Marking special occasions. Birthdays (some children won't mention theirs, so you need a complete list of dates).
- Different cultural holidays – collect the dates.

Managing conflict

What happened? Who is upset? How can we fix it? Just being heard and seen is often enough to defuse the upset or argument.

Jane, a young teacher talked about using restorative justice approaches in the school:

We brought it up a couple of years ago on yard. It was going to be like this thing of like, so say, John and Mary, you're fighting on yard, and someone hit someone or whatever, that they'd come in. There was five questions, or start of, how did you feel at the time? But I am sure you know them, yeah, and then, and then there was a sheet of paper, but I don't want to use the sheet of paper really. What I do is sit down outside the room with them. You know, outside, like we've an emergency exit and there's a bench outside it. So, we go out, we sit down, listen to both sides of it, chat about it, talk it out. I kind of think I do it innately, but you know, it's not, we're definitely doing it to maybe a 40%, 50%. Yeah.

The use of superheroes was something I saw at a happiness seminar. The children designed half a dozen of their own superheroes (obviously in the good-actor range!) and made posters of each, decorated with their superpowers and some helpful aspects of the superpowers expanded on by the class. So, if there was a conflict, the teacher would ask, 'What superpower do we need? Do we have it, or do we need another superhero?' The time machine operator might be called on to turn back the clock to before one child hit another, or happy humpty to bounce over to get the ball that was kicked in anger over the wall. This approach created such a buzz of suggestions and chances to act out the dramas that it usually sorted the original argument with ease.

(ii) Secondary school relationship building

Aim

- Recognising the common ground between SEL principles and TIP approaches, to build on the safe-space work to practise these skills in the classroom. The work is to create a supportive learning environment with positive relationships at the heart of it. According to Venet (14), the core competencies for helping students manage social toxicity coming

from trauma implicit in their living situation, or community, as recommended by Patrick Camangian, are knowledge of self, solidarity and self-determination. She suggests comparing these three, using a TI lens, with the five skills of the CASEL approach – self-awareness, self-management, social awareness, relationship skills and responsible decision-making.
- Transparency in the aims of the work: academic, personal development and communications.
- Leadership and the transfer of power and choice as a process, consulting with the group. One tutor noted that initial efforts to review the work caused anxiety as learners were not accustomed to being asked and didn't know what to say. She found that offering several options made it easy for learners to answer. Reviewing skills developed with practice.
- I have always found with older teenagers that an important part of enabling the safe space to emerge was in creating and keeping clear boundaries. As the leadership and communication skills develop in the group, you can hand over more control to the students. I had good discussions about this, which often began when we looked at job or training opportunities. They all wanted a handy, well-paid job close to their home and one where they wouldn't have 'bossy people narking at them'. After many logical attempts to clarify their chances, without knocking their confidence further, I ended up saying, 'If there were jobs as handy as that, would I be in here every day at 8.45 for a full day?' I used to follow up with a short one-handed drama of the boss letting me sack any of the staff I didn't like on day one of my job! This usually broke the ice for some talk about the reality of training and employment, and successful relationships with co-workers and bosses. Motto: *You are working together, not getting married!*
- Modelling relationship skills:
   o self-regulation
   o patience
   o kindness
   o respect
   o honesty
   o active listening
   o reflection
   o fun and laughter.

Building relationships that are positive and supportive

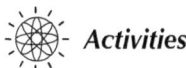 **Activities**

For concentration

- Breathing and counting five times.
- A set of simple stretches and some short movement breaks, which could involve going to sit with someone else.
- The ***Wayne Cook Posture** can be done sitting or standing. This is excellent for restoring focus. It may seem odd or awkward at first, but it's well worth trying – some people will like it, some won't! (15)

Self-regulation

We have different parts to our brain – the left brain focused on logical thinking and the right side on emotions (1). The old or 'reptile' brain is about basic survival and reacts instinctively to threats. This is how a person's sudden outbursts can be a response to triggers of trauma unseen by others. The importance of personal integration, staying in the flow, is likened to peaceful navigation down the centre of the river:

> When we're closest to the banks of chaos or rigidity, we're farthest from mental and emotional health. The longer we can avoid either bank, the more time we spend enjoying the river of wellbeing. Much of our lives as adults can be seen as moving along these paths – sometimes in the harmony of the flow of wellbeing, but sometimes in chaos, in rigidity, or zigzagging back and forth between the two. Harmony emerges from integration. Chaos and rigidity arise when integration is blocked. (13 p.20)

- Support students in staying regulated. Learning about emotions and where we feel them, how they are different from behaviours and how to recognise them in ourselves is important to process group and individual experience, and to avoid a blowout.
- If you are not the SPHE or pastoral care teacher, work these exercises into your syllabus. This can be done as oral language, practising for tests, group work and review of progress. The ideal is short, regular check-ins with yourself and how you are feeling, so you can restore calm and balance more easily.

- Students can design feeling volcanoes and measure the pressure and heat they assign themselves!
- If there are name-calling, racist, homophobic comments, it is helpful to remind the person that 'in this room we use first names only – that is how we speak to each other'. If you have a persistent serious issue, seek help from a group or organisation that specialises in providing workshops on the topic.
- Pre-empt upset by having smooth transitions and using group work to increase bonding and support in the class. It also helps with problem-solving and keeps students motivated. These sessions can be short – 5–10 minutes at first – until the pupils become accustomed to group work.
- Inform the class of changes before they happen.
- The cosy corner can be a more adult version, and you can have a ten-minute pass system, by agreement and within the school rules, where a student can leave the room and go to a safe place for ten minutes on showing the pass. Paula Flynn did a PhD study with students having behavioural difficulty and found no abuses of the pass cards – in fact, many never used them but loved having them (16).

Building bonds

- Comforting familiar rituals. Welcome and farewell. Celebration of stages of achievement. The group can develop their own celebration activities. This could be taking a bit of time for a game, a debate or group art project to acknowledge their achievements.
- Fun ways to talk and listen. ***The question game**, starting with easy, innocuous questions about favourite colours, pets, etc., progressing to ideas, beliefs and ethical questions.
- The ***Assertiveness training** (detailed in Chapter 6) is really effective. It includes discussion, drawing and acting, and can also be videoed if the participants want to. **Note:** Only use one video camera – no phones allowed – and delete the film section when you are finished with it.
- Marking special occasions. Birthdays (some pupils won't mention theirs, so you need a complete list of dates) are more sensitive at secondary level, so not a sure-fire success as in primary school. Maybe you could do a once-a-month celebration for the birthdays of that month.
- Different cultural holidays – collect the dates.

Managing conflict

- What happened? Who is upset? How can we fix it?
- Restorative justice has a full training package available for whole-school application. This is ideal, but if it's not available, you can use some of the principles in defusing conflict and finding a respectful solution (17). There are some helpful videos and research on the website.
- I got great training on managing conflict which I still remember. The first thing 'John', who worked with very angry and often violent young people, said was: 'Check yourself first.' If you're feeling triggered, angry, exhausted or upset, don't take it on. If there no one else who can do it, sit down near the situation of anger and say, 'I would like to deal with this tomorrow as I am feeling angry/exhausted/upset – does that work for you?' I often found the morning brought calm and a chance to talk it through.
- Always sit down and speak at a lower volume than the agitated person or people.
- If things are escalating, tell the rest of the class to take an early break, and if you need to leave for safety reasons, send someone to get help. State that is what you are doing and that you hope to help the upset person get calm again.
- ***Cartoons:** Four pictures for a given situation drawn by the individual and then discussed. 'What if' questions and third-party discussion are ideal with teenagers. Fold an A4 page in four and agree on a choice of several scenarios to be drawn. Do a bit of preparation with drawing stick figures. Most important: write the dialogue before drawing the box around it!

(iii) Adult education relationship building

Being aware that many adult learners are anxious and have multi-stress life situations

Aim

To reduce anxiety, personal and academic. To create a supportive atmosphere, enable positive relationships with the tutor and among the group. To build effective communications with the students to enable openness about needs, learning challenges and possible trauma triggers in the group. To encourage students to achieve their potential and support each other to do so.

Approaches

- Transparency in the aims and boundaries of the course.
- Clear information about the programme, its sections and learning objectives.
- Leadership and the transfer of power and choice as a process that is clearly defined.
- Modelling resilience and positive relationships, looking for new ways to do things when there are problems and setbacks. Asking the group for ideas.
- Always offer the choice to pass on any group round or activity.
- Clear boundaries about sharing personal stories – this is especially important with groups suffering high levels of trauma, as too much disclosure can be retraumatising for people in your group.
- Share the information around what extra supports, both for tuition and personal issues, are available in house, locally or online.
- Fun and laughter – celebrations of festivals and achievements of the group.

 **Activities**

Concentration

- Transition into class and closure. Some stretching and some relaxing breathing, counting in and out.

Self-regulation

- Free movement to take breaks as needed.
- Regular check-ins on how learners are getting on. Some people find this intrusive so they can work with a partner of choice and then just share whatever they are comfortable with the group.
- ***Breathing with longer outbreath** than the inbreath immediately calms anxiety.

Building relationships that are positive and supportive

- Modelling self-regulation and sharing with students some ways you use yourself to handle stress and anxiety.
- Energy exercises such as the Wayne Cook posture (15).

Building bonds

- Comforting familiar rituals.
- Fun ways to talk and listen.
- Marking special occasions.
- Different cultural holidays – collect the dates.

Communications

- ***The question game.**
- ***Walking debates.**
- ***Assertiveness programme.**

Managing conflict

- The communications work and the ***Assertiveness programme** will have provided experience and skills for managing conflicting views. The movement in the programme, like the ***walking debate**, helps reduce tension for sensitive discussions.

Movement

- Simple stretches can be effective to reduce tension:
  - Donna Eden's Daily Energy Routine – www.youtube.com/watch?v=Di5Ua44iuXc
  - Donna Eden's Connecting Heaven and Earth – www.youtube.com/watch?v=9OcnjqlqsMQ&list=PL7D41C4B25867E52E&index=1
- The work of Steele (18) on secondary trauma states you can reduce stress reactions in the body in a few minutes by movements designed to calm the physiological body's responses to perceived threat.
- Marching on the spot, then crossovers, elbow to opposite knee.
- If you have space to play a game, ***Cornflakes for breakfast** is always a favourite.

Managing the course workload

- Be clear about the learning outcomes and standards of work required.
- Visual charts are useful to show the timeline of the programme's work.
- Be transparent about the limits of your ability to support students, whether it is with the coursework or personal issues.
- Many tutors have found the restrictions of the curriculum and the need to complete modules in a short time affects their ability to engage with their students.

Managing assessment and exams

Anxiety about exam or assessment is a big problem for many adult learners returning to education. Different tutors have shared innovative ideas about revising material in preparation for exams:

- Making a quiz game with the topics for the exam as questions, playing the quiz game in teams.
- Interviewing previous successful students about how they managed the workload and showing these video interviews to incoming students.
- Having a practice exam and reviewing it with the group.
- Teaching some relaxation techniques to use before starting the exam.
- A matching card game with exam question words and meanings, to clarify questions such as:
  - Describe = tell me about it.
  - Compare = how are the things the same and different, better or worse.
  - Discuss = talk about it, tell me what you think.
  - Support your answer = show me why your answer is like this.

Cultural and language awareness

When I was teaching study skills to young adults preparing for an exam in a second or, for some, third language, I looked at their approaches to getting the information down on paper. The course tutor in the secondary school emphasised the need to write as much as possible and certainly more than one sentence for each answer. This was relevant for those writing in their native language, but it was causing these students to spend too long on second sentences and not complete the paper. We practised writing short answers with maximum information in them.

Collaboration and teamwork

You can start with easy, practical shared tasks such as rearranging the furniture or selecting activities and approaches to the work tasks. You can develop this approach to have the students work together on problems in the course material. They can share skills and concerns, and you can go around the groups to give input and support.

Review

- ***Group poster review** – this can be done at the start of a group process, during it or at the end.
- ***Unfinished sentences** – these are so simple and generate a lot of feedback. You can have generic ones and specific ones for certain times of the year or events.
- Asking the students regularly to give feedback with review techniques, and keeping in contact informally, will keep you informed about the reality of their lives. This will build trust so the learners can share concerns with you, before they have become stressed out about them.
- Review each section of the work before moving on, as per the layout on your visual poster guide.

Key points of Chapter 4

- Building a safe place and a supportive relationship is a gradual task, and it is about connection, consistency and regular communications.
- Every pupil/group is unique – there is no formula.
- Safe boundaries are important, and they need to be detailed.
- Predictable routines give security; changes need to be flagged in advance.
- Everyday communications and reviews are at the heart of the work. Ask and listen!
- Kindness and respect are the cornerstones of the safe space and supportive relationships.

References

1. van der Kolk BA. The body keeps the score. USA: Viking Penguin; 2015.
2. Ainsworth E. The Effects of Environmental Factors on Secondary Educational Attainment in Manchester. Manchester: Manchester Schools Council; 1974.
3. Bowlby J. Attachment and loss: Volume 2. London: Pimlico; 1998.
4. Picardi A, Fagnani C, Nistico L, Stazi MA. A Twin Study of Attachment Style in Young Adults. Journal of Personality. 2011;79(5):965–92.
5. Ainsworth MD, Blehar MC, Waters E, Wall S. Patterns of attachment: A psychological study of the strange situation. Hillsdale, NJ: Erlbaum; 1978.
6. Durlak JA, Weissberg RP, Dymnicki AB, Taylor RD, Schellinger KB. The impact of enhancing students' social and emotional learning: A meta-analysis of school based universal interventions. Child Development. 2011;82(1):405–32.
7. Walter MC, Wynard TS. Preparing educators to support SEL: The foundational role of trauma-informed training. Social and Emotional Learning: Research, Practice, and Policy. 2025;5:100071.
8. Substance Abuse and Mental Health Services Administration. SAMHSA's Concept of Trauma and Guidance for a Trauma-Informed Approach. Rockville, MD: Substance Abuse and Mental Health Services Administration; 2014.
9. Bailey S. Teacher-Preparation Programs and Trauma-Informed Teaching Practices: Getting Students to CHILL. Current issues in Education. 2022;23(3).
10. Sweetman N. A culture of silence: A study of a social emotional learning (SEL) intervention for teenagers affected by domestic violence. PhD thesis.Trinity College Dublin; 2019. www.tara.tcd.ie/handle/2262/86088
11. Nicholson J, Perez L, Kurtz J, Bryant S, Giles D. Trauma-informed practices for early childhood educators. London: Routledge; 2019.
12. Little People's Montessori Pre-School. Fun Brain Gym exercises and routines for children: Little People's Montessori Pre-School; 2022. www.youtube.com/watch?v=q-e0E1V5Ls4
13. Siegel DJ, Payne-Bryson, T. The Whole-Brain Child. New York: Delacorte Press; 2011.
14. Shevrin Venet A. Equity-Centred Trauma-Informed Education. New York: Routledge; 2024.
15. Phillips C.The Daily Energy Routine Exercise 3: The Wayne Cook Posture. www.youtube.com/watch?v=LPT19Im8vnU2011
16. Flynn P. Authentic Listening to Student Voice & The Transformative Potential to Empower Students with Social, Emotional and Behavioural Difficulties in Mainstream Schools. Dublin: Trinity College, Dublin; 2013.
17. Restorative Practices Ireland, Dublin, 2024. www.restorativepracticesireland.ie
18. Steele W. Reducing compassion fatigue, secondary traumatic stress and burnout. UK: Routledge; 2020.

5
The three Rs
Reflection, resilience and relationships

This chapter expands the focus on relationships to include resilience and reflection. It looks at some of the research around resilience and the current thinking on what resilience means in recovery from trauma. The use of reflective practice for educator and pupil will be explored. There are four sections in this chapter:

- Section 1 looks at the meaning of resilience and reflection, and aligns this with relationship building. Some personal experiences are included.
- Section 2 includes approaches and activities for resilience, reflection and relationships in a primary classroom.
- Section 3 details some of the activities that encourage resilience and reflection to become part of an approach to dealing with life's challenges, large and small, for secondary students.
- Section 4 provides approaches and activities for resilience, reflection and relationships in adult education.

'Approaches' are the attitudes, beliefs and responses we bring to the work of TIP in the classroom. 'Activities' are the materials we use to enact these methods of working and teaching in the class. These approaches and activities are all based on positive relationships and cannot be effective in a vacuum.

A personal story of reflection, resilience and relationships

My first job as a community facilitator was in a tightly knit inner-city community and was a personal development group for women on a local employment scheme. I had a strange start as I was stopped by the police as I was running down the road because I was late. I was wearing a hiking jacket of a brand that apparently had a certain connotation. Then I was asked by the police, 'Why are you running? And what is in your rucksack?'

It was my first intimation of the drugs trade that scourged the residents of this community. I arrived hot and bothered but determined to make a success of the group. I found the rooms and walked in, apologising for being a few minutes late.

'We're not f---ing doing this crap and you can't make us,' one very angry woman shouted at me. Others joined in, saying similar things, and the atmosphere was very negative and tense. I was taken aback as I had worked in many areas with different groups and always formed good relationships.

I took a couple of breaths and let it die down. Glancing out of the window, I saw a baker's van stopping at the local shop. Inspiration struck, and I asked, 'Do they sell cream cakes?' Someone said 'yes', and I suggested a volunteer go down and get some cakes while we arranged the room for tea and cake. The room got busy, and the cakes were bought, and we all sat down. (Fun fact: dairy cream is a natural sedative! My go-to when overwhelmed!)

After some general chat, I asked what the problem was with the programme. There was a rush of explanations concerning last year's programme. It seemed to have involved lots of personal disclosures that led to feuds and arguments in a group where many were related and involved in each other's lives. I asked some questions about the previous year's course, and then asked if it would be OK if I made some notes on the flipchart to help me understand the problem. This was agreed. It became obvious that the previous tutor had done some very inappropriate group work, exposing all sorts of issues with no resources or remit to cope with the disclosures.

We had a discussion about what the programme would be like if it was to be useful for them. We went from general themes like 'communication' to 'wanting to be more confident applying for jobs or courses'. I asked if it would be all right to show the group the plan I had made for the programme, and to discuss what would be safe boundaries for them and me. At this stage, the group was interested and began suggesting additions and changes to my proposal which was up on the wall. As the two hours were almost up, I asked them if it would work for them if I left the poster in the common room for them to study and add to, and we could look at it at the beginning of the next session if they happy to try the programme. This was agreed, and it went on to be a really productive programme with a lot of learning and laughter. Cakes became a weekly feature, with everyone bringing treats to the group.

Reflective questions

- What might have led to the inappropriate disclosures of the previous course?
- What could you do to maintain safe boundaries in any group?

As I analyse this experience under the three Rs, I see resilience on my part in persevering and initiating relationships while responding and taking the group concerns seriously. Some reflection on my part around the intensity of emotion in the group suggested some serious harm had occurred. On asking the group to reflect on their experience, a clearer picture emerged of their concerns. This respectful listening on both sides was the start of a trusting relationship. The women showed resilience in committing to an unknown programme when the previous programme had been harmful. This experience made me very aware of the vulnerability that can exist in groups and the need for checking in with participants at all stages that they agree with and understand the programme methods and process.

The fast period of reflection on my feet that day was developed further in the planning and review of other programmes. That is possibly more typical of the daily experiences of educators than the ideal of carefully planned reflection and review of your work! The use of choices for the learners at every step is very important and can seem a little artificial at first. These women were very fearful and felt what had been a deeply upsetting course for their friends was being forced on them.

The elements of choice and cultural sensitivity were important. As a very talented family worker told me once, 'People on benefits spend a lot of their time filling out long forms about every personal aspect of their life, so don't add to them!' He then told me how a student he took on placement into one of his sensitive groups lost half the group 'with a load of boring, nosey forms that no one wanted to fill out'. Another thing to be aware of for all ages is the community living situations and the vulnerability of those on benefits or allowances to the views and dictates of the authorities. In this case, it was a condition of their employment that the women completed my programme. Similarly, the children and young people in your classroom are legally obliged to be there – they have no choice.

Section 1: Relationships, reflection and resilience

Relationships, reflection and resilience are key elements in developing integration for everybody and particularly for those whose emotional, social and cognitive development has been harmed or delayed by traumatic events. These 'three Rs' are referred to frequently in the building of sound mental health and in the recovery from trauma and adversity (1).

Resilience in the physical world is the flexibility required of an object to return to its original shape after enormous strain has been put on it. The Oxford Dictionary defines it as 'the capacity to withstand or to recover quickly from difficulties; toughness' and as 'the ability of a substance or object to spring back into shape; elasticity'.

Resilience research

Research into resilience was originally focused on the individual. Resilience was viewed as a somewhat innate quality, with phrases such as 'the invulnerable child' being used by Anthony in 1974 (2).

Resilience is no longer considered an innate quality of the individual child but as something that is formed by the family, community and resources that are available to victim of trauma at all ages (3).

The work of Fleming and Ledogar (4) found that:

The three Rs: Reflection, resilience and relationships

Early resilience studies were concentrated on qualities of the individual child or adolescent – the resilient child. The resilient child was described as invulnerable (Anthony, 1974) or invincible (Werner and Smith, 1982). Gradually, researchers came to view these terms as misleading for several reasons and have broadened or sharpened the concept of resilience. (Abstract)

Later studies of resilience and recovery became more focused on the life situation of the individual. The family background, the community, the socioeconomic circumstances that people are living in are very influential in resilience. Writing in 2012 (3), Ungar stated:

I suggest that to account fully for the processes associated with resilience, we need to shift our focus. There is evidence that resilience is less an individual trait and more a quality of the child's social and physical ecology. This ecological understanding of resilience has the potential to resolve both definitional and measurement problems. (p.1)

In researching resilience, reflection and relationships, I found lots of material for adult skills, and many research studies into the importance of supportive friends and family, overcoming challenges and developing hope for the

Figure 5.1 It can be easy to bounce back!

future, for resilience and recovery. The support of family and friends and a home environment that meets the individual's physical and emotional needs are the basis for recovery from trauma.

The only difficulty with this advice is that those affected by trauma will have been betrayed by loved ones and often struggled to take part in education, leisure and work. This can be due to lacking concentration, social skills and confidence because vital steps in development have been damaged by trauma and intensified by the diverting of developmental energy to survival.

A study of outcomes for fostered young people in Ireland (5) interviewed 87 foster parents and social workers, four young people aged 12–18 and four people aged 18-plus, whose feedback suggested that:

> Factors promoting resilience: Participants referred to many different factors which they felt had either helped to promote their own resilience or had the potential to promote the resilience of children and young people in foster care in general. The majority of factors identified were either believed to be inherent in the individual child (e.g. 'ability to express myself' and 'being positive') or micro-systemic (e.g. 'feeling part of the family', 'foster carers who make an effort', 'feeling like I belong' and 'a safe environment'). Meso-systemic factors identified by the group included 'having a good social worker', 'foster family supportive of birth family' and 'support'. (p.3)
>
> Factors preventing resilience: Much of this discussion related to the presence or absence of protective factors (e.g. a young person 'having someone to talk to') and risk factors (e.g. 'having no one to talk to'). A number of variables were included among these factors, such as 'lack of control over their life', 'feeling different' and 'foster carer's lack of understanding'. However, the most commonly cited factors were those in relation to support from a social worker: the young people collectively listed 'lack of support from a social worker', 'no effort from a social worker' and 'lack of social work support for foster carers' as being factors most likely to reduce children's levels of resilience. (p.3)

Reflective practice

Reflection is part of what we have been doing in all these practices where we involve our students, whatever their age, in the process of planning the work, doing it together and reviewing the results.

The three Rs: Reflection, resilience and relationships

The **plan–do–review model** is an easy-to-remember method that works with TIP approach. The students are involved in every stage as much as possible. The time, the abilities of the group, the curriculum and the resources of the teacher or tutor are all the factors that will affect how this is put into practice.

Reflective questions

- How do you experience resilience among your students? How do they demonstrate it?
- How can this be supported in your education situation? Is there any discussion at staff level?

Reflection, consultation, building resilience and action

A committed tutor of an IT programme was very frustrated by the fact that he was stuck with a content-heavy curriculum that was stressing the students out massively. He still had to get it completed for them to gain the certificates that they had all signed up to achieve. He reflected at length on how he might change the programme and made the following adjustments in line with the students' concerns. He moved some parts of the work into the second semester and allowed more time in the first semester for students to identify their own needs and capabilities and work together in groups, supporting each other to complete the sections. Thus, when they hit the second semester, they were feeling more confident and had built up some support systems among each other and developed the habit of asking the tutor for support and explaining where their difficulties were.

Using the learning of past students

Another useful form of reflection that was used by a tutor whose students were feeling very overwhelmed and threatening to drop out was to interview some past students who had succeeded in completing the

> course, and then, with their permission, to show parts of these interviews to the new students. This action is not only part of reflection but also of building resilience – the feeling you can do something, the possibilities are there and seeing for yourself that other people, just like you, have done it.

As we all know, particularly in technical subjects, if you miss a section or can't understand it, you very quickly find yourself tumbling into confusion. As someone who has great difficulty with the computer, I know how this feels. A simple inability to remember a drop-down menu means that a whole process that you're in gets lost or mixed up. In the tech programmes, as in any other programme, communication with the tutor is very important. This needs reflection in action: plan out the changes, implement them and then review them yourself and with your students.

The University College Dublin (UCD) (6) reflection programme gives very practical approaches for the tutor to think about what happened, look back on it and learn from it. What was your experience? How did you cope with your own needs, feelings, hopes, approaches to the work?

Integration of memory and experience

Dr Dan Siegel produces various materials, from theory-based books on 'Mindsight' (7) for clinicians to practical guides for applying these principles to working with children and young people in daily life (8). The three Rs are central to his theories on Mindsight, which are about integrated experience and memory, and balanced responses to emotions. The analogy of a wheel explores the ability of the individual to retain a secure 'hub' of harmony at the centre, allowing the individual to deal with the ever-changing emotions and experiences on the rim and in the spokes of the 'wheel'.

The integration of the left logical brain and the right feeling and sensing brain is ongoing for children, teenagers and young adults until approximately 25 years old. So, much of the work in primary and secondary school is preparing the ground for this continual process of integration.

Previous chapters have looked at how relationships are the baseline where the important learning of security in needs being met takes place.

Support and love from carers is vital through all the developmental stages of childhood into adulthood. All the suggested approaches in the previous and following chapters are building up the tools to integrate experience and both types of memory – implicit and explicit – and to increase self-regulation and self-awareness.

Using the 'good for one, good for all' approach means using methods and approaches in the classroom (of all ages) that model and teach these SEL skills, with the extra layer of awareness of the effects of trauma on child and youth development offered by TIP. I also want to clarify that these approaches and supports in the classroom are very valuable and can be life-changing for some victims of trauma and neglect. However, these efforts and activities are not a replacement for therapy or professional interventions when they are needed. This is in line with understanding the different role of the educator and the therapist.

Exceptionalism

The study of the individual and the idea that everybody has free choice in how they do things and starts from an equal place was part of an equality approach to addressing disadvantage. This belief has been called 'exceptionalism', where the success of one person, against all odds, places the responsibility to achieve a change in circumstances on the individual. The supposition is that everybody starts from the same place, with small differences, and with a decent amount of effort, anyone can fulfil their dreams for a good education, a well-paid job and a secure home. Often you will read an interesting article in the newspaper, detailing the *amazing* journey of a young student who successfully completed their college education after a very difficult childhood in a violent home. This can be held by many as showing incredible resilience and bravery. But there are hundreds of young people who go to university in Ireland every year, the majority of them from middle-class homes. Nobody thinks this is a marvellous achievement; it's the norm that's expected of them.

Delayed gratification

Many parents ask teachers and childcare workers to teach their children resilience. This is a very difficult task because resilience requires challenge, which is not always easy or instant to resolve. Research suggests that the foundations of resilience are the ability to wait for things (delayed gratification), to continue and persevere with complex problems or situations, and to recover balance after taking hard knocks in life. Some studies maintain that these qualities can be identified very early in children and are markers for how they will manage to persevere and succeed in their goals in life. The 'marshmallow test' was an experiment conducted by psychologist Walter Mischel to analyse a child's ability to delay gratification, restrain impulsivity and regulate emotion to achieve a greater reward. In the 1960s Stanford marshmallow test (9), preschoolers were left in a room with a marshmallow for around 15 minutes. They were told that if they waited, they would be rewarded with a second marshmallow. So, instead of eating the one in front of them, they would get a greater reward of two marshmallows.

The experiment claims to show that the children who successfully resisted the marshmallow during that 15-minute test went on to be more successful financially and emotionally. Later research disputed this claim and noted that other factors such as socioeconomic status were not explored.

Resilience in the context of ACEs

In a society where families are small, and many people can gratify almost every wish of their children instantly, situations for resilience to develop can be rare. On the other hand, traumatised children often develop extreme resilience of a dogged type that enables them to support a great deal of suffering without flinching or expecting it to change. The ACEs research of the 1990s (10) and beyond showed very clearly that very difficult and traumatic experiences in youth affected the whole life – in health, in jobs, in relationships and in the ability to recover from adversity.

Resilience in its essence suggests an ability to bounce back and recover that may not be available to those who are traumatised, as their social skills and ability to relate to and trust others have been very damaged.

Articles about resilience and recovery from trauma always emphasise relationships, gaining support from those around you whom you trust, setting new goals for yourself, caring for yourself physically and being with people who understand you and want the best for you (11).

These are all things that would not be a part of life for someone who has suffered trauma or betrayal within the family home. As the ACEs research

(10, 12) shows, these emotional wounds continue into adulthood and make relationships difficult for many people who have suffered trauma.

Eimear, a family therapist, found that with her young clients trauma was normal:

> *One of the big things that struck me the most, I think, was how matter-of-fact children tell you about extremely traumatic incidences and situations that they have lived through as though they are very normalised. Say, one 12-year-old was taken away from their mother. The mother has a history of alcoholism, and they were responsible for getting two younger siblings up and out of bed, fed, dressed and into school, and the mother was physically abusing her as well. X talks about that story in a very well, 'That's just the way it is'.*
>
> *Drugs, alcohol addiction appears to be fairly prevalent in many children I have met through the system. You get the impression that, you know, an overuse of alcohol and drugs is very ordinary.*

If interventions and support have been made available, it's heartening to see how people can recover and go on to make happy lives and families of their own. But without interventions, it's very challenging to build relationships

Figure 5.2 Hard to bounce back if it's broken!

and trust if you haven't experienced positive affection and security directly in your formative years.

Skills and knowledge are built on positive experience and expectation that new events or items will be useful or fun to explore. This was something I learned when I taught catering in Youthreach and the students wouldn't eat my food. I reviewed with them the ingredients we had used to make the recipes they had asked for. Their feedback was that they wouldn't eat my food because it was 'too lumpy'. I realised most of my students were used to eating very processed food. If this is your experience of nutrition and mealtimes, you will not know how to cook, and it will not be part of your experience or expectation as something enjoyable, interesting or economical. The process of introducing fresh food and learning about nutrition and costs was gradual and successful.

The three Rs in trauma recovery

The psychiatrist and writer Dr Dan Siegel has written extensively about trauma and recovery (13). He suggests resilience, relationships and reflection as the cornerstones of integrating and recovering from trauma (14). Siegel's video on the topic is clear in placing relationships at the centre of integration and positive development. Reflective practice is important for processing experience and having the ability to live in the present, rather than responding from a place of trauma. The ability to self-reflect helps to understand one's own behaviour and emotions, and then be more empathic to others.

Self-regulation is the ability to calm oneself and return to balance after a shock, fright or highly emotional experience. This is also connected to delayed gratification in the integration of mind, body and heart. Reflection is important for the child in developing integration as a part of this is recognising their own emotions, feelings and behaviours, and regaining flow when overwhelmed.

All these elements are contained within the supportive communicative relationship; in isolation, they can become a meaningless tick-box exercise.

The value of the three Rs

Being able to use these to stay in the flow

Relationships, reflection and resilience are vital for healthy development for all of us during our lives, and these abilities all need positive safe environments to flourish. We all need particular skills to be able to use these three Rs as a resource.

For those young people badly affected by trauma in their environment, these skills may be scarce or unavailable in the home space. This is why it is so important to consciously prioritise these attitudes and activities in the school and education space. All the different elements of building and strengthening these skills are interlinked.

For example, the child who has gained awareness of their emotions and has some strategies for regaining balance and equilibrium (self-regulation) will have learned those skills through positive relationships and some reflection on different events and feelings. The confidence in a safe place gives resilience to try, fail and try again, and to view obstacles as something that can be overcome within supportive relationships.

The positive effects of movement, art, storytelling and all the various activities build the three Rs in all children, with an extra spoonful of awareness and support for those that need it.

I don't mean that you pick them out in the group as the 'trauma kids', but that you approach your work using a trauma lens with each individual pupil. For example, in the same activity, as the neglected child gets a hearty much-needed breakfast and supportive welcome, the well-cared-for child will enjoy their toast and chat at the breakfast club. The same menu is offered to all who attend the breakfast club. (The 'club' offers breakfast to pupils before school. Some clubs are targeted by need, and some are open access. My experience is that open access is more effective as it is less stigmatising.)

Section 2: Primary school – resilience, reflection and relationships

Approach: The attitudes, beliefs and responses we bring to the work

- Safety. It's very important to start from the *safe place*, especially for children who have been traumatised and have difficulty with frustration and a very small window of tolerance.
- The *window of tolerance* means the ability to cope with difficult emotions or challenges. If the window is narrow, it means that they can't cope

with failure, criticism or rejection. The only place to start is where they are – activities with built-in success that you can expand as their confidence grows.
- The safe place and positive relationships that you as the teacher build in your classroom will let you slowly introduce challenges that increase resilience.
- Any of the games and activities that are suggested can be expanded to have more complexity. It is the challenge and experience of sometimes succeeding and sometimes failing, and being able to accept this without blaming yourself, that build the foundation of resilience.
- The ability to look forward and accept that something has not gone well but has finished and something better could be coming tomorrow is a huge part of resilience. This is also lacking for neglected and traumatised children as they have rarely had their dreams come true in even minor ways.
- Modelling these attitudes and behaviours yourself is so important.

Another horrible legacy of the trauma inflicted on children is that they will frequently blame themselves for the abuse or cruel neglect they have suffered. Judith Herman's work addressed this in her book (15): 'simply by virtue of her existence on earth, she believes she has driven the most powerful people in her world to do terrible things. Surely, then her nature must be thoroughly evil' (p.105, quoted in Shevrin Venet (16)).

Figure 5.3 This is all your fault . . .

Developing empathy in the class is ongoing and widens the support network for everybody.

The child who has low self-esteem and blames themselves for everything can be supported by a child who is very relaxed about the tower of bricks that just collapsed or the paint that spilt and ruined the art project.

Activities: How we enact these methods of working and teaching in the class

- The skills you have been building all the time in naming emotions, practising calming and expressing emotions safely will be the foundation of this ongoing work.
- Movement: ***Walk on a line**, ***Marching on the spot** or around the line, simple exercises from ***'Brain gym'**. There are many types on the internet. I chose this as it is short and easy to follow (17).
- Identifying emotions: The matching games of emojis can progress to exploring the emotions and feelings of characters in books and posters in the classroom. This helps in learning the names of emotions and what effect they have on us.
- Locating feelings in the body, knowing what the physical sensation is like in the body.
- Social games: taking turns, winning and losing, inclusive chasing and skipping.
- Guessing games for concentration – an old favourite is having a number of items on tray, then the tray is taken away and you try to remember the things that were on it.
- Circles for sharing information and getting to know each other. Simple circle topics like favourite games, TV programmes and pets are a good place to start.
- Storytelling with objects, cartoons and props. ***Story bags**.
- ***Dressing up and acting out** small stories or dramas.
- Art-based activities, both individual and group. Art with a theme such as ***the tree of helping hands**.
- Self-regulation – dependable schedules and clear expectations in the environment. Building up the skills to regain balance – breathing, drawing the feeling, adding it to the *****feelometer**. Taking some time in the cosy corner. Name it to tame it!

- Puzzles and challenging tasks can develop more complexity as the children become more confident.
- Rewards can be delayed and need more effort to achieve, while keeping their inclusive quality of recognising and celebrating effort. Rewards work well when they are immediate or directly related to an activity in progress. Rewards/validation that benefit the whole group, and where the class has a part in choosing them, are effective in building relationships.
- Discipline/maintaining order and safe boundaries. Individuals can be held more accountable for their actions as their sense of personal choice and confidence increases. Use restorative justice questions: What happened? Who is upset? What can be done to repair things? (18)
- Cartoons and drawings of the different sides and functions of the brain can be interesting for the children and start their understanding of how emotions and feelings can bubble up and take over. The logical left brain is developing, but it can be offline in a big way with young kids as they are swamped by the big emotions and feelings of the right brain. The illustrations in Siegel and Bryson's book (8) are useful for showing this process.
- *Modelling is crucial for this age group.

As you deal with everyday frustrations and successes, you can share this with the children as appropriate. For example, you might share that you are disappointed that the coloured paper you ordered didn't arrive to finish the art project. You can be specific in describing how you feel cross in your throat with the shop and annoyed with yourself for not collecting it. Then, after some deep breaths or recording it on a card on the 'feelometer' (a large thermometer you have made with the pupils in the classroom), you can suggest some movement for all, and smile to show you are now happy again. Then the children can help to find another way to finish the work. You must include some of their suggestions, whatever they are, if you ask them to help you. When I was a young Montessori teacher, I let the infants paint old boxes and cardboard things they had made with a free hand. You guessed it! They all used black and went off delighted. Other classes emerged with tasteful paper flowers as their project. One lad went home delighted with his black Batman garage and came back upset when his mother threw it out as rubbish!

- All kinds of active and symbolic play, from games of shop to sand-play, express experience and emotion. While the educator avoids making a therapeutic interpretation of the work, the action of naming and expressing experience is in itself supportive for the child. Following a 'good for one, good for all' approach means these fit within the guidelines of the curriculum, with some extra sensitivity for the pupil who has suffered trauma.
- Games involving planning and guessing, reviewing activities and events, 'stick with it' challenges – all these approaches build resilience.
- The regular small reviews you do with the children about activities or situations in the class are a form of reflection.
- Discussion about what characters in fiction might feel or do are another form of reflection. These can be books or posters or their own stories from story time or ***A day in the life of. . .**
- Younger classes can draw a figure of any kind and add emotions or experiences to it.
- Simple ***cartoons** explore the outcome of situations. These are more suitable for older classes as they need to be able to draw representative figures.

Section 3: Secondary school – resilience, reflection and relationships

Approaches: Attitudes, beliefs and responses we bring to the work

- You will need your own resilience and reflection to introduce these ideas with resistant teenage groups. Many young people affected by trauma will have had multiple intrusions in their lives by different services – not always useful. It is essential to build trust slowly without making demands.
- Modelling the honest communication and respect you want to receive from the students is vital. I suggested to student teachers that apologising to students when you have made a mistake is important. One student smiled and said, *'I had a bad day and gave loads of homework. The next day I apologised for my mood and suggested we do the work together.'*
- Reflection can be applied to the progress of projects or phases of the work. All kinds of review can be reflective.

- Look for steps to success, resilience and possibility in students and situations.
- Reflection of more personal issues can be approached slowly through debate and 'what if' questions. ***The assertiveness programme** fosters these conversations. A third-party approach is safe for the students.
- Media stories can be useful to explore complex situations, especially those of resilience and perseverance in the face of adversity.
- Relationships in the group grow in kindness and empathy as the group develops.
- Conflict can be handled using assertiveness and listening skills.
- Remember that behaviour is a form of communication and expresses a need.
- Integration, or FACES as Dan Siegel calls it, is the ultimate aim: flexible, adaptive, coherent, energised and stable. He describes this state of harmony as being like a choir where each individual voice is driving the energy of the group forward to create the music (7).

Activities: How we enact these methods of working and teaching in the class

- All the relationships built up and skills developed in the group for communication and for empathy will facilitate developing the three Rs.
- Movement including simple stretches, marching on the spot and some yoga moves can be done in the room. Movements that stretch the neck and shoulders help release stress. If the hall is available, games like obstacle races, and running around to jump into a colour taped or box marked on the floor release energy. ***Cornflakes for breakfast** is a good one.
- Use technology to increase and deepen relationships, but not replace them. Creating word cloud to show results of feedback and using Padlet to gain information from the group are useful but never a substitute for live review and interaction.
- My experience of teenagers is that use of media, third-party questions and debates are really effective ways to address more sensitive issues. The old jokes about 'asking for a friend' aren't wrong!
- ***Making a magazine** is a way to incorporate art, debate, leisure, fashion, football, a problem page and whatever interests the group comes up with.

The three Rs: Reflection, resilience and relationships

Challenges around teamwork and overcoming obstacles to complete the project develop organically.
- The *assertiveness programme** gives a framework to explore feelings and behaviour and has shown profound effects on many young people I have worked with. The results ranged from minor to major.

> A boy yells at a teenage girl who has gained some weight, 'Here, have you got a bun in the oven or what?' She looks him up and down and answers, 'I don't think you're funny.' Silence fell and he slunk off!
>
> Another girl was accused wrongly of shoplifting. This could have ended in a rage with an assault on the security man, but she told us, 'I asked for a woman security to search me, and when she found nothing, I said I'm making a complaint. Hey, I got a voucher!'
>
> When I did final interviews with my group on my SEL intervention programme (19), I asked them about engagement with questions:
>
> Norah: So, are you OK with talking more directly about the domestic violence now we know each other better?
> Dylan: Yeah. . .
> Norah: If it's too nosy, would you tell me to stop?
> Dylan: Yeah, sure, assertiveness and all that! (p.230)

- A group effort by the class for other pupils. Older pupils can develop a game for younger classes. This can be paper-based or active like an obstacle race. The stages of **plan–do–review** apply and offer lots of learning points.

    All the stages of negotiating with the teachers involved, booking the hall, etc. are done by the pupils.
- Older students could consider a fundraiser either a cake/jumble sale or doing a run or walk in aid of a local group or foundation selected by the class. The most important thing is to make sure everyone has a role no matter how small. Designing the sheets to record the activity or sales that will be on display is useful, as is laying out the space, and keeping the lists of participants. The list of jobs needs to include everybody.

Section 4: Adult education – resilience, reflection and relationships

Approaches: The attitudes, beliefs and responses we bring to the work

- Reflection helps in making sense of your own life story and training. Many postgraduate learners on teacher education courses have said to me: 'It is just the way I have always done it – I never really thought about it, or how the students experience this.'
- How much is this three Rs work apart of your contract? In many adult education classes, there will be learners who are under pressure or have suffered serious trauma, such as homelessness, returning to education after negative experience in childhood, recovery from addiction, or refugees and individuals who have experienced violence and abuse. Of course, all groups are different, and you may have a middle-of-the-road group whose members don't report any significant trauma. The 'good for one, good for all' TIP approach means that you offer choice, safety, trustworthiness, cultural sensitivity, empowerment and collaboration to your students. This will be encouraging and supportive for all students.
- Transparency in what is involved in the work means being clear about the standards needed and the timetable of the work. Visual charts are very helpful.
- Review and reflection are essential around both the process of the class group and the progress of the work. Ongoing review will keep you up to date with students' successes and challenges, and help you identify blocks to learning for them.
- Small group work is very helpful for review as shy individuals can give feedback easily, which is then reported back to you and the full group. The ***group poster review** is ideal for this.
- Establish safe boundaries for you and your learners. It is very important to define the boundaries of your role and the purpose of your class and group.
- If you are able or willing to do it, you can offer some information on relevant in-house or local support services and allocate some time for queries or use a question box.
- Use TIP principles to make a safe space for your students where they feel heard and are part of the planning of the work as much as possible.

The three Rs: Reflection, resilience and relationships

 ## Activities: How we enact these methods of working and teaching in the class

- Greet students by name.
- Check in with a *****rose or thorn review**.
- Review the layout and process of the class on an ongoing basis. How do the learners prefer to work? When do they want to take breaks? Are there any particular cultural or individual sensitivities? Do they want to change the furniture around? Are people stuck on anything?
- Little and often – these kinds of review and reflection can be five or ten minutes.
- Small groups cooperate on problems that have arisen with the work – this builds a supportive atmosphere in the class and shares skills.
- *****Assertiveness programme: avoiding the 'bonio'.**
- Review sections of the work and process – review is always a form of reflection.
- Foster acts of kindness – *****bouquet of compliments.**
- Celebrate when a section of work is completed. A simple display of the work, a round of applause, some appreciation shared among each other for support given can be joyful and effective. A visit from another educator adds something to it as well.

Figure 5.4 Working together – repairing relationships

> ## Key points of Chapter 5
>
> - Relationships are the foundation of learning from infancy, and recovery from trauma is based on trusting, supportive relationships.
> - Resilience exists in the complexity of a person's life, not just within the individual's innate ability.
> - The person's life situation within the community, the family and extended family, and the level of trauma experienced, individually and in the community, all impact resilience.
> - Resilience can be celebrated and built on for all individuals as they share and experience it.
> - Reflection happens in the moment, after the event, and with another person involved – in, on and with.
> - Reflection can be an integrated part of classroom practice that is fast and easy.

References

1. Treisman K. Working with relational and developmental trauma in children and adolescents. London: Routledge; 2017.
2. Anthony E. The syndrome of the psychologically invulnerable child. In: Anthony E, Koupernik C, editors. The Child in His Family: Children at Psychiatric Risk. New York: Wiley; 1974. pp.529–45.
3. Ungar M. The social ecology of resilience: Addressing contextual and cultural ambiguity of a nascent construct. American Journal of Orthopsychiatry. 2011;81(1):1–17.
4. Fleming J, Ledogar RJ. Resilience, an Evolving Concept: A Review of Literature Relevant to Aboriginal Research. Pimatisiwin 2008; 6(2): 7–23.
5. Douglas D. Fostering Resilience: An exploration of the link between resilience, outcomes and foster care in Ireland [Masters]. Department of Children and Youth Affairs Scholarship Programme: Waterford Institute Technology; 2012.
6. UCD Teaching and Learning Resources. Reflective Practice Models. www.ucd.ie/teaching/t4media/reflective_practice_models.pdf
7. Siegel D. The mindful therapist: The clinician's guide to mindsight and neural integration. London: Norton; 2010.
8. Siegel D, Bryson T. The Whole Brain Child:12 Revolutionary Strategies to Nurture Your Child's Developing Mind. New York: Delacorte Press; 2011.
9. Navidad A. Stanford Marshmallow Test Experiment. Simply Psychology. www.simplypsychology.org

10. Bellis MA, Ashton K, Hughes K, Ford K, Bishop J, Paranjothy S. Welsh Adverse Childhood Experiences (ACE). Liverpool: Public Health Wales, Centre for Public Health; 2016.
11. Department of Education. Guidance for Primary School Staff – Using Psychological First Aid. Dublin: National Educational Psychological Service; 2022.
12. Felitti VJ, Anda RF, Nordenberg D, Williamson DF, Spitz AM, Edwards V, et al. Relationship of childhood abuse and household dysfunction to many of the leading causes of death in adults: The Adverse Childhood Experiences (ACE) Study. American Journal of Preventive Medicine. 1998;14(4):245–58.
13. Siegel D. Mindfulness and Neural Integration – blending technology, self regulation and education; 2009. www.youtube.com/watch?v=LiyaSr5aeho
14. Siegel D. Mindfulness and Neural Integration; 2009. www.youtube.com/watch?v=Nu7wEr8AnHw&t=199s
15. Herman J. Trauma and Recovery: Basic Books; 1992/2015.
16. Shevrin Venet A. Equity-Centred Trauma-Informed Education. New York: Routledge; 2024.
17. Little People's Montessori Pre-School. Fun Brain Gym exercises and routines for children: Little People's Montessori Pre-School; 2022. www.youtube.com/watch?v=q-e0E1V5Ls4
18. Restorative Practices Ireland, Dublin; 2024. www.restorativepracticesireland.ie
19. Sweetman N. A Culture of Silence: A study of a social emotional learning (SEL) intervention for teenagers affected by domestic violence. [PhD]. Trinity College Dublin; 2019. www.tara.tcd.ie/handle/2262/86088

6
Voice in the classroom

> This chapter focuses on the concept of voice and how it relates to the work of the educator.
> There are five sections in this chapter:
>
> - Section 1 shares some personal experiences around voice in my own work and two vignettes of very different experiences of self-expression by young and old.
> - Section 2 looks at some background to the development of this idea of voice and why it's important.
> - Section 3 includes approaches and activities for enabling voice in a primary classroom.
> - Section 4 details approaches and activities for developing pupil voice at the secondary school level.
> - Section 5 includes approaches and activities for empowering voice in adult education
>
> 'Approaches' are the attitudes, beliefs and responses we bring to the work of TIP in the classroom. 'Activities' are the materials we use to enact these methods of working and teaching in the class.

This chapter caused me to reflect a lot on my work and the meaning of 'voice' and what it is to be an individual or part of a community whose voice is silenced or misinterpreted. Many of the studies I read on developing student voice and the voice of those in marginalised communities focused on participative research. These involved working with children and young people who were active as co-researchers.

Section 1: Experiences of voice in the community and in education

As I thought of the reality of those years, I remembered so many individuals and families who could not speak for themselves. For example, I had various experiences of mothers asking my advice on court-ordered contact where there had been violence and the child was terrified of going to the father. Mothers described children vomiting and having nightmares before contact and the horror of forcing screaming children into the car or buggy for their visit.

The reasons for this lack of voice were varied and sometimes unexpected. Another thing I realised, which many people reading this know already, is that if you are not in tune with the voice of your students, you will not be able to do your work effectively or in many cases at all. I worked in one school that could be wild. It was my first job as a young teacher, and on day one, when I came down to lunch, there was no sandwich for me. I was a bit surprised, and then the staff all said, laughing, 'Don't be offended. We didn't think you would still be here. The shortest anyone has lasted was a religion teacher who left at elevenses.'

The person who had to find their voice in this case was me, and I did. I had to devise lots of ways around the curriculum and learn the dynamics in a class full of teenage boys, 90 per cent of whom had no interest in the exam curriculum and were there to hang out with their mates. For that class, finding their voice was in the debates and discussions we had, and in developing a critique of the English course. I remember distinctly the lads were in knots of laughter at the English poems glorifying nature: 'Yeah, not much of that around here.' We worked on a lot of ways to answer questions on the syllabus from their point of view. Particularly in English, History and Geography, we became co-experts on including opinions and any slim facts they could remember in their answers. This was the first time I had been confronted with the irrelevance of many of the materials to the students' interests and their lives.

As Conor, a young teacher, said of a disengaged class group he was supervising:

> I was just crestfallen about how badly served this particular class was, I mean, there was maybe 17 in the class, and 12 of them should not have been sitting in a room for two and a half, for an hour and a half

doing an exam – like it's just not the right recipe for those, those 12 students, and they don't – I feel like they don't feel like school – has the schoolwork that they have been offered any particular resonance with them? The schoolwork doesn't have any resonance with them. They don't really feel like they have anybody in their corner or anybody looking after their interests. So, yeah, they were in school, they weren't on the street, but they were in the room, and they were just like not sitting the exam, sat around, chatting in the exam . . .

The whole time, I just had a sad face. I just felt so sad for them. I felt terrible for them, and I didn't feel any rage or anger towards them, but I know how it feels to feel rage and anger towards that misbehaviour when you're sort of not able to provide what they need, and so you're just trying to keep the lid on it, and they're just looking to . . . They're just trying to get through the day. I'm not equipping them with malice. Yeah, they're in a crappy situation. And so, if they can wind up the teacher or wind up another student for a laugh as a sort of a way to release some steam themselves. They'll go for that.

Wider influence from research with young people

The groundbreaking work of Lundy (1) with young children, using a variety of materials, enabled their expression of their views around education. Houghton's participant-led work with young people affected by domestic violence (2) led to them making submissions to parliament in Scotland. The work of Holt (3) showed the powerlessness of children, and their silenced voice in contact arrangements post-separation. These studies are inspiring and demonstrate clearly that children and young people are very capable of understanding their needs and expressing their views when given support and space to do so.

Communications and confidence

In hindsight, much of the work I did was in working on developing confidence and communication skills in response to needs as they arose. The following vignettes illustrate the struggles of a young lad who didn't understand what was needed in communicating with teachers, and an older woman whose negative experiences of education left her illiterate. The scapegoating of her whole community because it had been dominated by drug dealers was another burden she carried.

'Come in right now or I'll knock the head off you!'

A secondary school form teacher expressed concerns about a pupil who was looking at rollover suspension with likely expulsion. I was very surprised as this lad, Al, was in school clubs. So were his sisters, and his mother, Carmel, was very supportive of the teenagers' education. I asked exactly what was happening, and it appeared that he was completely ignoring class instruction from female teachers and then reacting aggressively, including losing his temper and swearing at them when corrected. I met with Al and asked him what was going on. He got really agitated and angry and described how if any group was 'messing', he always got 100 per cent of the blame and that 'they' (the teachers) never told him to sit down before they sent him out or gave him sanctions. Al was convinced they had it in for him and just wanted him kicked out. I talked with his mother who was puzzled by the school reports. She confirmed he was a good lad at home and held down a part-time job. At that moment, Carmel looked out of the window and saw her youngest girl kicking a football at the fence. 'Come in right now or I'll knock the head off you!' she yelled out of the window. After a few more threats the girl trailed in and was sent to her room. Carmel was telling me how Al had ambitions for an apprenticeship that needed school exams and references, or he wouldn't qualify. We chatted over tea, and she shared something of the struggles of raising kids in a neighbourhood where drugs were an ongoing danger to youth. Local dealers used young people for deliveries and then kept them involved by threats and debts. She described the need to keep a firm hand on her daughters and son, make them listen to her and keep them out of bad company. I enquired how she did this, and she described facing them down and: 'keeping them in line by shouting at them and letting them know I'm still in charge here'. We had a long discussion, and this clarified that Al was accustomed to loud, threatening correction which escalated till he complied. He was literally 'deaf' to the more formal reprimands of his teacher – they didn't reach the required decibels. A shared effort between Carmel, the teacher, Al and the support worker (who offered some social skills training) meant he stayed in school to complete his exams and take up his apprenticeship.

My ****** project

A communications programme that I designed for a community group involved a short information-collecting project around local services. One older woman, Mary, had very little literacy and was thrilled that she wouldn't have to do a project. I suggested a young person in the family could help her as a scribe, and maybe use their experience for a school project. A grandson was duly roped in, and the study Mary did was amazing. The interviews she did with other older residents drew a picture of a friendly, supportive village environment that had been her early experience of family life in the flats. The current destruction of the community and the fear of violence and crime brought in by drug dealing was a horrible contrast. The government representative who came to our presentation evening was very impressed by her work. We hoped it would influence officials to understand the suffering of ordinary families as a result of the drugs trade in the flats. Every project was printed, bound and titled. Mary wanted to call hers 'my effing project' as she had found it initially very stressful to acknowledge her illiteracy and then to work with her young grandson. She agreed that it was too useful to be called that and chose another name.

These stories are examples of the many instances where those I worked with were silenced and excluded in many cases for infractions whose significance they were unaware of or powerless to influence.

Section 2: What does 'voice' mean for young people?

The question of voice for students of all ages has many different interpretations. The United Nations Convention on the Rights of the Child (4) made it clear that children have a place in deciding on their engagement in many areas of their life, including education. This same right is supposed to apply to adults, although, in many cases, people of all ages are excluded for reasons such as being part of a marginalised community, having a mental health issue, having a language issue or lacking the skills to make themselves heard and express their wishes and feelings.

The Laura Lundy model (5) states that to enable their voices to be heard, children need:

- Voice: Children must be enabled to express their views in a way that they choose.
- Space: Children need a space to explore expressing their views that is safe and inclusive.
- Audience: Their views must be heard by someone who has the ability to make changes.
- Influence: There need to be changes in response to their views where appropriate.

Laura Lundy and colleagues' work (1) with Children's Research Advisory Groups (CRAGs) focused on the ability of all children to express opinions and respond to complex questions given the appropriate tools. In this project, the children were aged four to five, so a variety of visual aids and verbal questions were used to ask what would help children settle in school on entry and various questions including what the reason for school attendance was, and what was hard and easy about school in their experience.

> [I]mages were used to stimulate discussion and thinking among the children on the issues surrounding the project: images of children playing together and sharing, children learning new skills . . . It was clear that the children had grasped the key concepts being discussed in that they articulated quite clearly their perspectives on the purpose of education, commenting that it was 'important to go to school' so that they could 'learn to share' and 'learn new things' such as 'reading, writing, and numbers' and that this would help them 'do other things'. (p.721)

The voice of young people who are traumatised was very clearly articulated by a group of young people who were discussing the effects of domestic violence on them, in a participative study conducted by Houghton (6). The young people said: we are the experts, and we know what we need and what we want. In many cases, those who are deemed *vulnerable* are not included in research, and their voices are not heard. So, you have this strange situation where we want to hear the voices of those who are marginalised and oppressed, but they can't be approached to take part in research because they're considered 'vulnerable'.

Hearing voices directly without imposing your values

Parental engagement is often viewed by academic measurement

A Scottish study of a primary school in an underserved area looked at parental engagement (7), using a participative research approach with the children and parents. The children identified important learning to include life and social emotional skills.

A total of 63 per cent of all learning experiences ranked 'Most Important Learning' referred to learning for self-development. Comments showing awareness of learning as part of growing up or learning for future adult life were most numerous within this theme.

- Pupil E: 'I learned how to cook dinner. Learning how to cook dinner is important because when you are an adult you need to cook dinner for everybody.'
- Pupil C reported on academic learning, not to do well at school, but for real-life future needs: 'And you need it [learning to read] to grow up.' Pupil C's high ranking of writing and spelling reinforced this: '. . . to be an adult, so you have to learn.'
- Pupil H stated: 'I think the football . . . because I can make a job out of them . . . and the football, I can make quite a lot of money by it.'
- Pupil B: 'Me going to my dad's work . . . It's kind of important seeing another person's work.' (p.1122)

The children shared hopes for the future and motivation to work, and reported that their parents involved them in household responsibilities to help them learn life skills and independence.

This study noted a tendency to middle-class prejudice against parents in underserved communities and suggested that future research should focus on what is valued in families as regards learning and how this could inform more links with the school (7).

This highlights the need to look to the strengths of parents and invite their participation in a respectful manner. I remember I used to call parents Mr or Mrs, and I later realised that, for most people, only those in authority or debtors call other adults Mr or Mrs. Later, I always started with: 'Hi, I'm Norah. How do you like to be called?' In 30 years, no one ever said 'Mrs Brown!'

Within your group, you need to be conscious of people's vulnerabilities, and this is why you start small. All the exercises that we've done previously in other chapters – to get people to review their own work, to discuss things that are going on based around the work we're doing, to listen to each other, to share feedback through all kinds of different methods, written, online, and in person – lead to students of all ages developing a clear and confident voice within the education system at any level that you're working in.

The importance of small steps and managing expectations to build trust is important. There may also be the challenge of including vulnerable individuals, suggesting the need for careful consideration of vulnerabilities and starting with small, manageable steps to develop a voice within the education system. In your own sphere, you need to follow through and only offer what you can deliver. For example, getting pupils to review a particular activity and share ideas for how they would do it differently next time will be a useful start. If you involve them in choices around the timetable or the curriculum, which you can't change, you will create disappointment and mistrust.

Section 3: Enabling voice in the primary school classroom

Approaches

The attitudes, beliefs and responses we bring to the work

- The work of building voice in the classroom is embedded in the values that we have discussed in every chapter so far. These are building trust, effective communication, relationships, resilience, reflection, and full transparency in group activities and curriculum.

- The work enables young pupils to express their views, problem-solve, use teamwork and develop some options to self-regulate.
- Enabling voice in the class is part of the safe space you are creating every day. Children feel able to ask for help, share their ideas, celebrate their success and ask lots of questions!
- Gentle inquiry: Some pupils may have difficulties with speech itself, and some may have trauma-related reasons for being electively mute, choosing silence. A caring young mother with a slight speech defect told me she didn't speak to her two boys much because she didn't want them to suffer like her, by having a 'weird' voice. Another child, the youngest in a family that all had a very distinct intonation that was hard to follow, had such muffled diction that it was hard to understand her at times. Intensive one-to-one work with sounding words and syllables saw fantastic improvement in a couple of weeks.
- See behaviour as a means of communication taking time to try and work out what is happening for the pupil in crisis or meltdown.
- Receive all contributions as equally valuable.

Activities for building voice in primary school

These activities are just a few of the many games and activities that encourage young children to play together, negotiate turns, resolve minor disputes and get to know each other.

- When you have explored the reasons for an individual child's reluctance to speak, the first task in building voice is enabling pupils to speak individually or with a friend or two.
- Many pupils are very reticent about speaking in public for any reason. This is where *circle time, *question game, rhymes, singing and other oral games are important.
- The second phase of speaking in a group is developing the ability to speak on a topic or share an experience or viewpoint. This needs an ability in the group to listen without interrupting or judging others.
- Games: *I spy: colour I spy, shapes I spy, numbers I spy.
- *Swapping games such as *What's changed?
- Story games: *A day in the life of a euro coin/a puppy/a teddy/a truck. This can be done in a group circle or pairs/fours.

- Matching games such as ***Matching emojis** – make and laminate two sets and then play Go Fish. With readers, you can match with words that name the emotion.
- ***Circle time**.
- ***Review** their work and their experiences in the class group in fun ways, using lots of visuals and movement. Thumbs up and thumbs down gives you an instant answer.
- Teamwork tasks can be curriculum-related or part of a game – doing a puzzle, solving a quiz, finding a hidden object.
- Problem solving can be of a particular problem in the class or a fictional situation.
- Offer a ***cosy corner** and/or objects and exercises to help the child regain emotional balance.
- Keep choice to participate as an ongoing part of all the work and support every effort as valid.

All aspects of the class curriculum can use choice methods to involve the pupils in expressing their voice in preferences. The Irish Primary PE Association's handbook for voice in physical education (8) has easy-to-use games and worksheets available online, which gradually increase choice in the sessions. Many teachers are doing these things already, but it is handy to have ready-to-use resources on an uninspired day.

Section 4: Enabling voice in the secondary school

What students need for participation and safety

Approaches

A three-year project with nine schools and 22 teachers on developing student voice in the secondary classroom was completed in Ireland (9). A partnership approach was used that reduced teachers' fears of being undermined in their classroom. Teachers became more interested in the work as they saw it improved pupil engagement and strengthened positive relationships in the classroom. The study found that the training of both partners – students and teachers – was necessary for the programme to have real significance.

Another effect of the project was that teachers who were not involved became interested as they saw the positive effects.

A research study with young people about the effects of trauma on their behaviour and the need for trauma-informed teachers and systems was conducted in consultation with young girls aged 14–18 in a court-ordered school in America by West and colleagues (10). The girls showed deep understanding of how trauma had affected their behaviour and their ability to settle to study and get along with others. The things they needed from teachers included patience, respect and understanding. Their request for teachers to take control is clear:

> Theme 6: [what the students want from teachers]
>
> 'I would definitely tell all the teachers like, if you see someone's having a problem in class don't just let it happen, you know, try to solve the issue right then and there. Don't keep stopping and "okay you guys need to stop talking", you know, pull them aside and let them know you can't keep doing this. You gotta do something about it. You can't just sit there in class and talk all day.'
>
> 'When the girls are cussing out the teacher and not letting the teacher speak . . . the teacher needs to, like, boss up [defend themselves] and put them [the disruptive student] out of class.' (10 p.61)

A further study by Crosby and colleagues (11) built on the work of West and investigated two schools with a comparable intake of females with court involvement issues who were all residents of a very underserved area. One school had a trauma-informed approach, and one had a traditional approach to discipline and classroom management. The figures are a powerful statement:

> [T]he trauma-informed school operates using a trauma-focused school climate intervention (described below), resulting in a 2% suspension rate (i.e., nine students suspended) during the observation period (Baroni et al., 2016). The comparison school utilizes suspension and expulsion as its primary means of behavior modification and student discipline. Approximately 79% of the comparison school sample had been suspended two or more times, and 67% were suspended three or more times during the school year.

These two studies are unusual in that the students were involved in a collaborative research project that used various methods to enable them to share their experiences freely. Many research studies into trauma-informed practice in education rely on previous studies and statistics, and the interviews are with teaching staff. The high value the students put on respect and understanding of their situation from teachers was the same in both schools and echoed the findings of West.

One important difference between the schools was highlighted by the young interviewees around their relationships with their teachers:

> Students at the trauma-informed school identified teaching staff as being useful in helping them to recover from difficult emotional states, with other students being the typical source of the conflict that triggers negative mood changes. On the other hand, students at the comparison school attributed these mood changes to the negative interactions with school personnel, while support from peers was often a source of comfort to overcome negative emotions. (11 p.72)

Maintaining a safe and boundaried learning environment was seen as essential by Gerry:

> *For a child who's experiencing trauma or has experienced trauma; they need structure. They do not need to be in a place where they are grandstanding. I'm thinking of a child now I worked with who went through a very difficult time in kind of middle childhood and was clearly at school in a primary school where she got a lot of support. And she went to secondary school, to a very big one, where she was, you know, a tiny cog in the wheel. And really the straw that broke the camel's back was kind of silly behaviour in the classroom throwing apples and stuff. Because that didn't feel safe for her. So, order is really important for children.*
>
> *They need to be safe. So, in other words, it means to be protected from harm. And they need to be secure enough that they know roughly what's going to happen and then when things go wrong. They need to be – what's the other word? – soothed? So, children need to feel safe coming to school. And they won't feel safe if there's bad behaviour going on. And they need to be reasonably secure. So, a child comes in . . . 'I know, it's Tuesday. I'm having PE, yeah, and this Thursday, I have art. And we always do maths first, and I always go after little break. I always go and see Miss Jones, and she helps*

with my reading' – *and they know it's a predictable environment. And they know that there's always going to be a teacher on the yard to keep them safe.*

- The challenges of strengthening voice in secondary school are very different. Traditionally, the secondary teacher supervises work and dispenses information in a more distant manner than the primary teacher.
- Teachers and students alike will often need some training and support to explore this way of working without adding more stress to the classroom.
- Awareness of what is needed for effective, useful learning – student voice research by Crosby (11) showed that students are aware of the need for structure in the class along with respect and understanding of their needs and experiences.
- Students may feel it is tokenistic or wasting class time to develop new interactive communication in the classroom, and teachers can have reservations about losing control and academic standards dropping.
- The small steps of reviewing progress informally and asking students what the most helpful way is to tackle a section of the curriculum are good starting points.
- Make connections with the students with unconditional positive regard. Alex Shevrin Venet (12) emphasises the need for unconditional acceptance while maintaining necessary structure. For example, greet a latecomer in a welcoming manner, and address the attendance issue at a different time, not in front of the whole class.

 ## Activities for building voice at secondary school

Older teenagers will need activities that aren't viewed as 'babyish'. Another important point is that teenagers usually dislike being asked individual opinions, so the following methods use a group or small group approach. These activities are a mixture of small group work, relevant to the curriculum, methods for review and whole-class activities to encourage communication.

Many of these materials can be adapted to review sections of the curriculum to find out where students are stuck or confused and learn about their preferences. This information helps you to know what can be done to increase student engagement in learning. All these things are designed to be short

Voice in the classroom

activities. The exhibitions and celebrations can be built into holiday periods – for example, before half-term or Easter – when work is winding down.

- ***Question game.**
- ***Assertiveness programme.**
- Small group work on tasks – these can be short, spontaneous responses to a challenge encountered in the work, or planned projects.
- ***Group poster review of work or activity.**
- ***Unfinished sentences (for review).**
- ***Walking debate.**
- Discussions in small groups will introduce the ongoing review method in a way that is not confrontational. If student voice has not been a regular part of school life, these exercises accustom students to expressing opinions in an easy way that doesn't put any one person on the spot.
- Building relationships that allow for open expression of needs and experiences by the students is vital. A young teenager mentioned he had to go to court, which sadly was not rare in our students. He told me that his cousin of the same name had been caught in a stolen car and ran away, and our student's name had been given to the police, who then arrived at his door. Following the very strict code of the area in which he lived, he was going to take the fall for the cousin. Nothing would convince him otherwise – this is the kind of dilemma you can be faced with.
- Listen to the student views by regular check-ins and reviews.
- For the curriculum and TIP to work together, supporting the students in approaching and completing the work, give as many choices as possible in learning and assessing the work.
- What does voice mean? Set clear boundaries about the purpose and use of voice in the classroom. The limits of expression are respect for others and hearing their views.
- Reduce discipline problems and interruptions by encouraging conversations and inputs from the students as part of the daily routine.
- Make space for viewpoints that are critical and don't agree with your views. It is vital that you model the behaviour you expect from the students.
- Encourage relationships that are supportive in the classroom, between yourself and the students and among the group.
- Reduce stress among learners by implementing their suggestions where possible. If it is impossible, explain why. Some members of a student group on a specialist programme requested football for an hour of each

session. I explained that the programme was to expand social skills and communication, so football didn't fit the bill, and it wasn't a unanimous choice of the group. If it had been, I could have negotiated a short session of football with some review of social skills on the pitch!
- Encourage students to take part in school forums such as student councils. You can set up some enquiry-based groups in your own class to investigate local amenities, for example.
- Provide information about local groups and forums for young people, including those that are working for equity in education.
- Some aspects of the curriculum involving citizenship will offer exercises that include public speaking and positive actions in the local or national area.

The *assertiveness programme

The visual and interactive **assertiveness course 'Happy head, Aggro head and Sad head'** that I used with all my groups showed great results with all ages. The extremes of behaviour from aggressive (Aggro head) to passive (Sad head) are contrasted with the assertive (Happy head) attitude. I didn't include the fourth category of 'passive aggressive' as it was a bit too complicated, but

Figure 6.1 Seesaw of feelings – finding balance

I have found that participants naturally include passive aggressive behaviour in their questions and scenarios.

This programme was designed in response to groups with low literacy levels or poor communication skills, where I knew assertiveness skills would be really useful for the group. In some cases, the regular programmes for learning assertiveness were too paper-based or moved too fast to direct personal scenarios. This cartoon approach has proved effective every time with many different types of groups because it is fun, and the indirect approach of the *heads allows expression of feelings and thoughts in a safe way. The participants usually get it quickly and add their own suggestions.

The initial discussion concerns the different moods and reactions we all have and the notion of the seesaw that we can get stuck on – being full of temper and frustration (Aggro head) or feeling helpless and hurt (Sad head). We want to learn some ways of staying balanced (Happy head), able to cope with things and get on with other people.

This programme starts with each person taking three templates – each has a big head, with a heart shape, a thinking bubble and a speech bubble. An A4 sheet gives space to draw and write.

The three heads are called Aggro head (aggressive), Happy head (assertive) and Sad head (passive). The programme can progress to acting out scenarios suggested by the participants, taken from media or cards supplied by the facilitator. Adolescents will enjoy being the teacher or parent standing firm to the demanding or defiant teenager in the scenarios. You may be surprised how they see the importance of boundaries and rules when they are in the responsible adult role!

The head templates, information on the principles of assertiveness and some initial questions are included in the materials chapter.

Section 5: Empowering voice in adult education

The adult education area has a much a wider reach. Some courses will be focused on personal development including rights-based issues and accessing supports and benefits. Other courses will be content-heavy to gain a particular skill or qualification. You as the educator will still need to know the needs and abilities of your group and build supportive relationships, whatever the content of your course. As mentioned before, don't offer anything unless you are sure it is possible, and establish the boundaries between personal disclosure and the work of the group at the start of your programme. It is useful to have information on supports available within the educational institution and local support services with referral methods to share with your group. This can be anything from computer courses in the local community centre to counselling services.

Approaches to building voice

- Welcome each learner.
- Learn about their academic, social and language needs in a respectful way.
- Demonstrate openness to learn about each person and their needs and experiences.
- See the group as a valuable resource that can support each member.
- Develop critical thinking and problem solving with the group.
- Use reflection and review as part of everyday practice.
- Share creative solutions, using teamwork. Use a variety of communication methods – oral, visual and movement-based – to encourage everyone to participate.
- Establish clarity in what is expected, both in the work and in the social process of the group.
- Lots of small choices in everyday matters build the habit of speaking in public, expressing preferences, showing talents and sharing problems around the work.
- Exhibit the students' work in the school and beyond. Local libraires and other educational institutions may host an exhibition of the students' work. Check out what are local issues and how your students can get involved. Some items on the curriculum require outreach and research by the student, especially communications modules.

Reflective questions

- What forums for students to express opinions are there in your institution?
- Are they used effectively? What can you do to enable student voice in your class

Voice in the classroom

Activities for building voice in adult education

This section is so varied that you will need to think carefully about the needs of the students, how you can find out what they need and the adjustments you can and can't make to the programme. All the welcoming, accepting approaches to the students are important.

Voice as a support and a link to safety was the issue raised by Elaine, an experienced therapist and yoga teacher working in mental health with traumatised patients. She noted that:

> *I use my voice all the time. So many of my clients can't do a lot of the yoga poses – they are too triggering for them. Like someone who was assaulted doesn't feel able to lie down – a lot of people use chairs. I talk all through the short meditation. This quiet space can be overwhelming for them, so, you know, my voice and directions to stay in the environment are kinda like a lifeline. It takes time to build a relationship and trust in the room, and when you do, it's great – but baby steps.*

- *Introductions such as the *paper ball throw.
- *Group poster review to share what people know already and what they want to learn.
- *Question game.
- *Assertiveness programme – especially using the *bonio.
- *Small group work on tasks – these can be short spontaneous responses to a challenge encountered in the work, or planned projects.
- *Unfinished sentences.
- *Walking debate.
- Researching local and national groups involved in issues of interest to the group.
- Conducting surveys in class/school or locality.
- Celebration or presentation for group completion of work or project.

Reflective questions

- Where have you seen the students using their voice? What encouraged this action?
- How can you enable this in your work with the students?

> **Key points of Chapter 6**
>
> - It is essential to check out the causes of an individual or group being reluctant to speak or showing difficulty in physically articulating.
> - People of all ages can use their voice with the right tools and a safe place to do so.
> - These skills can be built up gradually in lots of different ways and can be creative and fun.
> - All ages can share fears around speaking in public and can overcome them.
> - Finding their voice in the classroom, then the school, students can expand to wider involvement in community issues and equity in education.

References

1. Lundy L, McEvoy L, Byrne B. Working with young children as co-researchers: An approach informed by the United Nations Convention on the Rights of the Child. Early Education and Development. 2011;22(5):714–36.
2. Houghton C. Young people's perspectives on participatory ethics: Agency, power and impact in domestic abuse research and policy-making. Child Abuse Review. 2015;24(4):235–48.
3. Holt S. Domestic abuse and child contact: Positioning children in the decision-making process. Child Care in Practice. 2011;17(4):327–46.
4. Unicef. The United Nations Convention on the Rights of the Child. London: Unicef; 1990.
5. Lundy L. 'Voice' is not enough: Conceptualising Article 12 of the United Nations Convention on the Rights of the Child. British Educational Research Journal. 2007;33(6):927–42.
6. Houghton C, VAV: Voice Against Violence. Shaping the future: One voice at a time: Tackling domestic abuse through the voice of the young. Scotland: VAV; 2011.
7. Cameron T, Mowat J, Adams P. Understanding the value of parental engagement through pupil voice in a Scottish Primary School. Education 3–13. 2024;52(8):1116–31.
8. VOICE-PE Project Team. Getting Started with Student Voice in Primary PE. Irish Research Council; 2022. www.irishprimarype.com/wp-content/uploads/2023/06/Getting-started-with-student-voice-in-primary-PE-resource-final.pdf.
9. Macken G. Student Voice: Opportunities and Challenges in an Irish Context. ETBI Education Journal. 2019.

10. West SD, Day AG, Somers CL, Baroni BA. Student perspectives on how trauma experiences manifest in the classroom: engaging court-involved youth in the development of a trauma-informed teaching curriculum. Children and Youth Services Review. 2014;38:58–65.
11. Crosby S, Day AG, Soames M, Baron BA, Ford CB, Jones KV, et al. Exploring Trauma-Informed Teaching Through the Voices of Female Youth. Journal of Trauma Studies in Education. 2023;2(1):62–78.
12. Shevrin Venet A. Equity-Centred Trauma-Informed Education. New York: Routledge; 2024.

7
Trauma-informed practice in other disciplines
Equity in education

> This chapter will look at some developments in trauma-informed practice (TIP) in related areas like social work, medicine, psychology and in the classroom. The need for TIP in all the areas involving direct work with individuals and institutions is becoming clearer; it is not limited to education. The research into resilience and the long-term effects of ACEs are linked to social justice and equity in education. The meaning of equity in education and the application of this understanding in the classroom will be explored, and direct impacts on learners will be discussed.
>
> There are three sections in this chapter:
>
> - Section 1 offers a brief look at other areas of TIP practice, with some useful references for further reading.
> - Section 2 discusses the meaning of equity in education and the relevance of social justice in education, with a focus on the individual educator.
> - Section 3 asks 'What can an educator do?' and considers some of their possible actions at all levels of education.

Section 1: Aspects of understanding trauma-informed practice

Earlier chapters looked at the research into Adverse Childhood Experiences (ACEs) that laid the foundation for the development of TIP. ACEs research established the reality of the long-term and life-changing effects of childhood trauma on those people impacted by it.

Different workplaces and research areas developed trauma-informed approaches in response to this understanding of trauma and its effects.

Many people were already working with marginalised and traumatised people, as Gerry, an experienced teacher and principal, pointed out:

Our understanding of trauma from a neurobiological point of view has expanded so much in the last thirty or forty years. So, a lot of books have been written on trauma, so trauma-informed practice (in inverted commas) has come into all the caring professions and probably education was one of the last. But I think we have to be really careful that while we can explain it now, there has always been trauma-informed practice. There have always been teachers and nurses, and doctors and carers who have worked with people with a deep understanding of trauma. Because you see, there's two ways to learn. You can learn from studying and books, and you can learn experientially. And there are other ways too, but they're the two that are coming to mind. So, there have always been people who have a knowledge of how to be present to people in trauma. And some of those people have never done a professional training.

Some developments in understanding TIP resulted from research into trauma-informed approaches through all the disciplines, with education being a late adopter in many areas.

Medicine

The TED Talk by Dr Nadine Burke (1) about her experience working as a doctor in an undeserved area of San Francisco is moving and very informative. She describes the level of trauma she identified among young pupils as being a public health epidemic, and states that it is a challenge of this century to give young people the hope and healing for a positive future. Dr Burke found an everyday presentation of physical symptoms that were somatic, an expression of trauma among the children.

The individual view of trauma

The early studies of trauma focused on the individual experience, situating resilience in the individual for recovery from trauma. This dislocation from social, emotional and economic realities left the responsibility for recovery with the individual who had suffered the trauma. The obvious gap here is that all forms of trauma occur with an abuse of power by the perpetrator on the victim. This holds true from the individual who suffers an attack to the refugee from war, famine or persecution.

The recovery advice that suggests you 'lean on supportive friends and family' or 'look to the future' is useless to the person who has been violently betrayed by family or community and may have lost their hope of a better future. Ungar (2) writes of the importance of linked-in supports to enhance resilience:

> [Interventions] need to address three aspects of resilience-related programming: make social supports and formal services more available and accessibility; design programs flexibly so that they can respond to the differential impact specific types of interventions have on children who are exposed to different forms of maltreatment; and design interventions to be more focused on subpopulations of children who have experienced maltreatment rather than diffuse population-wide initiatives.

Socioeconomic factors

The shift in thinking from the exceptionalist view of those affected by trauma led to deeper analysis. Rather than a dewy-eyed response to the kid who made it to the winning team from the underserved community, researchers began to ask why are there no leisure facilities or pools in this area? Why is there a 'pipeline' from school exclusion to jail here? Catriona O'Toole (3) suggests that:

> ACE research treats the socioeconomic environment as a background factor, rather than an explicit object of interest. It fails to acknowledge a wide range of adversities associated with structural inequalities, such as being a member of a marginalized or oppressed social group, experiencing racism, poverty or homelessness, living in or having to escape conflict or war zones, experiencing or witnessing community or school violence, and being taken into care. (p.3)

The situation of any individual in their community, their family situation economically and in terms of stability, the resources available in the school or college to support resilience, and other traumatic events they have suffered determine how they will be affected and recover from trauma. If the trauma is located in the family, the community or the school, or is ongoing as part of the living conditions for a minoritised group, then recovery and support will be very challenging. The child in a secure home can recover from a traumatic event with the wrap-around support of a loving family and possible extra resources such as counselling. The family will typically have the funds to get private therapy if public services are unavailable or waiting lists are too long.

Eimear, a family therapist working in an underserved area, identified poverty as the main issue:

Yeah, poverty is, is the number one, lack of resources, hobbies like, even though there are some good community bases, there doesn't seem to be any sport after school there . . . So, there's, there's very little for the kids to get engaged in outside of school hours. So, and they're all, the ones I've met, anyway, out walking the streets every night.

Inclusive education

Research in the field of inclusive education suggests that the voice of the child has not been heard as professionals in special education made decisions based on their perception of the child's best interest. This rarely included the child's wishes or opinions, and is a deficit model which is focused on the child's difficulties, not their possibilities (4). Richard Rose wrote about the labelling and dismissal of children who came from an impoverished mining community and were struggling with formal learning. He developed this theme of the intersection of disadvantage with disability (4 chapter 11). The inevitable hardship that caring for a child with disability brings and the association of poverty with increased risk to health mean that, in his view, 'those of us who are concerned for the development of inclusive education cannot afford to divorce the processes of teaching and learning from the need to achieve social justice' (p.153).

Fovet (4 chapter 6) noted that the medical model for viewing disability sees it as a diagnosis of a difficulty belonging to the person. The institution essentially expects the person to 'fit in', with some possible adjustments being offered to them to compensate for their deficit or problem. The social model of disability suggests that disability is a construct and that it comes from the environments, activities or objects that are not accessible to all users by their design (4).

In the same chapter, Joanne Banks referred to her years working with excluded pupils with social, emotional and behavioural difficulties. She expressed a view that children were labelled, then excluded from a system which they didn't understand and didn't offer to meet any of their needs. The fast track she mentioned from minor disagreements to school exclusion is a common experience for pupils whose social and educational needs are not met in the school and who struggle with family and community poverty (4 chapter 6).

Physical factors

Research by van der Kolk (5) and Maté (6), among others, found that trauma effects and memories were stored in the body, and that prolonged trauma affected health and triggered biological reactions in the body. Neurological research into trauma is advancing and demonstrating the effects on all the interlinked stages of development, physical and psychological. The importance of all types of movement like yoga, dance and physical exercise was emphasised for regaining integration and becoming grounded within the body, for those affected by trauma. Van der Kolk describes the link between trauma and physical pain (5) and recounts the many specialists and diagnoses the person can engage with that never identify their symptoms as their effort to cope with trauma:

> [E]xperts in such self-numbing, they may become serially obese or anorexic or addicted to exercise or work. Half of all traumatized people try to dull their intolerable inner world with drugs or alcohol . . . [or] sensation seeking. Many people cut themselves to make the numbing go away, [or engage in]bungee jumping or high-risk activities like prostitution and gambling.
>
> When people are chronically angry or scared, constant muscle tension ultimately leads to spasms, back pain, migraine, headaches, fibromyalgia and other forms of chronic pain. They may visit multiple specialists, undergo extensive diagnostic tests and be prescribed

multiple medications [. . .] all of which fail to address the underlying issues. Their diagnosis will come to define their reality without ever being identified as a symptom of their attempt to cope with trauma. (5 pp.265–266).

The experience of Elaine, yoga teacher and therapist, highlights the importance of working with the needs and abilities of the person in front of you:

Yes, exercise and yoga can help with trauma, [but] you know they can also be frightening and overwhelming. Some people make it to do a couple of movements in the class and that's a big deal if they have been clutching a blanket on the side for weeks. I was given a class of people I didn't know a few weeks back and it didn't work well – it's not a cure-all. There has to be trust there. That's the main thing.

Psychological analysis

The British Psychological Society produced a new report (7) and a different approach to the assessment of patients presenting with many different symptoms of serious distress. The method is called Power Threat Meaning (PTM) Framework, and it aligns with TIP principles in recognising the unique experience of each person. This PTM approach also values all the responses of the individual to trauma and sees these as adaptations they have made to survive:

In summary, this framework for the origins and maintenance of distress replaces the question at the heart of medicalisation, 'What is wrong with you?' with four others:

- 'What has happened to you?' (How has Power operated in your life?)
- 'How did it affect you?' (What kind of Threats does this pose?)
- 'What sense did you make of it?' (What is the Meaning of these situations and experiences to you?)
- 'What did you have to do to survive?' (What kinds of Threat Response are you using?) (p.9)

Trauma-informed practice across the disciplines

The Innovate Project (8) in the UK prioritised respect and relationship building, based on trauma-informed practice. Their website has videos that discuss self-regulation and other key issues in plain language. The project also sees the broader view of TIP as being essential for all professionals to avoid pathologising trauma victims by diagnosing their trauma responses as a form of mental illness.

TIP is relevant across a range of disciplines and enables helping professionals to avoid pathologising trauma and, instead, emphasise the resilience and recovery inherent in traumatised individuals' best efforts to stay safe. This is particularly relevant for young people who have experienced emotional, physical, sexual, and relational trauma as a result of exposure to extrafamilial risks. In practice systems that are not trauma-informed, young people may be easily penalised for behaviours that result from prior trauma and their own best efforts to feel physically, emotionally, and relationally safe. The Innovate Project focuses on:

> prioritising the building of relationships, and working to avoid retraumatising whenever possible [. . .] A growing body of research indicates that working in a trauma-informed way does effectively reduce trauma symptoms and lead to positive behaviour change. This has led to significant, increasing interest in TiP in the UK from a range of sectors including health, social care and criminal justice. (8)

Section 2: Equity and TIP in the school setting

Research into trauma in education in mainstream and inclusive education settings has expanded from a focus on the individual student's difficulty with the system to an analysis of the systemic injustice that is frequently behind school failure. A report by the Organisation for Economic Co-operation and Development (OECD) (9) stated that:

> Equitable education systems ensure that every student can achieve their educational potential regardless of their personal or social circumstances. Governments need to prioritise equity and inclusion in education and recognise their importance in paving the way for students to have equal chances for success in the future.

What does unequal access to education look like?

Jake aged 13: The issue – domestic violence

Jake was a bright, cheerful lad who was regularly suspended for fighting. He missed a lot of school as well, and he explained to me that he had to be home to intervene in the violence towards his mother from her boyfriend. He was offered a chance to live with another family member, but said he couldn't leave his little sisters there alone. He often came to school with no equipment due to having run out of the house or moved to Nana's for a day or two. His focus was always on something else, and he had no spare energy to engage in school. He was very interested in history and natural science, and had a great memory for topics he was engaged with. He had no quiet place to do his homework and couldn't keep track of basic stationery and library books as his life was chaotic. Jake's role as protector of his mother meant that his responses were always on alert for aggression, and he fought with students and staff alike. The others were a bit afraid of him because of his temper, so although they stayed in his circle, he had no close friends. Jake was sensitive to others' emotions and knew he was not liked. His main source of pride was his strength and his ability to defend his younger siblings as much as he could. His sense of humour was fast and sophisticated, and he turned it on those who made any comments about his mother. Social services were involved, and eventually the younger ones were taken into care by a relative. Jake was already in trouble with police juvenile liaison services and was placed separately.

Reflective questions

- What type of support or interventions might have helped Jake? Socially, academically and with the family situation?
- How would you, as his class teacher, manage your feelings around his eventual removal from the area and separation from his family?

Jill aged 12: The issue – poverty and sub-standard living conditions

It was the attendance officer who noted Jill's permanent absenteeism. The class teacher thought she had moved house. The attendance officer visited the home and found a chronically neglected flat with broken windows and rubbish piled everywhere. Jill, her older sisters and her mother were living without basic services and lacked the ability to access the help they needed. It was Jill's final year of primary school, and she didn't attend as she had no way of washing her clothes and was subjected to bullying as a result. Family support systems started the process of applying for home repairs and services to be installed. A team meeting of resources in the school produced uniforms and books and some extra tuition. And Jill started coming to school. She was a quick learner and picked up her work, and eventually completed her six years of secondary school.

Reflective questions

- What skills do you think Jill had to help her persevere in her education?
- What would have happened if that attendance officer hadn't noticed her ongoing absence?

Methods of assessing support needs

There are many objections to the ACEs model being applied to pupils as a measurement tool in the education system. Catriona O'Toole (3) points out that each person experiences a significant event differently and will ascribe a different meaning to it. Alex Venet (10) describes this approach as a deficit assessment which leaves no room for the young person's resilience or survival methods to be acknowledged. Assessments can be a blunt instrument.

One young woman I worked with had a huge file of assessments and diagnoses. I was told that her 'case' was interesting as the level of specific difficulties in certain key areas was not consistent year to year. The teenager told me another assessment was due and that she hated them. We were talking about it, and she burst out laughing and said, 'I always make a mess of them, like answer all weird and mix it up.' I tried to contact the educational psychologist with this news and the suggestion that the assessment would be better used for someone on the waiting list. No reply meant another meaningless 'assessment of need' was added to her file!

Romy, a therapist working with traumatised people, highlights the individual nature of trauma and the ongoing challenges of adjustment for refugees, and finds:

> *The reality for those refugees or asylum seekers may be that the current situation of micro aggressions, racism, uncertainty about the future and very stressful living conditions may be the presenting problem and not the events that caused them to leave their homes originally. Struggles with identity can be unsettling.*

Issues using trauma-informed methods in the classroom

The challenges around supporting the child who is acting out a trauma while keeping the contract with the class group were described by Gerry, an experienced counsellor and school principal:

> *I remember a charge [pupil receiving support] was misbehaving once and I went up because I had a regular slot with him. And she [teacher] said, 'I don't want you to get to the root of his problems. I want you to make him behave.' Yeah, I completely understood. She had a big class – there was a lot of challenge. And actually, schools have to do both. Yes, life has to . . . you can't make a child behave. But you have to support a child to keep the rules and sometimes that's, you know, just incremental learning. Like you can't just tolerate children acting out. Because you have responsibility to the whole class as well as the one.*

Another challenge is when the TIP approach is not consistent or applied within the school framework for all staff, especially if staff training is needed in a new approach.

A young teacher, Pat, described a restorative justice approach that lacked full integration and training for staff in an underserved school:

> *The school's approach was restorative practice, was the whole school approach to any behaviour. So it is just about talking about it really, about why you might do something.*
>
> *No, no, not effective at all. Probably, because, well, I had no training in it, really, and it didn't seem like most of staff had proper training. It seemed to be just like someone had heard it was a good idea. Yeah, somewhat a half an understanding of it. And but there was no real kinda – and there's nothing behind it. And as well, the kid himself kind of knew what to say then after a while, so he wasn't really engaged in it. It didn't matter. It was just kind of like ticking the box.*

Social emotional learning (SEL) and trauma-informed practice (TIP)

There are some crossovers between SEL and TIP, but the main areas of contention are that SEL programmes do not address fundamental racism, socioeconomic issues and exclusion. Another aspect of SEL that is not necessarily part of TIP approaches is that SEL requires that the pupils be able to participate using communication skills and social skills for the training to be effective.

There are also concerns expressed by Alex Venet (10) that SEL can be used to pressurise young people to calm down, using conflict resolution techniques that don't acknowledge trauma caused by racism, embedded prejudice and violence in the community. 'SEL can become white supremacy with a hug' (p.61).

Gerry, teacher and principal, also cautions against well-being programmes being used to suppress the young person's traumatic experience and to make them responsible for their own healing:

> *I think there's a problem and it happens at all levels of education, that we need to focus on wellbeing now. So, what we do is we teach*

children to breathe, and we teach them yoga. And we teach them how to have positive thoughts. But actually, that child is going back home witnessing domestic violence. And by saying, this is how we're going to calm down, you're actually putting responsibility on a child to heal themselves, which they can't do, and ignoring the fact that the services in this country for domestic violence are abysmal, now; they are improving, but if you understand there isn't systemic thinking.

Equity in education

The theory of equity in education can be described by saying that equality gives everyone the same equipment and expects this to create equal opportunity, whereas equity gives everyone what they particularly need to create their equal opportunity. In Ireland, we have seen that this does not work in a straightforward manner. Schools are centrally funded by an allowance for each pupil, with extra hours of teaching and a range of supports available to schools designated disadvantaged by the Delivering Equality of Opportunity in Schools (DEIS) initiative (11). However, the gap in standards of achievement in national exams and access to higher education remains significant, although some progress has been made according to the OECD report (12).

Figure 7.1 Equal resources

The current economic situation of schools was reviewed by Kirk Eggleston and colleagues (13) in the USA where the funding of schools depends on the tax raised in the local area. This automatically affects the quality of education and resources available to pupils in marginalised areas. I was in the farmers market in Los Angeles one morning and saw a stall with placards raising money for a school. I went over to support the appeal, thinking it was for a new hall or trip away. I was amazed to see it was for teachers' salaries to prevent the school having to close two days a week.

In the Irish system, disadvantaged schools benefit from a range of support programmes designed to improve outcomes for pupils (11). These extra resources include extra teaching hours and small group work with literacy and emotional support. A meals allowance forms part of the package. DEIS support is allocated to the school. There are other individual resources allocated in any school following assessment of psychological or learning needs by the National Educational Psychology Service (NEPS). There are also specialist initiatives such as the School Completion Programme (SCP) which offers support to targeted pupils in the school system – in school and out of school – to encourage attendance. Even with this apparently equal opportunity, there is a gap in attaining higher education, and the pathway to lucrative employment is still dominated by the better-off. A study done by the Irish Higher Education Authority in 2020 found that only 5 per cent of students in Trinity College Dublin came from a working-class background (14). These statistics point to the wider issues around accessing academic third-level education for those students from underserved areas. The 'Growing up in Ireland' longitudinal study showed that the highest indicator for third-level education is that a parent had completed third level (15).

The UK system allocates funding to schools under two income streams – revenue funding for salaries and everyday expenses and capital funding for buildings, etc. The extra supports, such as the 'pupil premium', are allocated to schools on the basis of how many disadvantaged pupils they have in their school. This is determined by various criteria such as a pupil being eligible for school meals, being a looked-after child, or being identified at risk by social services. The school has discretion on spending this money. It can be used for targeted support such as tutoring or to support staff training or pupil issues with attendance, behaviour and social emotional well-being (16).

The systems have similar aims, and both have allocated extra resources to schools, acknowledging that the gap in academic achievement has widened since Covid-19. How resources are allocated appears somewhat differently. In the Irish system, the DEIS school receives centralised resources to benefit all the students, with extra supports for those with the greatest needs. The majority of Irish schools in DEIS would also have the SCP, and teachers work with SCP support staff to identify and engage the most at risk. However, how the schools attain DEIS status is a controversial topic, and allocation is complicated.

The UK 'pupil premium' system has several different aims such as encouraging schools to enrol less advantaged pupils to gain funding and create a more even mixture of pupils in schools. A review in 2021 by Gorard and colleagues (17) found the application of the scheme to be complex, and in some cases, funding was not reaching schools or was not ring-fenced for identified pupils. In some cases, figures for achievement were positive, but the report noted the difficulty in identifying the relevant factors in the improvements. The UK system of individual assessment may be more effective than the Irish system which requires the school to meet the level of assessed disadvantage.

Professor Emer Smyth, researcher with the Economic and Social Research Institute (ESRI) in Ireland, suggested that many pupils who were severely disadvantaged were not receiving supports as their school was not in the DEIS scheme. She stressed the need for these pupils to be eligible for supports. Her interview, in podcast form, details how inequity in access to education and other basic needs affects the whole of an individual's life (18).

A common result in the international research of supports is that lack of achievement in school is part of a web of social disadvantage that goes beyond the educational experience of the individual pupil.

Discrimination and inclusion

In the Irish context, until 20 years ago, society was very homogenous, and discrimination was typically practised against inner-city people and travellers. Travellers are a distinct ethnic group who are not Roma, but Irish, and followed a nomadic life till lack of casual work, loss of the horse-trading business and a dearth of halting sites or camping places led to many travellers settling in permanent accommodation. Prejudice is still very strong against travellers, and we now have a growing problem of racism with threats and, in some cases, violence, being directed at immigrants and asylum seekers.

Thus, awareness of and commitment to equity in education will become a broader issue as the diversity of the pupils increases. An international study of trainee physical education (PE) teachers (19) found that in every country there were issues around inclusion, exclusion, gender bias, cultural sensitivities and ability in the curriculum.

As Jay, the Irish interviewee in the PE study, pointed out:

> Ireland is becoming a more multi-cultural society. We're finding that we just need to be open to more inclusion . . . It's a worldwide thing. It's not just an Irish thing. (p.80)

It's important to see TIP as a lens, a way of looking at experience, and not a system that labels individuals and rates their trauma or upset according to a preset programme.

Romy, a psychologist who has worked a lot with trauma, finds that:

> *Trauma-informed care and practice and approach could be seen as a lens to view and try to understand the world, the experience and beliefs of others, not as a cure-all prescription. In my work, I see the important task is stabilisation – building trust and consistency, avoiding trauma labelling.*

Section 3: What can an educator do?

It is very easy to become overwhelmed with the levels of need and trauma among your pupils, especially if your institution is in a very underserved area with many dire problems. The awareness of further layers of discrimination, racism and social justice can seem like more waves of doom washing over you. Everybody has their own way of working and offering support for change and towards social justice. If you are a campaigner through the union or other forums, that is vital work, as are the individual struggles to meet the needs of pupils and carve out spaces for them in the system. The key thing is to take care of yourself, fill up on your own nurturing and avoid burn out. Some strategies for self-care and relieving stress will be addressed in Chapters 8 and 9.For me, the balance (when I could hang on to it!) was the starfish principle: the story is that a big tide washed hundreds of starfish onto the beach where they would die. One person walks along throwing handfuls into the sea, as another person says, 'Sure, that's pointless there are thousands more.' The first person throws another handful back in the water and says, smiling, 'They don't think so!' The other side of this was recognising that the wrap-around problems of deprivation suffered by the students were neither my creation nor my remit to solve alone.

Awareness of injustice

The fact of being aware of institutionalised discrimination and acknowledging it where relevant is respectful to your learners. This is part of trying to work for change individually and through broader action in the school or district where possible. Many of the changes I managed to make were related to individual needs such as getting local clinics to text our office the appointments for dental, speech and language, etc. for families who were consistent non-attenders. I had, of course, obtained their permission for this information to be shared. This meant we could remind people the day before, which was very effective in improving attendance.

The original aim of this book was to share the activities, materials and methods I used successfully for 30 years with people of all ages, to build confidence and communication skills. Apart from my initial two years teaching in a private Montessori school, all my classes and groups were based in very underserved areas. The many social and family problems that grow with deep poverty, stagnation and intergenerational unemployment were always woven through people's stories. The patterns of early school leaving and badly paid casual work left young people vulnerable to the only lucrative activities locally; these involved the drug trade and various levels of antisocial and criminal behaviour.

The reality of youth opportunity in an underserved community

The majority of people in any district are doing their utmost to provide for their family and keep them safe and well. Vulnerable communities are much more affected by the problems caused by lack of resources; working with young people and their families showed me this very clearly. I made many efforts to influence the young people away from petty crime and particularly the drug scene. Young people were frequently offered some 'party drugs' for a weekend to share with friends and they had to pay on Monday. The money was never there on Monday when 'the man' called for it, so making a delivery was how the debt could be cleared. Initially, the money was good and seemed easy till the young person wanted a way out or became more involved in the using and selling. There was a famous career criminal who terrorised whole districts of Dublin but was also a type of folk hero who evaded the police for years. Eventually, he was shot dead in a feud. One class of lads verging on criminal charges for joyriding were trying to convince me that it was harmless fun, and they would only get probation if caught. They were laughing and joking (16-year-old lads in a group – invincible!). I was giving examples of how lives were damaged by prison, and they began yelling at me, 'Look at yer man, he had loads of money – the cops couldn't catch him, huh?' I tried to point out he had actually been shot dead, but this didn't dent their fantasy. On another occasion, we were talking about taking ecstasy and how research at the time suggested it destroyed short-term memory over two decades. I said, 'Imagine when you're 40, you will be wandering around not knowing who you are or where you're going!' I paused to let my point sink in till one lad said with horror: 'Forty!! I want to be dead by then. That's too old!'

These kind of denial reactions to real consequences form part of standard adolescent beliefs in their own invincibility, but research suggests that traumatic events in youth exacerbate this tendency for taking rash decisions and making impulsive choices that bring negative consequences [20].

Working with individuals

In my various roles as a placement officer and a catering, life skills and literacy teacher, I worked hard with the young people to overcome obstacles to their chosen careers or training courses. The students taught me about the reality of exclusion and marginalisation. Things we did to get placements – such as always using an address outside of the inner city for applications – seemed ordinary routines, although, looking back, I wonder how it felt for the student to be unable to use their own address on a form. These situations demonstrated the clash between real-life needs and politically correct approaches. One of my classes was called 'preparation for employment', and various exercises made it obvious that very few students knew how to act in an interview, or how to deal with the public in the retail or hospitality sectors where they sought work.

We began to practise scenarios, and it was quickly known as the 'talking posh class' as we spent time practising 'Good afternoon. Can I take your order?' in our makeshift café, and then we got a few old phones to practise telephone manner. I was challenged on this by a tutor who thought I was disrespecting their culture and demeaning the students. This raised two issues. Did the students speak to their mothers in the way they often spoke to staff in the youth centre? And had this tutor ever worked in service jobs where speaking 'posh' to the clients is just part of your skillset that you put on with your uniform? The first was answered by running a survey which was actually funny and enlightening. It was very 'scientific' and it was called 'Would you tell your Ma to go f---herself?' Some answers were hilarious. One big, heavy lad, six feet tall, said, 'No way, she'd deck me with a sweeping brush!' The general consensus was a big NO. We continued working on the difference between street talk and work manners. I took a bunch of lads to an apprentice open day, and they were really on form, shaking hands with the instructors and holding the door open for me. The tutors in the workshop looked a bit stunned, and one of the lads whispered to me, 'OK then, will we go ballistic for a laugh.' Thankfully, they didn't.

What you can do in your classroom

A supportive approach for all ages

- Use your understanding of trauma effects on behaviour and development as a lens, a way of inquiring into the meaning of behaviour, while treating each student as an individual with their own story.
- You can work on creating a warm trusting relationship and a safe space for all ages.
- All the detailed activities and approaches of previous chapters can be condensed into 'caring trustworthy relationships and a safe, trauma-responsive environment'.
- When designing new materials, ask yourself if they meet Alex Venet's four priorities (10). Is it predictable and flexible? Does it foster empowerment and connection?
- You can be aware of the challenges faced by your students and acknowledge them, and adapt to them, even when it seems you can't change them in any radical way.

- You can get ongoing feedback from your students about their progress with the work and their experience of the class and make the changes that you can.
- You can inform yourself of wider supports that are available and make the information accessible to all.

The trauma-responsive environment detailed by Julie Nicholson and colleagues (21), which focused on the young child, can be applied as a principle in class groups of all ages:

> Trauma-responsive practices create safety for all children and for those children who are impacted by trauma, they become a lifesaving approach. When adults intentionally provide safe spaces for a child, can rewire their brain and body towards healing if provided in regular and predictable doses, repeated consistently over time, the result is the rewiring of the nervous system of a child to feel safe, present in the moment, and to have the capacity to listen, learn and engage. (p.78)

This idea of a trauma-responsive environment takes in the knowledge that, as humans, we will all suffer trauma of different severity in our lives, and a caring nurturing approach will benefit all of us, including the educator.

Eimear, a family therapist, acknowledged the difficulty working with angry neglected children and stressed the value of a positive connection:

> *And I do think that training into supporting teachers, caregivers, coaches, with some additional training in what a difference they can make. And they're not always likable children. They're very often difficult, rude, whatever. Yeah, and I understand it's very difficult in the class, and this one fella is at you every day, and you really find it hard to like them sometimes, you know. So I'm not trying to undermine that, what that is like, but somewhere, someone may be able to get through, yeah, if it's that one teacher, that one coach, that one person that actually sees them, hears them.*

She also suggests the importance of unconditional supports for traumatised pupils:

> *One of the things that often strikes me with supports for children who are causing trouble is everything is conditional. It's if you come*

to school every day we'll, you know, might give some money for Christmas presents, or the money to pay for a club. There was a school trip given, and it was taken away from the child because of being bold in school [. . .] but having something that's not always conditional on – that's just because you deserve it, because you're – I see you. And I do think that when you're given something that's seen as charity, that feels tough enough, and then it's taken away. It's, it's really doing a double injury.

Actions to encourage respect and equity within the classroom

Primary school

- Maintain safe boundaries and insist on everyone being called by their chosen name. (This helps to reduce name calling.)
- Avoid over-focus on holidays, birthdays, etc. as these can highlight extreme differences among the children's experience.
- Develop your own simple rituals for birthdays and major holidays, and have pupils make cards for each other.
- Do regular team tasks with the pupils.
- Play inclusive fun games that don't favour a particular skillset.
- Use story books and comics to encourage acceptance of difference.

Secondary school

- Your welcoming classroom with familiar rituals adds to the feeling of a safe space.
- Keep the format of *only speak for yourself, only discuss your own work, and call others by their chosen name*. This reduces teasing and name calling.
- If there are racist or homophobic slurs, respond with the format above. If severe or persistent, seek specialist help.
- The curriculum will include geography, history and political material that shows injustice – acknowledge it without over-focusing on any one student.
- Use media situations to discuss areas of discrimination. Keep it general – consult the student/s concerned if you are doing a session on another culture or ethnic group. They may be either interested or uncomfortable with a spotlight on them.

- Be led by your students as to their comfort around these issues – for example, if someone raises an issue like being followed in a shop because of who they are. Take a beat, look out some research or materials on this topic and have a structured discussion like a ***walking debate**.
- Be aware of opportunities for students to make their voice heard in school or in the community, and inform them about these.
- If you can link with local organisations, you can sometimes get resources that some students lack – such as sports equipment – and you can share them. Be discreet and respectful in your offers of help.

Adult education

- Set the boundaries early on of what support you can offer and where it stops.
- Get to know your group and you will become aware of issues they carry.
- Sometimes there will be a conflict – for example, an asylum seeker or an immigrant who is resented by another person. Use the format *only speak for yourself, only discuss your own work, and call others by their chosen name*. Depending on the group cohesion, you could have a workshop on the issue with support from a facilitator who is experienced in the area. Or you can maintain order with the format above and use the adult ***assertiveness training programme** to defuse tension.
- Keep informed about different initiatives that work for equity in education and share these with the students if they are interested.

Staff understanding of TIP

Many teachers and tutors have become tired of initiatives and new demands on their time, and a TIP approach can become either another burden or another box to tick. Schools vary enormously in their approach to pastoral care whether it is with TIP or not. In some institutions, a token day of training has been offered, whereas in others the whole school is working towards these methods of teaching, learning and classroom management (20). The need for teachers to find use and benefit in new methods was highlighted in a study into benefits and challenges in TIP:

The elements that contributed to successful and lasting reform were: first, that the reform offered solutions to problems educators were aware of and wanted to solve; second, that the reform identified an actual issue that educators were unaware of but engaged with on understanding it; third, that the reform correlated to public pressure on socio-political needs in education; and, fourth, that the educators were supplied with the tools and guidance to implement the practices in the classroom (Cohen and Mehta, 2017, p.2, cited in Sweetman(20) p.3).

The vital role of a principal who is committed to this work and encourages and resources the staff was mentioned by Anna, a teacher in a school in an underserved area, who said:

And then the SNAs (special needs assistants) have a timetable as well, that they go around, but you could call in an emergency and yeah, of course, or the principal, or in the class WhatsApp. Or the email to school email system. I need somebody and somebody will come. Yeah, you know, so that you don't feel alone in your class. And you need to not feel alone. Yeah, to see your principal is on board with this way of working. Absolutely. Yeah. That's very important in my experience. Because otherwise, you know, it's like just 'control your class, your classroom'. That 'my classroom' business.

Training and development for staff in TIP

It is just as important to remember that the staff will have their own experiences of trauma, so any training needs to be well structured and done with respect and awareness of others and their needs. As with your students, a relationship needs to be built up where staff are comfortable with the levels and intensity of the initial inquiry into TIP. The opt-out clause is vital and needs to be offered in an easy, unobtrusive manner at all stages of any training.

Venet maintains that the use of 'ACEs checklists' can be harmful for educators and pupils alike, as distress and confusion can arise when these lists are applied and used in classes or in training for teachers. This division into traumatised and non-traumatised is more labelling and a division that is not helpful to anyone (10). It's important to see TIP as a way of looking at individual experience and not as a system that labels people and rates their trauma or upset according to a preset programme.

Working effectively within your own staff group

- Build support slowly. Avoid judgement and preaching.
- Small changes that illustrate efficacy are the best influencers – showcase the work you do.
- Incorporate ideas of TIP with whatever is the established programme of SEL in your school/college.
- Do some networking in-house, especially with staff who are involved with pastoral care, career guidance and home–school liaison; they will be more likely to be receptive to TIP. Local services, such as youth clubs, often run specialised supports for young people who struggle and will be glad to make connection with you.
- Gaining support for these ideas is slow and steady – keep connected to your staff group as much as you can.
- Keep a sense of humour. In one of my first rookie teaching jobs, the class of teenagers were climbing the walls, and I had totally lost any semblance of control. I was close to tears when the door opened and one of the older, stricter teachers swept in. 'Ms Sweetman, there is a call for you in the office.' I learned later this was code for 'You have lost it, and we can all hear you!' I left a bit confused, and as I walked down the hall, I heard a few deep bellows and then silence and order, which held till the end of the day! This particular teacher ran several clubs in his own time and had endless patience for students who were struggling – but very little for those who he saw as destroying the education of others. I learned to appreciate each teacher as an individual in that school and gained a lot of experience. And those 'phone calls in the office' were a lifesaver!

Key points of Chapter 7

- Trauma-informed practice is a view and an approach in many professions – not a cure-all format.
- Equity in education is based in social justice; these are massive international problems. You can only work to your own capacity.

- Your awareness and acknowledgement of exclusion and discrimination is a worthwhile support for your learners.
- Build networks of support for yourself and your pupils. Keep an open mind on different approaches to supporting students and their families.
- Inform students of relevant supports and initiatives.

References

1. Burke Harris N. How childhood trauma affects health across a lifetime. www.youtube.com/watch?v=95ovIJ3dsNk
2. Ungar M. Practical strategies: Resilience after maltreatment: The importance of social services as facilitators of positive adaptation. Child Abuse & Neglect. 2013;37(2–3):110–5.
3. O'Toole C. When trauma comes to school: Toward a socially just trauma informed praxis. International Journal of School Social Work. 2022;6(2):Art. 4.
4. Banks J, editor. The Inclusion Dialogue: Debating issues, challenges and tensions with global experts. London: Routledge; 2023.
5. van der Kolk BA. The body keeps the score. USA: Viking Penguin; 2015.
6. Maté G. When the body says NO. New Jersey: Wiley; 2003.
7. Johnstone L, Boyle M, Cromby J, Dillon J, Harper D, Kinderman P, et al. The Power Threat Meaning Framework: Towards the identification of patterns in emotional distress, unusual experiences and troubled or troubling behaviour, as an alternative to functional psychiatric diagnosis. Leicester: British Psychological Society; 2018.
8. The Innovate Project. School of Education and Social Work. University of Sussex; 2019–2023. https://theinnovateproject.co.uk/trauma-informed-practice
9. OECD. Equity in education. Organisation for Economic Co-operation and Development; 2024. www.oecd.org/en/topics/policy-issues/education-equity.html
10. Shevrin Venet A. Equity-Centred Trauma-Informed Education. New York: Routledge; 2024.
11. Department of Education and Science. DEIS (delivering equality of opportunity in schools) an action plan for educational inclusion. Dublin: National Development Plan; 2005.
12. Department of Education and Skills. OECD Project: Overcoming School Failure. Policies that Work. Dublin: Department of Education and Skills; 2011.
13. Eggleston K, Green E, Abel S, Poe S, Shakeshaft C. Developing trauma-responsive approaches to student discipline. London: Routledge; 2021.
14. O'Shea M. Data covering 94% of all enrolments in 2018/2019 creates a socio-economic profile of Irish higher education students. Dublin: Higher Education

Authority; 2020. https://hea.ie/2020/12/07/new-hea-data-provides-in-depth-insight-into-the-socio-economic-profile-of-our-universities-and-institutes-of-technology
15. Williams J, Greene S, Doyle E, Harris E, Layte R, McCoy S, et al. Growing up in Ireland.National longitudinal study of children: The lives of children. Dublin: Economic Social Research Institute; 2009.
16. The Education Hub. School funding: Everything you need to know. Gov UK; 2024. https://educationhub.blog.gov.uk/2024/03/school-funding-everything-you-need-to-know
17. Gorard S, Siddiqui N, See BH. The difficulties of judging what difference the Pupil Premium has made to school intakes and outcomes in England. Research Papers in Education. 2021;36(3):355–79.
18. Smyth E. Inequalities in student experiences and outcomes. Let's Talk About Sociology of Education. A podcast with Melanie Ni Dhuinn; 2021. https://podcasts.apple.com/cd/podcast/episode-three-inequalities-in-student-experiences-and/id1560198605?i=1000518276434
19. Baek S, Dyson B, Howley D, Shen Y. Promoting an equity-based approach for social and emotional learning in physical education teacher education: internationalteacher educators' perspectives. Sport, Education and Society. 2024;29(1):74–88.
20. Sweetman N. What Is a Trauma Informed Classroom? What Are the Benefits and Challenges Involved? Frontiers in Education. 2022;7.
21. Nicholson J, Perez L, Kurtz J, Bryant S, Giles D. Trauma-informed practices for early childhood educators. London: Routledge; 2019.

8
Boundaries and emotional first aid

This chapter turns the focus back on you, the educator and the human being.

Previous chapters have looked at the application of the principles of trauma-informed practice in education and other disciplines. The meaning of equity in education and resilience in individual and community circumstances have been discussed.

I once called a little one of four years old 'pet'. She looked me up and down and said, 'I am not a pet – I'm a human bean.'

So, all you human beans out there, how are you going to care for yourself?

There are two sections in this chapter:

- Section 1 looks at the meaning and importance of different types of boundaries in the work of an educator.
- Section 2 explores the meaning of emotional first aid and psychological first aid. The practical applications of these will be discussed in three subsections:
  - Section 2(i) looks at emotional first aid for individual distress in the class situation.
  - Section 2(ii) looks at emotional first aid in terms of self-care and emotional health.
  - Section 2(iii) looks briefly at the use of psychological first aid (PFA) in disaster or group trauma situations.

Section 1: Boundaries

The most important thing to remember is never to promise what you can't deliver or follow through on.

The definition of a boundary is 'a real or imagined line that marks the edge or limit of something'. In the case of the class teacher or tutor, this means understanding what it means to offer support, empathy, a listening ear or a safe harbour to a distressed person (of any age), who may be affected or triggered by trauma – this is a trauma-informed (TI) response. Any further engagement, such as offering interventions or therapeutic advice, or working with the person (of any age) to explore circumstances or outcomes of their trauma, is crossing over into a counselling or therapeutic role.

The difference between being a TI tutor and being a therapist has at its base the contract entered into with the pupil/young person/learner. An adult educator on the tutors' course mentioned that in her class group with many embedded traumas, one person disclosed an intense trauma event. The next day, another person disclosed, and this became a theme and was causing serious distress for others in the group. The tutor in this case spoke to both students individually. She explained that the class was not the right place for these disclosures. She expressed empathy for their situation, checked in with them about the supports they were getting and offered referrals to in-house and local services for them. Then she had a discussion with the class group about safe boundaries and how she herself and others in the group could help and support each other with daily challenges or low moods, but emphasised that serious issues were not part of the group contract. She explained with the use of examples and some leaflets what kind of supports were available, and stated she could help with initial referrals to services.

For many in the group, this was a great relief as they were struggling to focus on education skills they badly needed and were becoming retraumatised by horrific stories that often mirrored their own.

The contract was for instruction in a skill. The disclosure needs an empathic response but a clear redirection to appropriate services either in-house or external. If it is a teaching situation, you have no agreement or permission to make therapeutic explorations or interventions. You have a statutory obligation to report abuse or violence to the liaison officer of your institution in the case of a minor. In the case of adults at risk, you are recommended to contact local health centres or, in extreme cases, the police.

At the start of the year or series of classes, take some time to clarify these boundaries. This information can be tailored to suit the age group of your pupils. Even the youngest pupils can be reassured by knowing the daily routine and what is expected of them in terms of social behaviour. Posters and charts are ideal for the younger classes, and helpful as an aid for all age groups.

Task related information

- The aim of the class.
- The standard of work needed – what is flexible and what is fixed and mandatory for completion.
- A rough plan of how the curriculum will be covered. Visual charts and posters are very useful here.
- The time frame of the sessions.
- The feedback methods you will use.

Group work information you can share

- Be clear how much help and support you can offer for class work and personal problems. For example, one adult educator found it was difficult to give feedback individually, with the group in the classroom, as students became so flustered that they weren't taking in information or participating in the feedback. So, after consulting with the group, they agreed on ten-minute individual sessions spread over two classes. The class chose to do revision exercises in small groups while individuals went out for their feedback session. Reports from the students suggested this ten-minute review was very helpful, and the discipline of completing the review in ten minutes gave focus to the meeting.
- You can help the student to access supports by using in-house services such as school guidance counsellor or pastoral care team referral. Also, links to community-based services can be displayed on posters and leaflets.
- There are limits of confidentiality: if someone is at risk or in danger, especially a child, there is a mandatory reporting system.
- Ensure appropriate sharing of personal information – start with everyday facts.
- Listen and show respect even in times of disagreement. The work around 'brave space'(1) is useful for setting some boundaries, which enable difficult conversations to take place safely. Specifically, we ask participants to give an example of how they might firmly challenge the views of someone else in a respectful manner. By further discussing the examples, the group can develop more clarity about ways to firmly and respectfully challenge others and how to respond when they themselves are firmly and respectfully challenged (p.148).

- Your commitment is to adapt the environment and pace of the work to their feedback as much as possible. You can give options and explain different methods that are available.
- Transparency about the work and the process will be part of your commitment – this creates confidence and security for the students.

Depending on the age and makeup of your group, your boundaries about the group's communications methods will vary. For example, with very young pupils, it may be necessary to take a strong position on behaviours like biting and scratching! Hopefully, this won't apply in your secondary school or adult education classes. Instead, you may have to address sexist comments or racist views, and this will be part of your group process.

I worked on a sexual consent programme, and we began discussions with the lads holding quite a judgemental view of girls' dress and freedom of movement. These were lads expressing concern for the girls they knew while holding some dated views! While discussing how sexual assaults occurred, the lads said, 'They [the girls] were stupid in their dress and where they walked at night.'

As we progressed through the weeks of the programme, we ended up with the lads saying things like 'I want to be that guy – that is sound, and anyone could come to me for support and advice' (about sexual consent or experiences around it).

The boundaries will change in any group as it develops its own character, decision making and leadership style. It has been my experience that clear boundaries and expecting a high standard of respect create a safe environment that allows all members to participate freely. When a group or class is new, you, as the tutor, are unaware of past history or current tensions in the group. By setting a clear and contained structure, you help to create a level playing field for the group. Simple actions like taking the time to find out what each person likes to be called can set the scene for this respectful approach. Young people may have been stuck with a nickname that is hurtful, and while their peers will insist it is 'only for a laugh and s/he doesn't mind', you set down a marker by insisting that the name preferred by the person is the one used. Following the basic rules of assertiveness means each person can only speak for themselves and comment on their own work.

The boundaries you set will also give you solid ground to retreat to if things are not going well. If group members use a discussion as a way to verbally bully others or undermine the group's work, you can call it and refer to the original agreements about respect and acceptance of difference without making a victim of any one person.

The boundaries you set for yourself will have some public aspects and some private ones. For example, I had an absolute rule about throwing things, and I told the students I would treat 'spitballs' of paper the same as bigger or heavier objects. I explained to them that a child I knew nearly lost their eye by someone throwing a hard crab apple at them. I still had books and, on one occasion, a small desk, thrown at me (luckily I dodged it!), but I referred to this rule and didn't change it. The child who threw the desk came in the next day with his dad and gave a genuine apology. The lad described it as a 'rush of blood to the head'. I went through my rule and why I kept it once more, and he offered his word, supported by his dad, that it wouldn't happen again. I accepted his apology and said that was a one-off exception. I never had a problem with him again, thankfully.

One smart lad once threw a ball of messy sandwich paper at me at lunch (which was a delicious roll, a yoghurt and a juice for €2), and the next day the lunch service was closed. I posted a notice saying I wasn't prepared to run around picking up supplies and paying deliveries on my own lunch hour to have things thrown at me. Sincere apologies and requests for reopening followed, and we did open it again.

Other decisions such as how much you will share about your own life with students are up to you. Sometimes some sharing about your own life can help to build a relationship and sometimes it can highlight for young people what is lacking in their own lives or lead to intrusive questions.

A vital aspect of the work is to avoid the saviour complex. Alex Venet (2) states that, for example, any student telling you that you are 'the only one they can talk to' should be a red flag for you. The important thing is to encourage connections for the student to other caring adults and/or services if needed. She maintains the teacher should be a bridge to these other services and adults. Ideally, this should be within the school and with other local agencies. In most cases, the class will have a new teacher each year, so fostering a dependent relationship will only lead to feelings of abandonment when the year ends and you have a new class. The group can be a resource to each other as a trusting positive atmosphere develops.

Apologies

Nobody is perfect, and everyone runs short on inspiration and patience at times. (If this has never happened to you, you are a perfect being and don't need this book!) If you feel you have let an individual pupil or class group down, talk to them and apologise for the specific incident where you felt you had a lack of patience or understanding. You can ask if they were upset or noticed it, and check with them that they are comfortable with moving forward. This apology can be a first-time experience for young people and models the respect you hope they will show each other. I once face-planted off the rostrum (an old-fashioned podium for the teacher's desk), and as I hit the floor, I dreaded the humiliating sniggers from my giddy class of 13-year-olds. There was complete silence and then a few scared voices said, 'Are you all right, Miss?' Three or four pupils came and helped me up. I started laughing with the shock, and we all laughed together in relief and acknowledgement of how funny it must have looked for them. I always remembered that moment for the kindness the young people showed me.

Boundaries around physical touch

Different countries and organisations have their own guidelines, including police clearance and completion of child protection training. This is compulsory for all professionals and volunteers who work with children or vulnerable adults in Ireland. The law that confirmed the Children First Act (3) and the mandatory reporting system in Ireland make reporting of harm or threat of harm to a minor obligatory by law. Although the law states that any person reporting in good faith cannot be held liable, it also puts an onus on someone who reports to share the concerns and possibly supply a written account. This is obviously necessary; positive action towards greater protection for children and more awareness among staff of how to make referrals where they are needed are essential. The downside of this is that many people who work with youth have become extremely wary of any type of physical contact. Even playing active games or actions like lifting young children onto a swing have become frowned upon, leaving neglected children even more isolated. I remember once walking through the playground with a big box of equipment, and five-year-old twin sisters ran over to say hello. We were all laughing because they were trying to hug me and ended up hugging my knees as I struggled to hold onto my box. I wished them a nice afternoon and said I would see them in the homework club later, and they ran off waving and still giggling.

Boundaries and emotional first aid

The next morning a teacher said to me, 'Are you not nervous being so friendly with the children? What if somebody got the wrong idea, or the children said you did something wrong?' I was lost for words (a thing that rarely happens!). I said:

They came over to say hi and remind me about their homework club. It was in the middle of a crowded playground full of children, teachers and SNAs, and I was standing there holding a massive box! I have worked hard to make a caring relationship with those little girls. Imagine what they would have felt like if I had pushed them away? They are both withdrawn and shy, so I was happy to see them in good form.

Another negative aspect of this mandatory reporting is that because everything must be recorded, many teachers have become very fearful of getting involved, which can lead to a reluctance to act on information or concerns. This issue was mentioned by Zoe, a special needs teacher:

Many of the teachers are really terrified of having to make a referral or a report. They're, like, obsessed with it and very afraid of getting involved. I pass on concerns, you know – because of my job the kids talk to me about stuff – although if I, like, ask too many questions, they just shut down completely and can ask to go back to their own classroom. I know that look – they are told not to talk about home in school. I do my best, but I am not sure the concerns are always passed on.

On another occasion in a youth work group, I overheard a lot of very extreme comments about sexual favours being given, and a local girl was discussed in graphic terms. When I heard this same topic again at another event, I was very concerned, and I went to my manager who said, 'We have no official grounds for reporting, and this girl is not a member of our groups.' I said, 'As an adult in a position of trust, I can't unhear this, so I am calling to the house to tell them what I heard.' You can imagine I wasn't a popular visitor, and at first her guardian was very angry and yelling at me: 'Are you accusing her of doing these things? How dare you!' I just repeated that I had heard these things more than once and was concerned, and said that 'maybe the young girl might like to talk to someone she trusted, maybe a young auntie or cousin or someone else?' I heard afterwards from her older sister that the girl attended a specialist service and received the right supports.

This was a situation using an approach that Venet (2) discusses in her study of boundaries. I am not a trauma counsellor, and I was not her key worker, but I helped to make her guardian aware of a concern, who then went and got the right support for her. It wasn't necessary for me to know all the details of the problem or be the 'bridge' to get help for this girl.

Working with children who have unsafe physical boundaries

I frequently had young staff and students on placement assisting with groups and outings. I always find it is necessary to be very clear and explicit about what you are discussing. For example, the young people and children we worked with were very often cared for by mothers, grannies and women teachers. Many other support services such as special needs assistant (SNA) and youth workers were frequently staffed by women. So, when the students or coaches were young men, our pupils frequently followed them around and clung on to them. Some of the men would have received excellent training through their own organisations, whereas others were very new to the work.

I used to do a full session on safe touch and what to do if it felt unsafe before we ran any events. Many young people studying to be teachers or youth workers are unaware of the prevalence of sexual abuse and how it can show up in behaviour. They may have had education on the topic but little or no experience working with children affected by abuse.

Staff training about working with children and young people affected by trauma

I worked on these basic aspects with the help of the full-time team, who shared their tips and experience.

- **Dress:** For both male and female staff, no sexy beach-style sportswear please! Save it for your holidays. Round-necked T-shirt, knee-length shorts.
- **Kind, safe touch:** Some of the young people will have had a range of inappropriate sexual experiences, and some will be hungry for attention

and affection. It is important that we show kindness and fun, and play with them without being over-intimate, so the dress code helps with this message.
- **Spreading the activity to the group:** Avoid any type of favouritism. If a child is consistently trying to push to walk with you, for example, turn it around to be sets of teams walking together, or if you have space, like a line holding hands crossing a pitch. They can take it in turns to call out 'stop', or 'hop' or 'run' to the group. All the lines will be tripping over each other and having fun.
- **Young person is too tactile:** Sometimes a neglected or abused young person will try to rub against you in an intimate way or push their cleavage in your face. Break the contact at once with an everyday comment: 'I need to check on the lunch/group/bus.' If you are sitting beside a young person doing anything like this, get up and change places at once. The reason for moving without comment is to avoid retraumatisation for the child or young person. Report your concerns with exactly what happened to your coordinator or manager.
- **Persistence:** Particularly in the middle of an activity where you can't leave the group, and the young person is saying or doing overly personal things, you can state it clearly to them. I saw a young instructor saying to a 12-year-old who had a crush on him: 'Mary, you need to stop standing so close to me. I am married with kids of my own. I am here to help you all and teach interesting stuff, so no more messing – OK?' Mary accepted this and kept to her personal space afterwards. When he discussed it with me, I decided to pass on my concerns to the school counsellor, as the instructor said Mary's behaviour was very inappropriate.
- **Follow your gut instinct:** If it feels off, it is off! Cutting the contact without embarrassing the child leaves space for an individual check-in by the person responsible for referral, to find out if there is cause for concern.

Boundaries to keep a space safe

Steele and Malchiodi (4) see ground rules as essential for an effective trauma-informed relationship:

> In order to help you and other children feel safe in this room, there are a few rules. There is no hitting or breaking toys or games. No hitting or hurting yourself or me.

The issue of confidentiality is also mentioned:

> [I]f you might be hurt or hurt someone else, I will need to tell someone (case worker, social worker etc.) about it because I want to make sure you are safe and OK. Before I tell someone else, I will always tell you first. (p.146)

Boundaries around safeguarding

Different age groups and institutions have their own code of conduct. For example, working with preschoolers will by necessity include more physical contact, and all staff will have received training in safeguarding. The primary classes aged 4–8 will typically be more engaged with the adults and sometimes want to hold your hand, for example. Then you will find that as they approach puberty, young people become more distanced and want to maintain their private space more. At this age, a high five or an arm around a shoulder is a friendly way to encourage or console a child who has had bad news or is feeling lonely. The use of ***cosy corners** in classrooms gives the children the ability to soothe themselves.

Each school or centre will have their own approach and boundaries. If you are new and these things are not clear to you, ask for information. Some overarching rules include not being alone with a pupil without another adult, who could be the other end of the room, busy with something but still present. Always have other adults present, especially when supervising changing after PE or swimming with younger groups. One male sports coach told me that if a younger child needs the toilet, he just calls a toilet break and gets the whole group to go to the bathrooms.

Boundaries for the educator with their students

Information sharing

Venet (2) wrote about the need the teacher can feel to know the pupil's trauma:

> Maybe if I knew the trauma they had experienced, the adverse circumstances, and the family makeup, I could avoid unintentional triggers

and create a safe environment. Our clinical director, John Grimm, would remind me that I didn't need all of that information to provide quality care: 'The frames can guide the work with anyone.'

The frames he referred to were the larger ideas that drove our work: unconditional positive regard for each and every student; restorative approaches to discipline, rooted in relationship; an orientation toward slowing down and considering student motivation; skill and capacity when designing learning experiences.

When using these overarching approaches to our work with students, we create safe and caring environments for all students. (p.2)

> **Reflective questions**
>
> - Are there individuals or aspects of your work where you feel your boundaries are pushed/crossed?
> - Have you ever shared these concerns or received support or training in this area?

Boundaries between work and home

Some rituals to cut links between home and work can be linked to your reflective practice, which can be a quick five minutes, or something more elaborate such as mindfulness exercises or other methods that work for you to ground yourself.

Having a photo of loved ones, maybe on your keyring, and taking it out as you leave the building is easy, and a reminder to let go of the day and focus on your own life.

Say an affirmation as you leave:

- 'I have done my best and my workday is now finished.'
- 'I let go of today and have my evening for myself.'
- 'I am well and happy, and I deserve it.'
- 'Today was hard and I was struggling, but I did my best and I will begin again tomorrow.'

This may seem artificial, but working with people of any age who carry anxiety, stress and trauma can be debilitating and can stick with you. Affirmations need to resonate with your true feelings, so if you're feeling upset or discouraged, express that and add some kindness to yourself. Sometimes you can feel almost guilty for the happiness and privilege you have in your own life. That's why it is vital to cut the emotional ties with work as you leave. Many educators have preparation or reading to do in the evening, but try to keep this task-based, assign a time to it and then stop. If you are always way over your time, there is a problem with your workload. Either you have taken on too much or you have been given too much to do. I know this sounds simplistic, but these are all things I learned the hard way!

Boundaries around your workload

A friend of mine who was getting buried under lots of small, slightly relevant tasks to her role eventually made a spreadsheet of all the conflicting demands she faced and the time they took. She analysed this in terms of the ratio of her own scheduled work for her boss versus lots of small tasks others could do, but which landed on her. Her boss took one look at it and gave her an office with a door and a clear remit of what her role was! If, as teachers or youth workers, you are spending endless time on form-filling and repetitive paperwork that takes time from your engagement with the children, record it, add up the hours and bring it to the principal/manager and to your union. You are an educator, not a data entry worker!

Reflective questions

- What boundaries have you put in place for yourself to keep work in work?
- How do you mark the changeover from work to home?

Section 2: Emotional first aid and psychological first aid

(i) Emotional first aid

This has several meanings. The most obvious is the offering of instant support to someone of any age who has had a shock, an accident or a trauma trigger response. This can be in your school or workplace, or in a public setting. One winter's night in the city centre, I dropped my bike and gashed my foot on the edge of the pedal. I remember clearly wondering what the squishy feeling in my shoe was and noticing in a detached way that it looked like blood. I was determined to take my bike home, afraid of it getting stolen. I was trying to get on it in a wobbly fashion when two young men approached me. 'Hi there, are you OK?' 'Yes, I just have to get home with my bike.' I think they noticed the blood and that I was as pale as a ghost, because one said, 'There is a great place to lock a bike around the back, I could take the key and lock it for you, and then we could wait for a taxi with you?' His friend agreed, and he helped me wrap a scarf around my foot. They offered to come with me when the taxi arrived, but I had come around by then.

This is a very common reaction to an accident or event. The person is in shock and makes nothing of it in their desire to get out of the situation and get home. So as the first-aid person, take a minute to check things out and help the person to regain calm and make a safe decision. On a walking trip, a young woman fell and hurt her ankle. She was all set to walk back to the start, which wasn't far, and was so determined that no one should go with her that people were uncertain whether to let her go. 'I don't want to cause any fuss; you carry on. I will be fine, I'll wait for you.' When I asked her what the pain was like on a scale of 1–10, her eyes filled with tears. She had to go to the hospital to get it x-rayed as she had a serious fracture.

I am often asked, 'What will I do if someone gets upset?' If the work you are doing or an interaction with one pupil or among the group causes someone to become severely distressed, what should you do? Sometimes it is an unexpected trigger that upsets someone. As it is impossible to know every traumatic trigger of every person, your response needs to be kind and respectful. It comes with acceptance of what the person is experiencing and a readiness to listen if needed.

I usually answer this question, first of all, by asking what you would do if someone you knew became very upset talking about a bereavement or a hard time in their life. The first thing is to acknowledge they are upset. Give them a minute and ask them if they would like to walk a bit or sit quietly. Check how they are feeling and what support they would like. Often, people will say something like they were just reminded of their mother's death, or a time they felt lonely, and they will tell you they are all right. If the distress continues, and especially if their breathing is heaving or they are sobbing and not settling, ask them if they want to continue to sit in a cosy corner or a quiet room or to move around. That way, you can get them some privacy and a quiet place to sit. If it's a classroom situation where you can't leave the class, you can send someone to get another adult to help you. Offer a hot drink, or water, and something to eat like toast, biscuits or that useful energy boost, a banana. If your group have become worried, reassure them that, for example, the other person got sad thinking about someone they miss, but they are going to be back and they are fine. The detail you share should be age-appropriate and with the consent of the person who is upset; often a person becomes embarrassed about causing an incident, and they will tell you what information they are happy to share with the group.

I have ornophobia (fear of birds) which I can normally manage unless threatened by large birds. I was sitting in the sun outside a bar waiting for coffee when a big seagull swooped down and stole a pastry right in front of me. I ran screaming into the pub, and then I heard this manic screeching and realised it was me! I felt very embarrassed until I realised nobody took any notice. I was told it happens all the time and that children can't eat anything walking along the street. The manager also asked me what I wanted him to do about it. It wasn't quite the trauma-informed response I was hoping for.

If the person is not settled and able to return to balance and rejoin the group after a few minutes, or settle where they are, you might need to ask them if they would like to go home and if there is someone who could collect them. In the case of a child, you would contact their parent or guardian. An adult will usually tell you what is going on and what they need. Sometimes it is a physical reaction like severe migraine, which can make someone feel very sick and dizzy. If the person has never had anything like this before and has no explanation, you should recommend they check in with their doctor. As the guidance for psychological first aid for primary teachers states, you are a teacher not a medical professional, so your support is in line with what any kind person would offer another in distress (5).

These are extreme situations. In many years working with groups and classes in all kinds of situations, I have had lots of upsets and distressed reactions, sometimes to unlikely triggers, but the response of checking with the person at each stage and meeting their need to be heard, seen and supported is the same. It is important to check in with the person how they feel and not to presume you know. Some people cry with rage or frustration, so your soothing words could make them feel silenced. Others are quite open with their emotions, and becoming visibly upset is comfortable for them. Another person could have serious shame issues about letting out feelings in a public space. There is only one way to know, and that is to ask.

(ii) Another form of emotional first aid is self-care

Guy Winch gave a TED talk (6) where he discussed loneliness as a condition that not only causes unhappiness but contributes to illness and shortens the life span. He noted that when humans started to practise physical hygiene, overall health improved, and he suggests the same improvement in well-being would come from caring for our emotional health. Guy speaks about caring for your own emotional well-being and avoiding rumination on failure or rejection, and he describes self-criticism as like taking the knife and digging it deeper into an open wound on your arm. He uses techniques like redirecting negative or fearful thoughts, which he says is effective in changing the downward spiral.

Exercise

Wendy Suzuki (7) found that exercise had all-round positive effects on brain power and energy. She describes it in a TED talk:

> I noticed in myself, better mood, better energy, better memory, better attention, and the more I learned, the more I realized how powerful exercise was.
>
> I've come to the following conclusion that exercise is the most transformative thing that you can do for your brain today, for the following three reasons. Number one, it has immediate effects on your brain. A single workout that you do will immediately increase levels of neurotransmitters like dopamine, serotonin and noradrenaline, that is going to increase your mood right after that workout . . . Finally, studies have shown that a single workout will improve your reaction times.

William Steele (8) maintains that when we are stressed, we need to calm our physical reactions to the stress and that movement of the simplest type and changing posture can relieve serious stress responses. This is also part of the recovery programme of van der Kolk (9) which focuses on movement to help the client to ground in their body and find a safe place within their own body.

This approach was used by Zoe who said that she used a variety of ways to manage vicarious trauma:

> *I walk in the park every day. I listen to some music, stuff, some podcasts. No, I think I'm experienced enough to mostly leave it behind. I mean, there is sometimes you wake up at three o'clock in the morning, like on a Sunday, you know, you know you might have one or two children in your brain.*

Movement

The sympathetic nervous system is the one that responds to stress and kicks in the extra alertness and energy for perceived or expected stress and emergency. The parasympathetic system calms things and restores balance after the incident has passed. Simple sets of movements can calm the arousal of the sympathetic nervous system quickly, as can making your outbreath longer than your inbreath. You can also stroke your arms down the outside of your upper arm, or sweep the tension off your hands, or stroke down your face to release it from the body. This is one method used in 'Havening', a form of healing that releases anxiety from the system.

> **Reflective questions**
>
> - What methods do you use to calm yourself in a stressful situation, in the moment?
> - What actions do you take to maintain your own well-being?

Supporting a distressed pupil

The following is taken from an Irish handbook for teachers (5) prepared by the Department of Education (Ireland):

> When a child's sense of safety is threatened, a secure and trusted relationship with key adults will help them to process and manage how they are thinking and feeling. Adults can help support children and

young people during this time by fostering resilience and promoting recovery using the five key principles (adapted from Hobfoll et al., 2007) that were outlined by NEPS over the last number of years in supporting all members of the school community during Covid-19. These are:

- Promoting a sense of safety
- Promoting a sense of calm
- Promoting a sense of belonging and connectedness
- Promoting a sense of self efficacy and community-efficacy
- Promoting a sense of hope. (p.2)

This handbook also suggests a 'Look, Listen and Link' approach to becoming aware of pupils who could need supports for recovery from trauma or severe distress. This involves *looking* at the behaviour of a pupil to see if they are acting differently from usual or seem more disengaged, *listening* to their worries and how they feel they are coping, and *linking* with specialist service if needed, in consultation with the pupil and their guardian. These are all actions that a teacher is familiar with and qualified to take.

(iii) Emotional first aid or PFA for groups

The Psychological Society of Ireland produced a booklet called *Not ReLIVING – But LIVING* (10) intended for ordinary people welcoming Ukrainian refugees. They gave the following definition of psychological first aid:

> Psychological first aid (PFA) is humane, supportive and practical assistance to fellow human beings who recently suffered exposure to serious stressors. It is not counselling or psychological debriefing, neither of which is recommended for people in this situation. PFA is a way of providing support from one human to another human who is experiencing distress.
> It involves:
>
> - non-intrusive, practical care and support
> - assessing needs and concerns
> - helping people to address basic needs (food, shelter, transport costs)
> - listening, but not pressuring people to talk, comforting people and helping them to feel calm

- helping people connect to information, services, and social support
- protecting people from further harm

It is NOT asking people to analyse what happened, drawing out their experiences or looking for details or pressuring people to tell you their feelings or reactions to an event. (p.3)

The National Child Traumatic Stress Network and National Center for PTSD (11) describe their PFA:

Psychological First Aid is an evidence-informed modular approach to help children, adolescents, adults, and families in the immediate aftermath of disaster and terrorism. Psychological First Aid is designed to reduce the initial distress caused by traumatic events and to foster short- and long-term adaptive functioning and coping . . .

Psychological First Aid is designed for delivery by mental health and other disaster response workers who provide early assistance to affected children, families, and adults as part of an organized disaster response effort. These providers may be imbedded in a variety of response units, including first responder teams, incident command systems, primary and emergency health care, school crisis response teams, faith-based organizations, Community Emergency Response Teams (CERT), Medical Reserve Corps, the Citizens Corps, and other disaster relief organizations. (p.5)

As the above handbook is designed for supporting victims of disaster, it is not part of the usual work of the classroom. There is a lot of information about logistics and managing groups of displaced people. However, it is interesting to see that all the same guidelines needed to support others in any trauma or distress are emphasised – approaches such as making sure the victim can decide how much they want to talk (or not) about what has happened, staying in the moment and providing whatever immediate comfort you can. There are some useful reminders, for example, not to give out soft toys to comfort children if you haven't enough for everybody. The recommendation is to share whatever reliable information you have, but to be careful not to falsely reassure or promise resources that you don't have or that may not arrive. Another useful point was that if a child's parent is visibly overwhelmed and unavailable to comfort the child, you could check if there is another family member who could care for the child until the main carer feels able to. The sharing of accurate information is very important and should be adapted in appropriate ways to a child's age. Sharing information about available supports is another action to take.

Key points of Chapter 8

- Clear and meaningful boundaries are helpful in building a safe environment.
- There are many aspects to creating safe boundaries for you and your group of learners. These include clarity around the standards and timing of the work, and limits around confidentiality and group sharing of sensitive personal information.
- Boundaries change and develop with the group, and as bonds develop, the participants will take more initiative in what is important for them in order to have a safe, supportive group.
- Emotional first aid is based on a kind and helpful response to another person who has suffered shock.
- Emotional first aid means taking care of yourself to maintain emotional health and well-being.
- Psychological first aid for a group following a shared disaster follows the same principles as for an individual.

References

1. Arao B, Clemens K. From Safe Spaces to Brave Spaces. In: The Art of Facilitation: Reflections from Social Justice Educators. London: Routledge; 2013.
2. Shevrin Venet A. Role-clarity and boundaries for trauma-informed teachers. Educational Considerations. 2019;44(2).
3. Minister for Children and Youth Affairs. Children First Bill 2014. Dublin: Department of Children and Youth Affairs; 2014.
4. Steele W, Malchiodi CA. Trauma-informed practices with children and adolescents. New York: Taylor and Francis; 2012.
5. Department of Education. Guidance for Primary School Staff – Using Psychological First Aid. Dublin: National Educational Psychological Service; 2022.
6. Winch G. How to practice emotional first aid; 2015. www.youtube.com/watch?v=F2hc2FLOdhI

7. Suzuki W. The brain-changing benefits of exercise; 2017. www.ted.com/talks/wendy_suzuki_the_brain_changing_benefits_of_exercise?subtitle=en2017
8. Steele W. Reducing compassion fatigue, secondary traumatic stress and burnout. UK: Routledge; 2020.
9. van der Kolk BA. The body keeps the score. USA: Viking Penguin; 2015.
10. Martin E, Carey A, Cowley-Cunningham M, Rogers E, Ryan M, Miller I, et al. Not ReLIVING— But LIVING: Psychological First Aid for Refugee Care: Helpful Do's and Don'ts. Psychological Society of Ireland. 2022.
11. Brymer M, Jacobs A, Layne C, Pynoos R, Ruzek J, Steinberg A, et al. Psychological First Aid: Field Operations Guide; 2006. www.ptsd.va.gov/disaster_events/for_providers/PFA/PFA_2ndEditionwithappendices.pdf

9

Overwhelm, compassion fatigue, vicarious trauma and supervision

> This chapter looks at the effects on the educator of working with high levels of trauma and distress in their learners and explores ways to reduce the stress and remain engaged in the work.
>
> There are four sections in this chapter:
>
> - Section 1 focuses on the effects of the work on the educator.
> - Section 2 looks at the different ways this can manifest itself and how to recognise them.
> - Section 3 explores approaches to self-care and why we so often neglect it.
> - Section 4 discusses the use and benefit of supervision.

Floods of sad stories and traumas – I feel I am drowning!

I said to the principal in one school, 'It's hopeless – there are just too many kids and too many problems. I can't take any more. It makes no difference what we do.' She answered in her usual proactive way: 'Now look, all these children we are retaining in school, years ago they wouldn't have gone to school or would have left at 12 years old. Now they are here, and we are helping them. Here, have a bar of chocolate!'

Section 1: The effects on teachers of working with traumatised students

William Steele (1) offers a reality check on stress:

> Reality: you cannot expect to work with at-risk traumatized individuals or for an organization or program that services trauma victims or those experiencing emotionally challenging situations and not experience some form of stress. There are different forms. What is important at this point is acknowledging that stress comes with what we do. (p.5)

The weight of the suffering and trauma that your students bring to class every day can become overwhelming. This depends a good deal on the catchment area of your school or institution. A well-resourced school in an affluent area will have individual upsets and traumas affecting the pupils, and some children with extra social or educational needs. A school in an underserved area with endemic issues like addiction, unemployment and deep poverty will have a school population who are living with trauma on a daily basis as their version of normal. Then, in addition to this reality, which has been called 'being marinated in trauma', the pupils will endure the individual suffering around bereavement and loss that we all experience. There will be

Figure 9.1 Feel like I'm drowning in problems and trauma stories

pupils with extra educational and behavioural needs in every class, with the individuals in underserved areas having less access to private resources and possibly presenting more complex needs in the classroom.

The stress on the staff involved is very real and must be taken seriously. It is important to support the staff effectively to avoid burnout and compassion fatigue. The educators may be working hard and achieving positive relationships and academic progress with the children, but it is a tough energy-draining process.

Conflicting responsibilities

Teachers mention the ongoing struggle with caring for the whole class and the children who have extra needs. Jane works in a school in a wealthy area, but still must find this balance between the class group and those needing more attention:

This year I have one child that needs a lot of my attention in the class. Last year I had a little child with special needs and the other child who had a lot going on at home. So like, you try your best, you listen as much as you can. But yeah, those two. And then I had 27 others. Yeah, who were all entitled to be cared for as well. And I found, like, because I . . . because it was too draining on a lot of my resources last year, I didn't have time to listen as much.

Another teacher, Anna, in an underserved school described the struggles to keep on top of it all:

Just you always feel like that you're never doing enough or you're never – there's just too many bases to cover. Yeah. And it's just – I'm in the classroom on my own. She [a traumatised child with educational and emotional needs] doesn't have a special needs assistant. She gets two short movement breaks and three 15-minute movement breaks in between every part of the day. And then there's other classes as well [for this child], but it takes me to do that, to deal with meltdowns, to manage all the time, but then I have other children in the class – 20. And then I've got a few of them that are way above average, four to seven with average, and pupils that didn't score academically. Yeah, and I've tried to deal with them on my own. And this explosive behaviour, and then other mini explosions in the classroom. You just think somebody's getting let down somewhere. That's what I feel. Yeah, it's impossible. Yeah, not gonna beat all that. Yeah, that's what I feel.

A lack of training for trauma-informed approaches

The study by Oberg and colleagues (2) of compassion fatigue and burnout found that teachers were working with a population of children and young people with increased levels of anxiety and other mental health challenges, with numbers rising every year. Covid-19 has increased the level of trauma among pupils, and their findings suggest that:

> Conclusion: The lack of trauma-specific training reported by pre-service and current teachers indicate a need for higher education institutions and schools to better prepare teachers to support traumatized students while safeguarding their own wellbeing. (p.1)

In engaging with trauma-informed practice (TIP), it is vital to remember that staff at all levels are also dealing with real-life stress in their own lives and, as human beings, will have suffered traumas, which they may have worked with or not. This work can be triggering for many professional, administrative and logistical staff, as well as those we perceive as 'victims of trauma'. The training and application of TIP needs to be mindful of the sensitivity and needs of all the staff. Any type of interaction that asks people to reflect on their own experiences can produce positive and negative results.

For example, when supervising students doing research for their Master's, I remind them to check in with their interviewees that they are comfortable with the questions and, after the interview, that they are feeling fine with no unpleasant reactions. For example, a teacher interviewed about discipline methods in the classroom could be triggered back to a memory of a public humiliation in her own school days.

Maintaining a safe place and avoiding retraumatisation for students and staff

The previous chapters have detailed many of the practical steps and attitudes that support a safe place and enable learning to be a positive experience. The most important is what a mother in my parenting group called 'a bit of loving kindness'. It is impossible to know everything that could upset a person, so the important thing you can do is build a trusting relationship with yourself as educator and among the group. You will be aware of students' anxiety or discomfort in relation to certain activities or materials that are in use, but it is not always obvious. An atmosphere that makes it easy for people to ask for what they need and say if something bothers them is the key ingredient. Teachers in many different countries report feeling unprepared to work with traumatised pupils and having had little or no training in the theory of trauma affecting behaviour, or the practical classroom management needed to work with these dysregulated distressed students.

The National Education Association (NEA) of America (3) reports that:

> Until recently, the discussion around compassion fatigue focused on mental health professionals, first-responders, nurses, and other professionals dedicated to the relief of individual emotional and physical suffering. Over the past few years, researchers began to include teachers in their surveys and analysis. With nearly half of U.S. children having experienced adverse childhood events, poverty and trauma, how could educators, in their supportive role, not be affected? Overall, the available research indicates that compassion fatigue among teachers is prevalent and disproportionately impacts those in underserved schools.

Reducing trauma triggers and responding to the unexpected

Karen Treisman (4) gives a list of triggers she has experienced with young people that are school-related, which include a range of emotional responses around feeling crowded, excluded, ignored, shamed by the inability to do tasks, rejected, or abandoned by a change of teacher. The autobiographical triggers include family days, family tree work and in one case, snow, as this was the day the child was placed in foster care (p.150).

One Christmas, we were making some decorations in an art session, and teenagers were discussing gifts and whether they would buy something for their parents, granny or siblings. One young person talked at length about the beautiful gift they were saving to get for their dad – 'the best dad in the world – he will be getting all the family great presents'. The children were taken into care the next day due to dangerous levels of violence and alcoholism in their home. It is not always obvious what is going on.

Loud voices and noises, arguments in class, the lunch line – will there be enough food? Will it run out? This can cause real distress for a child that knows hunger regularly. Sudden changes in routine can lead to pupils feeling unsafe and acting out. This list illustrates the known and unknown nature of trauma triggers. A reduction in noise, including your lowered tone of voice, and warnings about sudden noises such as bells are easy to implement. The relational emotional triggers are harder to pre-empt, as they can be subtle and build up unseen. Memories of abuse can also be triggered by sensory experiences. The effort of trying to make the classroom environment and activity trigger-free can be a challenging task without support and training.

As the teacher, you are working with these traumatised children every day. Whether you are fully aware of the details of their life or not, you are living with the behaviours, the emotional responses and difficulties in learning caused by trauma. The triggers that can cause the pupil to become angry, upset or withdrawn may be unknown to you. Living through the trauma-affected behaviours and experiences of your pupils impacts you in using up your energy and the empathy you feel for the young person. The helplessness to create meaningful change can feel like revving the engine at a red light!

The change comes in the view – the trauma-informed lens – that helps you to deepen the awareness and understanding that you are using already to care for your pupils in a way that makes them feel safe. This is a gradual learning for all of us, educator and pupils, in a new class. Shielding the pupils from all possible triggers and negative experiences is just not feasible. As you get to know the young people and develop trust, they will be able to let you know what they need, and you will become more aware of their triggers and what their behaviours mean. This enables the pupils to settle and learn.

The build-up of pressure on teachers, educators and support staff

Working with high numbers of traumatised children or young adults, whether it is in groups or individual sessions, carries risks for the educator. The focus can be on the children to the extent that it is all-consuming and can literally

Overwhelm, compassion fatigue, vicarious trauma and supervision

burn you up. If you are continually nurturing others and not replenishing your own source, the well runs dry. This overwhelm can spread among the staff, as described by a recently qualified teacher, Pat:

And the school, it was in a tougher area, maybe had something to do with it, but it kind of felt like the kids were running the school. It was like people were bending over backwards to try and do their best, but it was just kind of letting the kids do whatever they wanted, really.

Yeah, and there was a lot of us, sixth class teachers, and I don't think we had a meeting together all year, so there was no real kind of cooperation, or nobody really trying much. Yeah, that seemed to be the whole kind of atmosphere of the school; most people wanted to leave the school, and they were looking for a way out . . .

Once the principal came up and couldn't deal with him [a difficult pupil with extra social and educational needs], so he just left and left me with the kid, like there was no support. They were down about seven or eight staff, so there wasn't the support to go around, really.

Another instructor in a practical skills workshop for teenagers, Stephanie, found the same lack of specialist support:

There's a guy at the moment, he's on suicide watch. I find that very hard. I don't have the tools to – I can't, I feel I can't push him, or if he doesn't want to do an exercise, doesn't want to do something, yeah? So, there's no supervision for the staff, and dealing with these nine students in my class today . . . there's no extra support because we're severely short-staffed. There's no resource teacher. The resource wasn't replaced from last year. We're down two other staff. So, and I know I said that to other people, and I know people said that to me as an instructor of practical skills [using tools with safety risks] two years ago, 'What, you have eight students?', we can't manage them in a class.

Stephanie highlighted the pressure of low support from the manager in dealing with students:

In all fairness, my boss, who has been there years, is always going to reiterate that [that traumatized children actually need routine and boundaries] but reiterates it to us without support. If that makes sense, you have to follow through . . . I don't even discipline now, because I feel it goes above my pay grade. You know, if I'm to remove somebody from the class, then it was met with [her manager] two seconds later, bringing the student back in. There were no repercussions for their actions. Yeah.

Zoe, a specialist support teacher, spoke of the continuing problems that weigh on her:

The most, the most awful part, really, is in 2024 there's so much of, you know, poverty, addiction and families – you know, families just not coping. And you know children, year after year, still being like undernourished, underdeveloped. You know there's no assessments for their educational disabilities, and you can see that they're struggling. So, you know, in the school that I work in, they're only allowed to have two assessments a year out of a school of 200+ that's just not enough, two in total for the whole school. And Covid-19 made everything so much worse for the less well-off. Families that had room in their houses, access to laptops, books, puzzles, toys and back gardens, had some interesting times and more family time. In communities where parents depended on the school for structures, extra meals, after-school clubs and materials for learning, many parents were not able to cope at all and they have stayed switched off from their kids. I have kids coming in at six years old telling me to go and f--- myself and fighting in the clubs! This used to be sometimes, now it's every day.

Section 2: What are compassion fatigue (CF), secondary traumatic stress (STS) and burnout?

Charles Figley, writing in 1995 (5), believed that **compassion fatigue (CF)** affected lots of different caring professions including veterinary, although the original research was conducted with nurses. He also distinguished between CF and **secondary traumatic stress (STS)**, stating that STS was more significant for those working with trauma populations. In his work on supervision and support, William Steele (1) aims to reduce compassion fatigue, secondary traumatic stress and burnout. These states have elements in common but are different in origin and in their effects on the person. Steele sees stress as a subjective reaction and suggests that self-care practices need to be resilience-based and trauma-sensitive, while having a calming effect on our subconscious reactions to stress. He also emphasises that each individual will have different practices that work for them, and that you need to try a variety to see what suits you.

Compassion fatigue

Caring professions, such as teaching, nursing and caring, require empathy from the practitioner for their client, and then compassion motivates the desire to help the person's situation and meet some of their needs. CF results when the person is overwhelmed by the demands made on their caring or compassion (1). When this happens, your resources are so depleted that you just feel you can't respond in a meaningful way to clients or pupils. You may start avoiding difficult clients or situations or start blaming the clients for their problems. The cynicism and judgemental views expressed concerning struggling pupils that can be found in some staffrooms are a part of compassion fatigue. You might find you are working harder but getting less done, feeling irritable and shut off from others. If people notice your different attitude and behaviour, your reaction is denial or offence.

The overarching emotion and physical feeling are ones of absolute exhaustion.

Secondary traumatic stress

STS occurs when a person becomes deeply upset and develops trauma symptoms from hearing or witnessing the traumatic experiences of others. The signs can be similar to those of post-traumatic stress disorder (PTSD). The clients' traumas and issues, current and previous, become triggers for the worker, who may begin to have nightmares and intrusive memories of the clients' experiences. Other symptoms, such as being very jumpy, nervous and expecting bad things to happen, contribute to poor sleep and feeling isolated from others.

Burnout

Burnout is not specifically related to the caring professions or associated with those who work with a traumatised population. It is associated with workplace policies and practices. It is characterised by intense overwork with a narrow focus on task completion, and leads to total exhaustion; physical collapse can occur. The ability to focus on work, complete tasks and concentrate is reduced, and work and the workplace can become a source of dread. A study of how burnout can be 'contagious' among 578 teachers by Meredith and colleagues (6) suggested that personal interactions were very influential in increasing burnout risk over time. Both conscious discussion of stressful issues and unspoken emotional expression had effects on others, and the stronger the relationship, the more powerful the effects.

A study by Corbin and colleagues (7) describes the added stress on educators post-Covid, and also notes that TIP remains a theory if teachers are not equipped to use it:

> [T]he effects of trauma can wreak havoc on educator well-being. Unfortunately, educators experience STS and burnout, likely the result of the unrelenting responsibilities placed on their plate, including having to address the external manifestations of childhood traumas in the classroom. Few educators have adequate training on how to address the complicated behaviors associated with childhood trauma, leaving many feeling helpless and ineffective. Trauma-informed pedagogical approaches are helpful in the classroom [but] are rendered useless unless educators are physically, mentally, and emotionally available to implement the practices. (p.7)

Christian Brandt and colleagues (8) looked at stress symptoms and how they related to the dropout rate of teachers:

> STS is defined by stress reactions or symptoms that mirror Post-Traumatic Stress Disorder (PTSD) and may be experienced by teachers or other helping professionals who hear the stories of others affected by trauma (Caringi et al., 2015; Hydon et al., 2015; Stamm, 2010). STS has been conceptualized as a type of burnout by some (Figley, 2013), while others have characterized STS as one aspect of 'compassion fatigue'; burnout being the other aspect (Stamm, 2010). (p.2)

Reflective questions

- How do you know you are becoming overwhelmed? What feelings or actions make you aware of this?
- What is the attitude to CF, STS and burnout in your workplace? Is it taken seriously? Can you talk about aspects of it and get support?

Section 3: Self-care

Learning about your own needs, immediate and ongoing life choices

I just had a very frustrating morning. Computer skills, tech matters and maths – all my weakest points conspired against me! I kept struggling to do something that wasn't working until I took my own advice. I used to always say to trainee teachers if a pupil doesn't understand the principle or method, there is no point repeating the question/problem to them. Yet here I was, repeatedly downloading an article that presented itself as lines of numbers and symbols – I kept on trying even though I know I have missed some (simple) vital step. I realised this morning that stopping the frustrating task and doing something productive (I went for a quick walk) was a vital piece of self-care for me. This got me thinking about self-care and stress reduction.

The huge question is why most of us don't do, and enjoy doing, the things that keep us well and energetic. Maybe it's because 'self-care' and 'reflective practice' can seem like another chore to do in a busy life, or perhaps we are over-givers and literally do not have time to care for ourselves. That is, until 'The Body Says NO', according to Gabor Maté (9), and we become ill or develop some kind of pain symptom. Most people don't need to train themselves to wear warmer clothes when it's very cold or close the hall door to keep in the heat. These are instinctive types of self-care built up over time. The process of strengthening the minute responses to our stress build-up is individual, different for all of us. The good news is that anecdotal and research evidence shows that the more you follow these habits of supporting yourself, the easier and faster it becomes. In a lecture on resilience and reflectivity, Rebecca Finley (10) stated:

> We should encourage meaningful reflection as an important habit that promotes resiliency. Reflection gives us pause to process emotions and cognitions such as appreciating multiple perspectives, and it provides protection against stress and burnout. Similarly, we should encourage informal practices to promote self-awareness, such as slowing down when necessary and clearing one's mind; setting boundaries regarding one's job; and establishing enough time for sleep, exercise, relaxation, and personal relationships with family and friends. (p.1187)

Self-care

Know it and do it!

There are two important aspects to self-care. The first is recognising the warning signs of overwhelm. The second is developing strategies that fit your everyday life and work for you to stay integrated.

This first part of self-care is learning about yourself and how you recognise the signs of stress in your body, your emotions and your relationships, professional and personal. As your awareness grows, it will become natural to you to check in with yourself regularly during the day. The second part helps you adapt your daily programme to fit, as much as you can, to your own emotional state.

Learn about your own stress responses

What physical sensations, thoughts and emotions go with overwhelm for you?

- What sensations do you feel in your body when you are overwhelmed – whether it's anger, frustration or sadness or any other feeling?
- What responses do you have when you are emotionally overwhelmed? Are they feelings of hopelessness, sadness, anger or any other feeling?

- How do you know the feeling of stress or overwhelm is growing?
- How do you clear it?
- What are you saying to yourself? Is it negative or self-blaming? Say it out loud –would you ever say this to a friend who was struggling with something? (I was saying to myself today, 'You are just a real messer.' My crime? I couldn't find my glasses! I switched to 'I am very busy and doing my best!' – instant smile and I found the glasses.)
- How do you calm and quieten yourself?
- Who else would notice? Would they be supportive or critical?

Signs of stress for you (they are different for everyone)

- **Physical:** Loss of appetite, headaches, unsettled stomach, disturbed sleep, food or alcohol cravings, rashes, hair loss, stiff joints, back pain, nausea, exhaustion.
- **Emotional:** Crying easily, upset by outside events like the news, feeling guilty for being happy or privileged, feeling ashamed of your low state, feeling vulnerable and easily offended, feeling hurt, quick to anger.
- **Psychological:** Feeling scared by your sad feelings, feeling less than others who seem to be coping better, blaming yourself for your upset ('Other people are much worse off than me'). Ruminating on problems or past events over and over. Forgetting things, mixing up dates and worrying over small details. Using negative self-talk, putting yourself down.
- **Relationships:** Feeling isolated, finding it hard to talk about your feelings or what is going on, keeping away from people, being cranky or snappy with people, feeling no one cares or understands, over-sharing and then feeling embarrassed, refusing help or invitations.
- **Professional:** Trying to hide your feelings and difficulties from colleagues, feeling like an impostor, avoiding groups or social events.
- **Personal:** Keeping to yourself, making light of your problems when asked, becoming irritated with close friends and family. Lacking energy to join events, giving up things you enjoy.

How do you regain your balance and get back to what Dan Siegel (11) calls FACES: Flexible, Adaptive, Coherent, Energised and Stable. This is when positive energy is flowing, and your energy is integrated.

The second aspect of self-care is focusing on what makes you feel happy and relaxed

People, places and plans that make you feel happy and energised

This is looking at real enjoyment, passion and laughter. It doesn't include the essential decompression things you do after a hard day. For example, a run around the park to burn off the helpless and frustrated feeling you have about being unable to help a student is not the same as an enjoyable hike with those you love, or a long, lazy lunch with old friends.

What makes you laugh? What makes you feel happy and carefree? When was the last time you did this?

You want to thrive, not just survive. You're doing a demanding job, and probably looking after people in your home life as well. Where's the fun time?

Things that make you happy and energised

- **Physical:** Any kind of exercise that you like – that's the key thing. Don't sign up for things you don't enjoy because you won't do them. Go for a walk around the park or to the coffee shop, do yoga or dancing or swimming or ride your bike, take up badminton, hill walking or bowling. Once you like it! Breathing exercises like *box breathing can increase calm in a few minutes.
- **Creative:** Colouring, painting, gardening, sewing, knitting, carpentry, baking – any level.
- **Emotional:** Spend time with those people you care about. Accept help and kind gestures and enjoy them. Notice what brings your mood down and avoid it! Eat with friends and family as often as possible; it's one of the best ways to boost your well-being. It can be a toastie and a coffee – no need for anything fancy.
- **Psychological:** Take up healthy habits of self-care. The first one is the easiest and the hardest. It is: *Stop being so hard on yourself.* Let small mistakes go without a sigh – so what if you burnt the cake, lost the key or forgot that birthday? For bigger, more impactful mistakes, clear up the damage as best you can, make any necessary apologies and remember that nobody will care in a year's time. If you find yourself being cranky and critical of yourself and others, take a breath and say something nice to yourself, like: 'I'm feeling a bit down, so I will take it easy and do my best.'

You would never inflict the nasty criticism you give yourself on another person, so stop right there.

- **Relationships:**
  - Professional: Sharing with colleagues, having a support network. Having a laugh at life. Learning how to deflect mean or belittling comments. If necessary, learn how to protect yourself against negative people. Celebrate small successes and occasions at work.
  - Personal: Putting time into the relationships that nourish you. There are some fixed duty-type relationships that we are bound to in some sense, such as family, in-laws and neighbours. If you're lucky, these are part of your happy supportive network, but if they aren't, you need the rest of your friendships and all kinds of relationships to work even better for you.

    It's always helpful to do an occasional inventory of your relationships that take up your time and energy. You know that person who is very negative and critical? You always feel exhausted after meeting them, so why are you doing it? Why spend your precious energy? The friend who always makes you laugh and has lots of ideas to discuss with you, the person who thinks about your needs and supports you – when did you see them last?

    An inventory of family life can be informative and relieve a lot of pressure when able-bodied family members are helped to realise that they are no longer young children and can shop, cook and clean along with the regular staff! That's you! Remember: if you can walk safely with your plate, you are the right height to put it in the dishwasher.

    Quick tip: These changes take persistence. It is unlikely that those who have enjoyed hotel service will spring into action after a single request. Subtle and less than subtle encouragement may be needed – like withdrawal of services or spending the 'treats' portion of the shopping budget on a night out for yourself as you have not received a fair amount of help. 'There is nothing to eat in this house'! Faint cries as you exit stage left.

Strategies to know and calm your stress and stress/trauma triggers

- **Aware:** Become aware of the immediate uncomfortable stress reactions in your body and emotions. Learn them, so check-ins and adjustments become habitual.

- **Act:** Have short-term ways to restore calm:
  - Yourself: Breathe, move, change the activity, speak kindly to yourself. Start an action that feels good to you – a stretch, drawing, looking at a beautiful picture or photo.
  - Your class group: Extend these actions to a group. If you are the leader in the room and are feeling overwhelmed or uneasy, it is likely others are too. So whatever the age of the group, you can own the feeling and lead a minor change for everyone. For example: 'I am feeling a bit fed up and frustrated with this issue/topic/task. How are you all feeling? (If they are all keen to finish the task, just take a minute or two and get back to it.) Let's all stand up and stretch and take a few big breaths.'***Drawing to music** – 'Now I will play some music and we can all draw and doodle whatever it feels like to us.' Play some beautiful music and give everyone a sheet of paper and colours to draw with.
- **Appreciate:** Practise looking for the positive even in a tough situation. Get rid of self-blame and say kind things to yourself. This sounds fake, but it is very powerful. (This can be challenging when you lose the key to the post box, break into it, buy a whole new kit and then find the key in your pocket. Grrr.)
- **Ask** for help if you need it. It doesn't have to be a crisis.
- **Acknowledge** that you are doing the best you can and more. Look for the ways you have coped, and the strengths you have.
- **Accept** that life is full of challenges – most of us are sailing along, tacking in the wind as best we can.

Self-care plan with a commitment

- **Transitions:** Mark the end of your working day by a change of clothes, playing music, doing a bit of exercise, yoga, tai chi, a quick walk or dancing in the kitchen. Do the crossword or a puzzle, some colouring in a mandala-type colouring book or sketching. Something that changes the energy and lets your body and mind know you are finished work for the day.
- **Stop and swerve:** Learn to read the clues that you are becoming overwhelmed and head off the path. Cards that give you a thought for the day are useful, or any change to the action or feeling as mentioned in 'Act' in the previous section.

- **Store up laughter:** When someone tells you something funny, remember it and you can share it with someone else or laugh yourself again.
- **Do one thing** you enjoy every day. Keep it simple and you will do it. Ring a friend – no texting! Or send a card, have a bath, or make something in the kitchen.
- **Practise saying 'no'** in front of the mirror – essential for those who take on too much. You will laugh at this, but when you are about to commit to something unwanted, you may remember and utter the word 'No!'
- **Create reminders** to do these things – visual, audio on your phone, journal.

> ### Reflective questions
> - What could you do to reduce the level of your work stress?
> - What support do you have in making positive choices around self-care at work and at home?

Section 4: Supervision and the buddy system

This section will look at the meaning and purpose of professional supervision. This is a support that all those who work closely with others, meeting their needs in social care, education, medicine and therapy, should have as part of their work. However, if you don't have access to supervision, you can commit to a sharing support with a friend. It works best if you both have some understanding or common ground in your work, but it can also be effective if you are both facing the same challenges in very different fields. If you are reading this book, it is down to the buddy support system that I was able to finish it.

What is professional supervision and why is it important?

I had professional supervision at several stages in my life and, in two out of three situations, found it very supportive and a wonderful chance to learn from somebody who is an expert in the field. In two cases, it offered support for the work and managing the workload, and helped me explore the inevitable dilemmas that come from working with people. On one occasion, however, I suffered from bullying and found that my confidence was destroyed by sarcasm and negative criticism. On another occasion, I experienced someone on a management committee attempting to set up an 'assessment system' of our team – which they were not involved with and had no authority over. We were lucky in that we had a supportive board member who definitively vetoed this person's idea. These incidents only occurred to me when I was interviewing professional supervisors and one of them mentioned the power imbalance in the relationship. It is an example of how we can bury and make light of our own negative and distressing experiences, as I thought I had forgotten all about these events. In the supervision relationship, it is important for the supervisee to feel safe and heard, and to experience it as helpful and empowering.

The fact that professional supervisors in the therapy world also receive supervision makes for a different approach from situations where the supervisor has not received specialist training and there is no accountability. In hierarchical systems, the only supervision employees receive is often a performance review, which usually has implications for your prospects in the organisation. Student teachers are supposed to receive mentoring in the school placement and from the education institution they are studying with. This appears to be very variable according to the school situation and the approach of the supervisor, or inspector as they are often called. According to recently qualified teacher Pat, the emphasis is on aligning with the inspector's views:

> *I think definitely, you would have to kind of suit the inspector. And they probably, yeah, I wouldn't have gotten the impression they would have appreciated it if you were doing something that they didn't agree with.*

This was echoed by Conor who became a teacher as a second career. He described the trauma-informed training they received as:

> *vanishingly little, and my college is very paperwork-heavy. They're very, very serious about paperwork, about having lesson plans and again, kind of a roadmap for how the class was going to go in the first five minutes, like, they want all of that paperwork, all done long in*

advance of the class. And that's a huge overhead. I think as a teacher, I found I was a little bit resentful for how paperwork-heavy it was. So, you know, my experience of being on placement is that for seven weeks I was preparing a lot of paperwork, which wasn't terribly relevant once you got into the class. And then I had three visits, three random visits, yeah, where I didn't know where, I didn't know they were going to show up. And someone sat down the back of the room and gave me some feedback. And that feedback was very valuable.

As regards supervision and reflective practice, Conor found that:

And then after the lesson you are supposed to write a little reflection on how the class went. So you're supposed to journal after every class. And then after every placement block. So there is quite a lot of expectations on you to reflect. But there isn't really . . . you kind of feel like you're reflecting into the void. I would say you feel like it's busy work. Really there's no collaboration . . . I felt like it's more of a surveillance thing.

This need to suit the inspector seemed to cause anxiety in new teachers and led to them presenting very traditional approaches, and being nervous of sharing ideas or innovation, according to the study by Weiss and Weiss (12):

Therefore, if the supervisor and co-operating teacher differ in their directives or disagree in their assessments, the student teacher often tries to appease both so as to assure both an excellent academic grade and an outstanding job reference. This process perpetuates the status quo. As a student teacher in a traditional program told one of the authors regarding her method for resolving a conflictual experience, 'I want to graduate and get a good job in a good school. So, when they talk their talk, I try to walk their walk.' (p.127)

This is very relevant in the education sector as any complaints from a lower rank about those in powerful permanent positions will negatively affect your chances of freelance work or advancement of your career. Currently in many organisations, like the education system, accessing the counselling service is seen as a sign of weakness and take-up of available hours is low among teachers. When used effectively, professional supervision is a private space for people, either individually or as a group, to review and reflect on their work and learn from each other and their supervisor. It is not necessarily connected to the management structure of the organisation where the supervisees work.

Supervision of trainee and practising teachers

A study by Loomis and colleagues (13) on the use of reflective supervision to support early childhood educators (ECE) found that:

> [B]oth reflective supervision and trauma-informed approaches have been identified as promising practices for professionals to address children's challenging trauma-driven behaviors, while simultaneously addressing pathways to burnout that teachers face when responding to children's trauma-related behaviors. (p.267)

The use of a reflective, collaborative model was the focus of an action-based research study into the supervision of trainee teachers by Weiss and Weiss (12). The study found that the hierarchical nature of the traditional model fostered insecurity in the trainee teachers and a tendency to follow the methods they grew up with.

As Marina, an experienced supervisor, explained:

> *There were three headings that I was thinking under, and one was reflexivity, which is a very important issue in therapy, and important if you're working as a supervisor, or if you're working one to one with people, and so I think most people coming for supervision would see it as a safe place for them to bring up a dilemma that they have, so that if something arises, with a family, with a couple, with an individual. I was talking to one of my supervisees the other day, and she was saying, 'Oh, I was so happy, because I knew I'd be coming to talk to you on Thursday', and this was on Tuesday, you know that she'd had a very difficult session.*
>
> *So generally, I think if supervision is not seen in that way as a supportive area of somebody's work, then obviously it's not doing its job. So, the sharing of skills and ideas, clearly, some of those who come to supervision have been working for many years in the area,*

> so they they've got a lot of skills, a lot of ideas, and it's a requirement for therapists to do a certain amount of supervision every year. Not the case with other professions, it's beginning to be used a bit more now. But as a supervisor, you can learn, obviously, from the people you supervise as well, because they've been to some interesting workshop, they've just read something interesting. They've done a piece of work.

The lack of training in trauma-informed practice was mentioned by Melodie, a nurse and therapist working in primary care mental health. This was in response to the question 'Is there any training or awareness around trauma-informed practice in your field?'

> It's, yeah, like, I mean, the mental health services, people are starting to use the word [TIP] but it's just a word they're using. Yeah, you know – how much does it inform people's practice? To be honest with you . . . and it's almost seen as if it's something that's separate or new. So, it's like people's perception of what trauma is. So, it's like, if you've experienced domestic violence or you've experienced sexual abuse, you've experienced trauma, but not really. And I would just see coming into attend the mental health services as a trauma in itself, but that would never be taken into consideration. Or, you know, you'd work with a lot of people, maybe who'd been hospitalised, maybe have been hospitalised against their will, and really no, no conversations around that.

Melodie receives regular supervision as she works as a therapist, and when asked how she maintains her well-being, she said:

> Like I say, I go to supervision and I've the great supervisor that I've been seeing for a long time and it is just that bit . . . I am actually going to supervision later today.

Supervision in different professions can have other aspects, according to Marina:

> Well, I think definitely that's an aspect of perhaps, not within therapy so much, because I think within certain professions, I know talking to

> *social workers, there's a quite a hierarchical structure there, and so they would be nervous about being, you know, being criticised, being undermined, being found out, and that supervision for them might not always feel like such a supportive space. So, yeah, I do think that can be an issue for certain people.*

So, what about the teaching profession? Have you ever supervised teachers?

> *I would be talking to teachers who are teaching within the therapy world, OK, but I do think that that's really an issue, that practitioner's fear of criticism, and therefore they won't feel easy about bringing up an issue. So I think, you know, that's maybe where peer supervision, where group supervision, can be helpful. You know that people feel safer if they're in, say, a group of young teachers of their own level of experience, and they could challenge each other and challenge the supervisor, if necessary. You know which, maybe creates a safer space, but I think it's something that really needs to be developed within areas like the teaching profession, that people will feel, will see supervision as a resource, not as a threat.*

Access to supervision support for teachers and educators

Research and feedback from teachers and other professionals show that supervision provides a place for learning, discussing dilemmas and reducing stress and burnout. Currently, teachers in Ireland and many other countries don't have access to professional supervision. Ways to increase awareness of the value of supervision being available for educators include:

- Making a request through the union.
- Using counselling hours that schools or education boards have available, and asking to transfer them for group supervision.
- Looking for supervision workshops as part of continuous professional development (CPD).
- Groups sourcing their own supervisor.
- Buddy system.

Buddy system

Essential elements in a buddy system

- Agree at the start about confidentiality. Make your choice and take it seriously. Some people prefer to keep the whole arrangement private; others just keep the content personal – that is, the content is never to be discussed or referred to outside this time. This must have two levels for it to work. The first is that each speaker chooses their topic each week in turn, and the listener doesn't refer to any other issues known to them or mentioned in previous chats. The second has caught out many people in general conversation. A third party mentions, 'Oh, Mary seems very stressed in her job; I hope she is OK – I am worried about her', and to calm their worries, Mary's buddy says, 'Oh, don't worry, she has some ideas for working on it' or 'She is thinking of leaving – it's not worth it.' This is something that is important to clarify in groups – that confidentiality extends through the group itself, not just outside it.
- A regular appointed time, every two to three weeks, is a good length of time. Any more frequent, it becomes another chore; any less, it loses its energy.
- Commit to a time and stick to it. You don't change the times of your important medical or family appointments, so make this buddy support a priority and do it.
- Be flexible. You can add extra time if you need it in a time of pressure.
- Have a defined time for each of you to talk while the other listens before making any comment. It is better to have a fast ten minutes either way and stick to it than have a long session that you end up cancelling because it is too tiring.
- Use the assertive approach to expressing yourself. Speak in the first person and own your feelings and experience. Avoid moaning about others or blaming others for your feelings.
- A buddy support is not just a cosy chat about how fabulous you both are (though I'm sure that's true); accountability is a big part of it. This means that you can speak freely about your concerns and successes and learn from them, with the help of your buddy's insights. You can have things you want to do or explore and commit to them.
- As you get used to it, you can develop your own formula – something like 'one thing that worked well this week, one thing that didn't, one area

I want to work towards a change'. Be specific, and start small. Finish on a positive affirmation that is real to you. For example: 'This week: I am going to use my own method xxxx, to reduce stress and it will be easy. I let go of last week and move forward at my own pace.'
- If the sessions are always running over and full of intensity or distress, you need to seek further help. This mirrors the way you support your students; you offer empathy and a listening ear, but when this is not enough, you look for a referral.
- In the event of one person showing signs of serious distress, it is important to be honest about what you see, and if the person needs to access some specialist help, the buddy can support them to get this and keep meeting about whatever is going on if you both want to.

Figure 9.2 Flexible, adaptable, coherent, energised, stable (11)

Key points of Chapter 9

- Stress is a part of working directly with people, particularly with traumatised groups.
- Learning to recognise signs of overwhelm – mental, physical and emotional – in yourself is vital.

- Developing immediate ways to change the energy for yourself avoids build-up of toxic stress.
- Building healthy self-care habits into your life on a long-term basis is an ongoing process.
- Supervision offers learning, support and reflection to keep a happy life–work balance.
- A buddy system can offer support when supervision is not available, within agreed limits.

References

1. Steele W. Reducing compassion fatigue, secondary traumatic stress and burnout. UK: Routledge; 2020.
2. Oberg G, Carroll A, Macmahon S. Compassion fatigue and secondary traumatic stress in teachers: How they contribute to burnout and how they are related to trauma-awareness. Frontiers in Education. 2023;8.
3. Walker T. 'My Empathy Felt Drained': Educators Struggle with Compassion Fatigue. NEA, USA; 2023. www.nea.org/nea-today/all-news-articles/compassion-fatigue-teachers
4. Treisman K. Working with relational and developmental trauma in children and adolescents. London: Routledge; 2017.
5. Figley C. Compassion Fatigue: Coping with secondary traumatic stress disorder in those who treat the traumatized. New York: Beunner/Mazel; 1995.
6. Meredith C, Schaufeli W, Struyve C, Vandecandelaere M, Gielen S, Kyndt E. 'Burnout contagion' among teachers: A social network approach. Journal of Occupational & Organizational Psychology. 2020;93(2):328–52.
7. Tirrell-Corbin C, Bart Klika J, Schelbe L. Using research-practice-policy partnerships to mitigate the effects of childhood trauma on educator burnout. Child Abuse & Neglect. 2023;142(1).
8. Christian-Brandt AS, Santacrose DE, Barnett ML. In the trauma-informed care trenches: Teacher compassion satisfaction, secondary traumatic stress, burnout, and intent to leave education within underserved elementary schools. Child Abuse & Neglect. 2020;110(3).
9. Maté G. When the body says NO. New Jersey: Wiley; 2003.
10. Finley R. Reflection, resilience, relationships, and gratitude. American Journal of Health-System Pharmacy. 2018(75):1185–90.
11. Siegel D. The mindful therapist: The clinician's guide to mindsight and neural integration. London: Norton; 2010.

12. Weiss EM, Weiss S. Doing Reflective Supervision with Student Teachers in a Professional Development School Culture. Reflective Practice. 2001;2(2):125–54.
13. Loomis A, Coffey R, Mitchell J, Musson Rose D. Reflective supervision as a vehicle for trauma-informedorganizational change in early childhood education settings. Reflective Practice. 2024;25(3):267–85.

10
Working for change at different levels

> This chapter looks at some of the elements and stages of working towards TIP and equity in education, for the individual educator, in the school and in the wider community.
> There are three sections.
>
> - Section 1 looks at the background and theory of effects of trauma on abstract thinking and decision making. Some changes and practices you can use to integrate these TIP approaches into your personal and professional life are included.
> - Section 2 looks at working for change in your workplace or school.
> - Section 3 explores the bigger picture of social justice and where this can intersect with your individual work for justice and equity in education for your students.

The primary aim of this book is to provide the educator, who has a class to manage and a curriculum to complete, with an understanding of the effects of trauma and neglect on children and young people's development, abilities and behaviours. The trauma-informed practice (TIP) games, activities and approaches in this book are designed to meet the different needs of those affected by trauma as listed in the SAMHSA report (1). This material is designed based on research, professional experience and interviews with those working currently with young people.

This chapter will integrate some of the learning and adaptations to practice available to the educator with research on the value of TIP. This will keep the focus on the TIP and supply some useful research to discuss with other staff. This includes both those who are interested and those who are resistant or dismissive. I have done workshops with staff where some people have expressed anger and criticism of new initiatives to retain

Figure 10.1 Working for healing

and support difficult students. In a facilitated discussion, a concern for the well-being of all the students and a commitment to deliver high-quality education is usually the basis of this viewpoint. It is also important to remember that teachers are at risk of assault in their workplace in increasing numbers internationally. So a 'safe place' needs to offer educators the same guarantee. Each institution has its own rules and boundaries, and while an individual educator can soften the edges and offer more space to students who suffer, the maintenance of the agreed structure is essential for everyone.

Section 1: All about me!
Developing stability and flexibility

It starts with you. If your intention is to include trauma-informed aspects in your teaching, it is important that you know how to create emotional stability and flexibility in yourself. The skills and understanding that allow you to regain this emotional equilibrium when you are upset or worried about a pupil or something in your own life, is the other half of this action. Your modelling of self-regulation will pass on this skill to your students. This forms part of your daily work with all students and especially if your student group are experiencing a lot of trauma in their lives due to war, displacement, neglect, abuse or extreme poverty. The previous chapter looked at ways to keep balance in your life with a mixture of on-the-spot responses and full commitment to your own self-care.

Now, all you have to do is start practising these awareness and supportive behaviours for your own self-care as part of your everyday routine! Easy, isn't it? (*Not!*)

Integrating theory and daily practice

Skills and approaches

Self-regulation (SR) is frequently identified as an essential ability that enables people of all ages to manage emotions and behaviours, make good decisions and persevere with tasks and challenges. It is a survival skill for those who work with other people to avoid being affected by the rage, fear or panic of others. What is SR and how can we develop it in ourselves and enhance it in our pupils? A review of longitudinal studies (2) of mothers' level of warmth in parenting and children's long-term self-regulation found that:

> The current study examined the longitudinal and reciprocal links between two key parenting processes (i.e., maternal warmth and maternal harshness) and children's self-regulation across early and middle childhood.
>
> Results demonstrated significant bidirectional associations in middle childhood, such that maternal warmth at age 5 predicted children's self-regulation at age 9, and children's self-regulation at age 5 predicted maternal warmth at age 9. (Abstract)

This study supports the consistent theme of TIP theory that poor attachment or neglect in childhood has long-term effects on the child's development at all stages. This is especially noticeable in the damage done to social emotional skills which affects relationship building. This includes self-regulation, a key building block of executive function. It also makes sense of all the TIP games and activities for students of all ages to improve concentration, reduce anxiety and build relationships in a safe environment.

The work of Diamond (3) identified self-regulation as an important basis for developing executive function. Her work explained executive functions as the processes that involve abstract thinking, problem solving, delayed gratification, creativity and flexibility in perception and planning. These are essential skills for concentration and learning, whether it is for academic or practical tasks. The damage done by traumatic events and/or persistent neglect means the secure base for developing these higher-level skills is often lacking in those affected. Executive function is needed for abstract thinking and analysis but also for the tasks of everyday life – managing emotions and conflict, making positive decisions and delaying gratification for a long-term aim.

Executive function, sometimes called higher thinking, has several elements:

- **Inhibitory control:** To be able to control behaviour, attention and thoughts. Self-control is a part of this, such as being able to resist temptation. For the child, it might be to resist hitting or biting another child or grabbing something. For an adult, it could be a minor temptation to eat too many sweets or a major action like harming another person for your own gain or being dishonest at home or work.
- **The ability to complete tasks** involves commitment and delayed gratification. Allowing time to respond to questions or puzzles is part of this ability to stay tuned in to the task or activity at hand. This can be difficult for children and more so for children who have not experienced self-regulation from their carers.
- **Short-term memory** just holds the current and very recent information. This develops much earlier in children than working memory. The stages that move to working memory are things like the child's ability to find a hidden object. This develops from the initial pulling it from under the cushion to going to search on a shelf that is out of sight. These early stages of development are damaged by trauma and neglect, so the puzzles and problem solving you do for your pupils will benefit all of them. The pupils who lack this skill can learn it in a relaxed way and all of them will enjoy the games and improve their concentration.
- **Working memory** is the ability to work with information no longer present in front of you, so you can relate past events to current ones. This is needed for planning, adapting to change and relating different

information to get the answer. It is also part of creativity, bringing conceptual (abstract, logical) and perceptual (seen, experienced) knowledge into decision making.
- **Cognitive flexibility** also comes later in development and allows the person to change their perspective or view. This is essential in planning and problem solving.

What does TIP mean in your daily practice?

How does TIP impact the way you work with and relate to your students? Some teachers find it fits with their natural way of working and the skills they have gained through years of teaching.

As Anna who is teaching in an underserved area said:

This is from my own understanding, reading. Yeah. Talking to people. So no, I didn't get any [training in TIP] – nothing formal. No, no. I haven't actually heard that term [TIP] before, only in narrative conversations. I think it probably comes from my own philosophies and my own personal thinking and comes from things that I brought myself through childhood, some difficulties I experienced . . .

And I didn't want – I don't want children in my classroom to feel like that [like an outsider]. I want to always try and understand them better, or see if I can help them better or, you know, understand them better, I think.

Jane expanded on this point and felt the patience and understanding came with time and confidence:

And I suppose, like I never got training in anything like this before, don't get it in college at all. But as the years have gone on. I – this might sound bonkers, but like, I feel like I've taught myself how to do it, because over years, it's just I didn't have, I'd say 5 per cent of the patience ten years ago as I have now. I just like- that all came with time, because I came out of college and it was, you know, you got to get this done, this, and like, if everything, if everybody wasn't on the same level, I would think that the things aren't going right.

And if everybody wasn't on the same level in terms of behaviour or quiet, that was me doing my job wrong, whereas now I realised there's not one of them are the same, and specifically, you're going to have to exercise ten times more patience for a couple of children. But I just didn't have that. And that's only experience that has helped that.

Awareness of your own emotional and physical state and that of the group

Are you aware of the triggers for upset in your own life? If you are not, they will be affecting your moods and behaviour in ways you are not conscious of. This is because responses to trauma and trauma triggers often happen at a physiological level not in our control. We move from conscious awareness to responses and actions that subconsciously driven. A woman in a group I worked with described being in the hairdresser when she got news of a relative's sudden tragic death. She developed an instant allergic rash to the hair dye and her head began burning. This reaction developed into an allergy that lasted. In this case, she could stop colouring her hair, but more serious reactions like panic attacks or agoraphobia can severely limit a person's ability to live a full life. The trigger response you have may be unnoticed by others, nothing dramatic. You might notice you stop engaging in the conversation or lose your appetite or feel unreasonably irritated by others. The infectious nature of emotion means it is important to build up resilience and tools to help you use co-calming and grounding actions that will work for you and your group.

Gabor Maté, whose work on understanding trauma and addiction is world renowned, has a website – https://drgabormate.com. He has videos, articles, books and podcasts available on trauma effects and recovery. One interesting video (4) is an interview on the topic of 'the power of saying No'. This refers to his book *When the Body Says NO* (5) and discusses how trauma causes a disconnection from our authentic selves. Dr Maté describes trauma as 'an invisible force that shapes our lives. It shapes the way we live, the way we love and the way we make sense of the world. It is the root of our deepest wounds' (https://drgabormate.com/trauma).

What does being in the flow of your life mean for you? Dan Siegel (6) calls it FACES: flexible, adaptive, coherent, energised and stable.

This is the central concept of the book *The Whole-Brain Child* that he co-wrote with Tina Payne Bryson (7), which stresses the importance of all the parts of the brain working together. This builds strength and resilience in the child where they can respond to challenges and setbacks with some choices and problem-solving skills. Otherwise, the child is at the mercy of instant reactions and floods of emotions. Siegel has many examples and exercises to the develop this approach he calls the 'Yes Brain'.

Key elements in your own learning and self-care

Make the three Rs – relationships, resilience and reflection – the centre of your work.

- Knowledge of trauma and its effects on development and methods of supporting healing in children.
- Awareness of your own sensibilities – how do you know you are getting frustrated or upset?
- Actions – short- and long-term – to regain your balance. You can share some of these with your group where appropriate.
- Approaches – how will you integrate these TIP methods into the group? Start small and slowly.
- Plan–do–review. A method that never lets you down. Can be five minutes or an elaborate plan.
- Reflect *in* the moment, *on* the activity or incident later, *with* the other person or group, then or later.
- Support yourself with supervision or a buddy system.

Section 2: Change in the school setting

Maintaining relationships and working for change

Gerry commented on teachers who receive training in different approaches:

I think that teachers should absolutely go away and inform themselves, and the teachers that do that, what they have to do then, when they

> come back, their task is to try and gradually have an influence on the school culture. They can't start doing what's against the school protocol. So, it's, I think of it as kind of a process of osmosis, you know. Something travels from one area to another.

Research into the benefits of teachers receiving TIP training suggests that having the knowledge and skills to work with traumatised students and some approaches to support their distress and calm their reactive behaviour promotes the teacher's feeling of self-efficacy (8).

> [B]oth reflective supervision and trauma-informed approaches have been identified as promising practices for professionals to address children's challenging trauma-driven behaviors, while simultaneously addressing pathways to burnout that teachers face when responding to children's trauma-related behaviors. (p.267)

Changes in the students

Working with pupils, you aim to increase their integration and balanced experience of life, using the activities to build concentration, expand windows of tolerance and enhance self-regulation. What does it feel like for young people who have endured major trauma and are expected to come to school to sit and listen for hours? Maybe they are hungry, tired, scared and dreading more trouble when they go home. Maybe they are relishing just being in a safe warm room and feel scared when they are asked to do a task they haven't understood. They can't do their work because they have no school equipment and never get help with their homework.

As your class settles and you can complete more tasks, have some mini exhibitions and ***celebrations**. These are great to demonstrate the pupils' achievements and get other staff involved. One or two other teachers – better still, the principal – coming to view the work and making a short speech of praise will do wonders for their confidence and reputation. Always get the pupils to make and deliver the invitations themselves if you want family attendance. Let the child select the guest – brother, Nana, auntie or anyone they choose. Other people from the local area – sports coach, youth leader, community worker – can also be helpful and get involved with your events.

Through your ongoing review of work and process, the pupils can see their own accomplishments, and you can have regular updates for them on these changes, which may be minor to someone else and huge to them – for example, someone insulted them, and they kept their temper. *Cartoons are a good way to explore these mini situations in an impersonal third-party way.

Attitudes of other staff

As Julie, a teacher in a school in an underserved area, once said to me:

> I get what you're trying to do with the school retention and the family support. The thing I find hard is almost all the pupils here are disadvantaged, and some are trying really hard to study and pass exams with very little support from home. It's hard for them to see extra privileges, supports and rewards being given to students who were always disrupting the class and are often the local bullies.

Research into social emotional learning and ACEs

This was a valid concern from a dedicated teacher and is something many of those working with marginalised groups will be asked about. One response is some light – and I mean light: don't bombard them with research facts – interesting facts about school retention and the lifelong effects of a traumatic childhood. Most teachers know these things in some sense but may not want to acknowledge or discuss such issues. Always include some true and hopeful examples of healing and recovery from trauma.

Resources sharing

Class teachers are often very short of resources, so sharing materials and equipment, such as giving out photocopies of quizzes and games, will help your integration, whether you are in a different role or you are a mainstream teacher. For example, our school support project had built up some quality sports equipment and games, and we had links with local sports clubs.

In the summer term, we held a sports day with an open invitation so any pupils could join for that day.

It is important to keep an open, respectful attitude to other colleagues who may have different views and tread gently while expressing your views or new ideas about teaching.

Gerry warned against a heavy-handed approach:

> *I do think teachers can inform themselves but then I think they can't go in . . . that they have to gradually influence their peers. And sometimes the way to do that is by other people witnessing them, but you can't come in – 'I've done a course last week now, and we're all doing it wrong'. And yeah, you can't come in all guns blazing. That doesn't do anybody any good.*

Refer to previous changes that were resisted initially and are now valued

The Irish education system identified the need for special needs assistants (SNAs) in the classroom to facilitate inclusion of children with special needs in the 1970s. It took time for this system to become accepted, and even in 2003 in mainstream schools, some teachers still objected to having *untrained* people in their classroom. Historically, in Ireland there has been a culture of 'my classroom' as a private domain of the teacher, run under their direction and method. However, by 2017 there were 13,969 SNAs working in schools, and they had become an essential part of the team as all schools were applying for more SNAs. There are currently approximately 21,000 SNAs working in our schools (9).

Marina, a therapist and supervisor, reflecting on the caution around supervision expressed by some teachers suggested:

> *So, it's really interesting, isn't it? So, they [teachers] changed from seeing them [SNAs] as a threat, to them being seen as a resource. And yeah, that would be the cultural change as regards supervision, to see it as a resource and not as a way of undermining or criticising or judging. Well, I think that the strength that supervision can create is to keep that continuous, curious voice there, you know – tell me more about*

what's going on and how is it impacting, and what have people done, and what's the impact on you?

Other approaches influenced by TIP include the use of sensory rooms in some schools and what are commonly called safe corners or quiet spaces, either in the room or another area. These facilities with soft toys, weighted blankets, games and art materials have become mainstream as teachers see them working to calm distressed pupils.

Zoe, specialist support teacher mentioned:

It's to have that little toolkit, where you have fidgets, you know, like, ask the right questions, you know, like, what has happened today? You know, what can we do now? How can I help you now? Like, you know, very specific kind of, do you need a minute, you know, do you need a soft toy? Like, what would help you in this moment, right now – do you want to, kind of kick it out? Do you want to go to the yard and, you know, kick a football around? Some of the teachers see the quiet space working and it is much more common than before.

Like all the youngest, younger students are more aware that kids need quiet time or soft spaces. Their classrooms have a soft space, where you know more of the older style, it's more discipline – like, go to the head, go to the principal.

Jane expressed a similar appreciation of the 'soft space' spreading through her school:

When I had a very, quite difficult child, and I had one [a soft space] in my room because it had been recommended. I know it was brought up in a couple of meetings. And I know more people started doing it. And then last year, it was kind of a thing that, like, this isn't just for one or two children in every class. It should be there for all children.

Being a part of the school community

Venet (10) looked at how teachers of colour were blocked in their career promotions for addressing racism and discrimination in their teaching, and this can happen to any teacher who seeks to make changes and challenge the status quo. Your career is one issue, but day-to-day social indifference or dismissal of your ideas can be very disheartening. It is important to find common ground when you can with all the staff. Try to hold on to the attitude that we are all doing our best and that the concerns of others can be well founded and based on worries about standards of education dropping. The school rules require all staff to follow them, and while you might give leeway to some students in your own class on some issues, you will make life awkward for others and lose the respect of the staff if you ignore the rules.

Gerry, experienced principal and therapist, explained this clearly:

You can't make a child behave. But you have to support a child to keep the rules and sometimes that's just incremental learning. Like you can't just tolerate children acting out. Because you have responsibility to the whole class as well as the one. Well, unless there is some procedure in the school where when somebody is so distressed that they're causing distress to others. Yeah, there needs to be a plan of action other than just sending them to the office. And then very often, it's not punishment they need. Sometimes they need sanctions, but they don't need punishment because they have probably been punished already. Yes, but they do need to understand, they do need a psycho-educational process to help them understand that you can't do that in school because it's eroding other people's safety. There's always that balance, I think, between supporting the child, the vulnerable child who may be acting out, and keeping everybody else safe.

Building support among the staff, creating common ground to move forward, respect and listening are key elements of relationship building.

The sharing of information on training by a peer presentation was suggested by Jane's principal as a way of giving feedback to the staff group from a short course she did:

A few of us went on that training [about managing emotional behaviours and attunement to the child] and I know when the next one is free [a training hour], that there's nothing on the agenda comes up, I know she'll [the principal] ask us to deliver basically what was delivered to us. Yeah, very short synopsis . . . But I'd say she'll ask us then to deliver.

> **Reflective questions**
>
> - What is the culture around change in your workplace? Is it negative or interested?
> - Do you feel able to offer new ideas? Is dialogue part of the system?
> - Is there a way to share experiences and discuss a range of different approaches, where staff may have very different or opposing views?

Section 3: The wider community action and awareness

How does this fit with my classroom work?

Getting to know what works for me – in direct involvement with the class group, wider engagement with the school system, links with education policy, local initiatives.

In my work with adult groups and young people, I was very focused on opening doors to all kinds of opportunities for the people I worked with of all ages. I did this by a variety of approaches:

Meeting the needs expressed by the students

- Developing specific workshops in response to needs expressed by learners of all ages. This included everything from interview preparation to sex education to assertiveness. If this is not your area, can you swap with another teacher, or is there a departmental service or voluntary organisation that does this work?

Widening horizons – new experiences

- Visiting any free cultural sites in the city – museums, art galleries, exhibitions.
- Finding speakers to come and share life stories around resilience and accessing opportunities for training and employment.

- Using media stories to expand views and experiences around life choices and consequences.
- Organisations working for social justice and educational equity frequently have toolkits and sometimes workshops they will deliver on the wider aspects of inequality in education.

Making contacts/building relationships

- Building relationships with local police to introduce the police in another light. Some 'community garda' (police officers) were very tuned in to the young people. We had some funny moments. For example, coming back from a day out in the Garda (police) van, two lads were lying on the floor while others were playing the siren – a massive treat. The two lads on the floor said, 'If our nana looks out and sees us in here, she'll have a heart attack.'
- Developing relationships with tradespeople and workshops that take apprentices.
- Working with local sports clubs to help to engage pupils in the clubs. Some clubs have resources for community and local outreach, and will supply coaching for your pupils.
- Arts groups including drama and dance can have workshops available for little or no cost.

Expanding and developing services in the school

- Setting up school breakfast and lunch clubs to supply healthy food.
- Setting up homework clubs with food for after school.
- Running a *parent/guardian and child club** in school hours which had an hour with parents to discuss their concerns and then an hour to do simple craft and art with their child.
- Setting up a *family therapy service** on site in the school in the evenings.

I would recommend any of these activities as being immediately beneficial to the pupils and families. Many of them have a mainstream application and benefit to all, such as links to sports clubs and breakfast clubs.

On occasion, I had presentations or brief involvement from local councillors or TDs (members of parliament), but the majority of my outreach was focused on immediate needs. I haven't experience of a wider involvement in advocating for changes in the curriculum or school discipline systems at a higher level.

Some avenues to work for change at a systemic level include involvement in curriculum development. There are ongoing working parties on various aspects of the curriculum and behaviour management approaches linked to the Department of Education. In most schools, there are in-house committees that work with school policy on topics like bullying. These committees are frequently linked to national initiatives.

Advocating for training in TIP, restorative justice or topics of interest to the staff for CPD is a way of broadening the awareness of the staff. Forming links with local or national organisations working for change, availing of their materials, training or initiatives for the pupils is another resource.

Whatever your approach, the centre of the work is relationships – between you and your students and among them. Kindness and patience are the glue that holds it together.

Key points of Chapter 10

- Your own awareness of your own stress points and reactions is very important. Your triggers can be unconscious and cause difficult relationships with students.
- Having short-term and long-term ways to maintain your emotional and physical well-being is vital. As you practise them, they will become habitual.
- You will be modelling behaviours for your students, so they need to be part of your daily life and actions.
- Change is gradual and best accomplished slowly by agreement. Aim to avoid isolation and conflict with staff who disagree with you. Stay engaged with social and group events.
- Everyone has their own level of engagement and way of working. You will find your own path.

References

1. Substance Abuse and Mental Health Services Administration. SAMHSA's Concept of Trauma and Guidance for a Trauma-Informed Approach. Rockville, MD: Substance Abuse and Mental Health Services Administration; 2014.
2. Liu Q, Merrin G, Razza RA. Reciprocal Associations between Maternal Behaviors and Children'sSelf-Regulation during the Transition from Early to Middle Childhood. Journal of Child and Family Studies. 2024;33:1602–17.
3. Diamond A. Executive Functions. Annual Review of Psychology. 2013;64.
4. Maté G. The Power of Saying NO, 2022. www.youtube.com/watch?v=x6l-eJNvqAY
5. Maté G. When the body says NO. New Jersey: Wiley; 2003.
6. Siegel DJ. The mindful therapist: The clinician's guide to mindsight and neural integration. London: Norton; 2010.
7. Siegel DJ, Payne-Bryson, T. The Whole-Brain Child: New York: Delacorte Press; 2011.
8. Loomis A, Coffey R, Mitchell J, Musson Rose D. Reflective supervision as a vehicle for trauma-informedorganizational change in early childhood education settings. Reflective Practice. 2024;25(3):267–85.
9. SNA Workforce Development Unit, Department of Education. Report on National Survey of Special Needs Assistants. Dublin: Department of Education; 2024.
10. Shevrin Venet A. Equity-Centred Trauma-Informed Education. New York: Routledge; 2024.

11
Activities

This chapter details the materials, activities and approaches.

- There are some suggestions on useful materials and sourcing them. Instructions and templates are included.
- There are 12 different sections including movement exercises, art activities and others, some of which intersect.
- The self-care supports for the educator are included.
- Each activity will be marked with P, S or A or a combination of these. P = suitable for primary school level (5–12 years); S = suitable for secondary/second level (13–18 years); A = suitable for adults (18+ years).

The asterisk * shows the item is included in the main text of the book.

Section 1: Useful materials for development activities, arts and crafts

- Ask friends who buy newspapers or magazines to save them for you. Ask anyone who works in an office for discarded card, paper or coloured brochures. Pupils of all ages can bring in card, paper, teabag boxes, for junk art, which is a big favourite. **NO food containers!** (Or you will be presented with half-washed yoghurt pots . . .)
- Contact travel agents for brochures including nature and animal pictures. Local animal shelters and zoos will have brochures and pictures. Writing to ask for them is a team task.
- Any organisations local to you that support Global South development, youth services or social justice will have materials for teaching. Many sites

offer a wide range of excellent, easy-to-use materials for schools and colleges. There are presentations, projects, videos photos and quizzes.

There are many sites for teachers which have projects, templates and suggestions for all kinds of learning materials games and crafts.

Selection of individual names for group tasks

This is a vital part of building relationships and group integration in your class. It is important that it is seen to be genuinely random and that students don't rearrange the groups. If you just call names aloud, they can quickly mix it around – defeating your purpose of mixing in small groups. Inviting students to select teams creates a power dynamic that works against weaker or vulnerable students.

A set of laminated names is needed and then a way to show the teams drawn. Putting Velcro strips on a board and the other half of the Velcro on the names is the best way – you can put them up as you draw them from the pile and no one can argue.

Otherwise, a box like a chocolate box with divisions will do – you place the names in groups as you draw them. Later a student can be invited to do this – with your help.

Supplies for the class

- For each group of four students:
    - 1 set of markers
    - 1 ruler
    - Pencils
    - Erasers
    - Paper glue
    - Paper (a ream from the office!)
    - Colouring pencils and crayons, especially for younger children, will last longer.
- Have a pencil case/box to hold the materials set for each group. Ask one person in each group to set out the materials and return them to the box or case complete after each activity.

Activities

- Value supermarkets and pound shops are good sources of art materials.
- Great work has been done using flour-and-water paste and old paintbrushes to make collages from old magazines newspapers and brochures.
- A laminator – this is the most important thing! It will save any materials you create for reuse and preserve work done by the students. Your school may have one you can use.

I know it seems hard to have to buy materials out of your own money, so try to secure a small budget in advance from the institution or local support service. Either way, I always found it well worth the investment.

Section 2: Welcoming environment

- **PSA** Your welcoming greeting and smile for students of all ages.
- **PSA** Plants – you can use photos and posters of plants if live plants are not available. One of the group may be a gardener and be happy to take on the watering of plants.
- **PSA** Age-appropriate pictures or symbols that say 'welcome' – rainbows, sun, smiley face.
- **PSA** Involve students in how the furniture is arranged.
- **P *Cosy corner:** soft cushions, some fidget toys, soft toys, art materials, a weighted blanket, soft warm covers, some books or cartoons. If you have some self-regulation reminders, they could be on a poster – such as the ***feelometer** (see Section 3: Art activities). You can collect other items from staff and friends as requested.
- **SA** Time-out space: According to the boundaries and rules of the school, you can have a cosy corner in another space, in a space allocated by the school, or a cosy chair or library corner at the back of the class. This is to allow rebalancing and avoid blowouts in the classroom for the overwhelmed pupil.

Section 3: Art activities

- **PSA** Make a ***name plate:** Each student decorates their name on a sheet of paper; teacher collects and laminates them and gives them out each week.

247

Copyright material from Norah Sweetman (2026), *Trauma-Informed Practice in Education*, Routledge.

- **PSA** Make a ***wall frieze** of a word that means something to the group. Each person does a letter, and then it is laminated and put on the wall. This is a good 'get to know you' exercise and relaxing as well.
- **PS *Feelometer:** Use a big rectangular sheet with sections from cool blue at the bottom of the sheet, moving through orange and heating up to red and boiling over in a thermometer shape. Feelings about certain incidents can be done first as an individual drawing, using the feelometer as a reference point. As the group gets to know each other, they may be happy to share their thoughts and add to the main 'feelometer'. If it's a group exercise, you go first and model appropriate sharing. Each person draws or writes something that keeps them cool, something that bothers them and finally something that makes them angry or upset. They stick their small drawings on the sheet. Explain that you only speak for yourself, not blaming others and no name-calling.
- **PSA *Tree of helping hands:** Each person draws the outline of their hand and writes or draws skills and supports they will bring to the group, one on each finger. Then all the decorated hands are cut out and stuck on to the tree trunk (already drawn on the big sheet) to form the leaves and branches.
- **PSA *Cartoons:** Fold an A4 page in two or four depending on the age of the student. Then ask them to draw a short story. Younger pupils will tend to go for two pictures: 'I fell off my bike, I hurt my knee.' Older teenagers can draw four or eight pictures (two pages) on their own theme or a suggested theme. Do one yourself with stick people, to show it is easy and fun, and remember to write the words first, then put the box around them!
- **PSA *Making a magazine:** Small groups each make a page – it can be football, food, jokes, interviews, stories, poems, true adventures, surveys of group preferences, or their own choice.
- **PSA *Drawing to music:** Play some relaxing music without lyrics, handout paper and colours, and ask each person to doodle, draw or make patterns in response to the music.
- **PSA *Visual charts:** Layout of the work or day's activities. Time and sequence on the poster. *Individual ones** for pupils who need more detailed timetables and more support with any change or transition are helpful. For example, a pupil who has difficulty focusing on packing their

bag after sports could have a sequenced visual list in their bag reminding them of the order of dressing and packing.

Section 4: Communications

(i) Introductory

'Good for one, good for all', in the context of this book, means that activities and attitudes that promote feelings of safety and acceptance will benefit all the pupils and be essential for those who are affected by trauma.

- **P *Circle time** and news sharing. Keep this very simple and structured till the pupils are accustomed to it and understand the boundaries of sharing. You can ask a simple circle question like 'What programme did you watch on TV last night?' or 'What is your favourite food/colour/animal?' Teacher starts: 'My favourite animal is . . . because . . .' and it goes around the circle – real or dream pets can be included.
- **PS *Can't say no or yes:** In response to questions of a partner, pupils can't use yes or no in their answer.
- **PS *Swapping games** such as ***What's changed?'** One person leaves the room or wears a blindfold while something or things are changed in the room. Person comes in and must notice the change. Start with easy, obvious things.
- **PS *Hunting an object in the room** using 'hot' and 'cold' for how near they are to the object.
- **PS *Story bags** have a well-known book for younger pupils and a wider range for older. The bag holder tells the story, turning the pages of the book for younger pupils and using a few props that they pull out of the bag. Animals, dolls, toys, food, clothes – whatever goes with the story. You could ask the teacher of an older class to make the bags as a project with their students.
- **PS *Dressing up and acting out:** These can be well-known tales or ones they make up. Essential for the dressing-up box are glasses, umbrella, handbags, cardigans, baggy dresses that fit over clothes, hats, jackets,

shirt, tie and sleeveless jumper (for being the teacher). A request to friends and family should fill the box fast! (Some teenagers love this and some like to act out scenarios but not dress up.)

- **PSA *Introductions** such as ***Paper ball throw:** Each person writes or draws something they like doing and something they want from the class. All the papers are scrunched up and thrown in the centre. Everyone takes one and shares what is on it without knowing whose it is.
- **PS *Matching emojis:** These can be found online or on sticker sheets. Cut out and laminate two sets; mark the back of one set before cutting out. You can use these to play matching games. This leads to naming emotions and role play of emoji by one player to be guessed by others.

(ii) Sharing ideas and listening

- **PSA** Story telling – ***A day in the life of a euro coin/a puppy/a teddy/a truck** – can be done as a circle, with each person continuing around, or as an individual or small group game.

SA *The Question game: This is for all ages that can read – if some can't read, they can partner with another who can. In this case, the game will be played in pairs so as not to pinpoint the non-readers.

The cards are divided into three levels:

1. 'bus stop conversations'/trivia
2. more personal but not intrusive
3. issues of the day, 'what if' questions, ethics, beliefs.

You will need to do the 'brave space' work before level 3. Start with level 1 and one card for each player to introduce the game.

To play the game, you need a group of six or seven minimum and ten maximum. If the group is bigger, split in two groups. The questions are laminated paper cards. The cards are dealt one, two or three per player.

The player to the right of the dealer starts by reading their question and answering it themselves – no one else joins in. Always it is the cardholder only who speaks. Go around the circle till all the cards are read and answered. The cards below are examples of each level. You can suit them to the group,

Activities

and as they become accustomed to the game, you can invite them to add questions. Always check the questions first before adding their suggestions – I have had some whoppers in my time!

Mark the back with a colour for level 1, 2 or 3, laminate your set of cards and add in more questions.

Level 1: Easy, general, non-embarrassing, not personal or related to any culture

What is your favourite colour?	Which TV show makes you laugh?	Do you like animals?	What is your favourite dinner?
What music do you like?	Do you have a pet? If not, would you like one?	City or countryside – which would you like to live in?	What snack is your favourite?
What TV programme makes you laugh?	What do you think of video games?	What is something you learned this year that you didn't know before?	What movie scared you the most?
What team do you follow?	Do you like sport on TV?	Do you like Art in school?	If you could have a superpower, what would it be?

Level 2: Some opinions, but still general, not controversial

Should pupils wear school uniforms?	Is AI – artificial intelligence – useful or dangerous? Why?	Would you use a driverless car?	What makes you laugh? Is any subject OK for comedy?
What's your best way to relax?	What makes a great friend?	Who do you admire and why?	What is better – health or wealth?
What makes you laugh?	What do you think of electric scooters?	What is your favourite day of the week and why?	Did you ever get a nice surprise? What was it?
What's your best way to have a laugh?	What makes a great teacher?	Who do you think is famous and why?	Do you play a sport?

Level 3: Opinions that may be controversial and lead to discussion

Would you give up TV and computer for one year for €200,000?	What century would you like to have been born in and why?	What is the most important thing in life?	If you were in government, what one thing would you do?
What would you do if you won €10 million on the lotto?	If you could be anyone else, who would you be and why?	Would you give up family, friends and country to live away for ever for €3 million?	If you could save a friend's life by giving up TV and all computers and games for one year, would you?
If you knew a friend was robbing their granny, what would you do?	Would you like to travel? Where and why?	If you could have any job, what would you do?	Do you think dogs should be muzzled?
What makes a happy family?	What is the most important thing about being a good parent?	Why do we have wars? Are they necessary?	Should people have to work for their dole/benefits from the state?

Always start with level 1 and stay there until the group has established relationships and respectful communication. Only the person answering the question is allowed to speak. Others are not allowed to express an opinion. As the group bonds, you can move towards levels 2 and 3, and sometimes include a card 'Ask Group'. This allows the cardholder to go around the group and get opinions. The same rule of no comment applies to each contribution.

You remain the facilitator/moderator of the activity. If it becomes awkward or overly personal, you can note that and close it down with a commitment to explore the difficulty arising.

PSA *Quiz

Some important points:

- Aim for something that will give around 90 per cent success the first time. Remember that many of the students of all ages may have very different levels of general knowledge. So have a mix of general questions and some specific to the district.
- Work in groups of two or three. Move fast so that no one feels exposed or foolish. Swap with the nearest group, and they correct each other's quiz! (In a colour agreed to avoid confusion or marks changed!) You check and read out the results. If some have hardly any correct, just read top three and hand them back.

Activities

- Keep your quiz questions so you can see which ones were popular. You can start to increase the challenge and include relevant classwork and current topics. Write out the answers you will accept before you begin, so there is no confusion.
- After the first time, when the students are accustomed to the quiz, you can pull the names randomly for the teams to keep it equal.

Primary level

Eight starter questions – two sets of four:

- Set one – general questions:
  - What is a baby cow called?
  - Name four types of ice cream.
  - What is the capital of England?
  - What is a baby horse called?
- Set two – local questions:
  - What's the name of the local park (swimming pool/shopping centre)?
  - When are we getting our next holidays? (What days do we have school?)
  - What is the longest holiday from school?
  - What's the name of the school principal (the school/the road the school is on)?

Secondary level

- Set one – general questions:
  - What is a baby deer called (Baby rabbit? Baby goose? Baby swan?)?
  - Name six vegetables (or other question related to studies).
  - What is the capital city of France (Spain, Italy, Poland, Sweden)?
  - Name four types of energy on the power grid we all use.
- Set two – local questions:
  - What is Dublin's main street called? (or local city)
  - What river is the city built on? (Or another local feature)
  - Who won the FA Cup this year? (or other major event)
  - Name six types of transport (bonus point for any extras – e.g. camel, donkey, skateboard).

Adult

- Set one – general questions:
  - Where does spaghetti grow?
  - What seas are around Ireland (or other country)?
  - What are the two official languages of Ireland?
  - What is the capital city of Norway (other countries)?
- Set two – local questions:
  - What is a mammal?
  - Who wrote the novel *Ulysses* (or the play *Romeo and Juliet*)?
  - When is the longest day of the year?
  - Name four types of cheese (e.g. fruit, pasta, flour).

(iii) Expressing ideas and experiences

SA *Assertiveness programme: The visual and interactive *assertiveness programme 'Happy head, Aggro head and Sad head'** is effective with all ages. This programme was designed in response to low literacy levels where I knew assertiveness skills would be really useful for the group. In some cases, the regular programmes for learning assertiveness were too paper-based, or others moved too fast to direct personal scenarios. This cartoon approach has proved effective every time with many different types of groups. The indirect approach of the 'heads' allows expression of feelings and thoughts in a safe way. The participants usually get it quickly and add their own suggestions. I didn't include the fourth category of 'passive-aggressive' but I have found that participants naturally include passive-aggressive behaviour in their questions and scenarios.

The initial discussion is around the different moods and reactions we all have and the notion of the seesaw that we can get stuck on – being full of temper and frustration (Aggro head) or feeling helpless and hurt (Sad head). We want to learn some ways of staying balanced (Happy head), able to cope with things and get on with other people, by becoming more assertive.

This programme starts with each person taking three templates – each has a big head, with a heart shape, a thinking bubble and a speech bubble. An A4 sheet for each head gives space to draw and write.

Activities

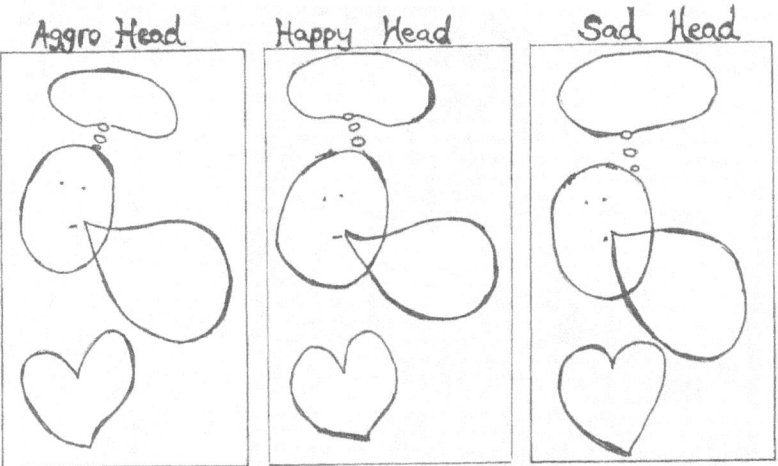

Figure 11.1 Heads

The three heads are called Aggro head (aggressive), Happy head (assertive) and Sad head (passive). Below is a blank example of the three heads – what the head *thinks*, *feels* and *says*, how it looks will be created by the participant.

Each participant writes what they think each of the three heads are *saying* in the speech bubble, *thinking* in the thought bubble and *feeling* in the heart shape. Each person decorates their head as much as they want.

Then, in small groups, people can discuss questions like: Why do you think Sad head is always down? Does Aggro head have any real friends or are people just scared of them? Why is Happy head happier?

You can use cards like the samples of behaviour types below to ask students to identify which behaviour is which, and also to ask them what would happen if different combinations meet up – like Sad head and Aggro head or two Happy heads. Everyday scenarios can be suggested by the educator or participants. This programme can develop into people practising the skills of assertiveness on real dilemmas or fictional situations. You can get the participants to make cards of different situations.

Note: Use of names in the group or those known to us is not allowed – these are all hypothetical situations. If people want to use the 'I know someone' approach, that's fine, but no names as this can stir real existing conflicts.

Here is an example from one of my groups.

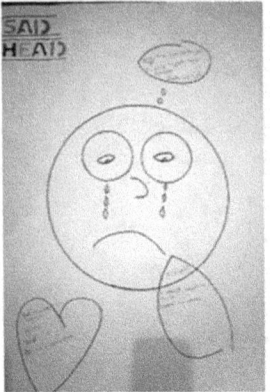

Figure 11.2 Sad head, Happy head and Aggro head

Sample cards of behaviour types:

Aggressive I know what I'm doing. Get out of my way.	**Aggressive** Shut up now . . . or else you will be ***** sorry.	**Aggressive** You're always like that – you're thick.
Assertive I want to be called Jim, I don't like being called the ******.	Assertive Actually, you didn't pay me back, you still owe me €20 and I need it today.	Assertive Let's sit down and talk it over. I want to explain how I feel.
Passive It's always me. I never get to pick . . . It's not fair.	**Passive** Nothing works out, no point, it's always ****.	**Passive** She is always making me depressed.

The skills of assertiveness in the simplest form

- Keep to the issue at hand. Ignore distractions brought in by the other person who says, 'But last year I did xx for you'. Stick to your point.
- Speak for yourself – 'I feel upset', not 'You upset me'. Take responsibility for your own feelings.
- Repeat your point, don't digress. Don't make excuses for why you are not coming, don't want to join something, lend something or do something!
- Look for an agreement that works for both parties.
- Ask for what you want. Understand you may or may not get it.

Activities

Further use for awkward adult conflicts you are drawn into unwillingly – the bonio

- The use of the *'**bonio**'. Some adult groups that have a lot of family or community connections find that they are being drawn into other people's petty arguments and asked to take sides in neighbours' squabbles. We talk about these as 'bonios' – chewed dog biscuits left on the ground. The question asked was 'Would you like to dive on the bonio and chew it?' Lots of laughter and the following weeks many participants said things like 'When they asked me what I thought or would do in that situation, I just visualised that bonio and let it go!'
- **PSA *Walking debate:** This needs some space, although it also works if you can clear a central pathway in the class. You select topics about recent events or sections of work – 'Do you think we should have to wear school uniforms?' 'Was the English test fair compared to what we studied in class?' – and ask the pupils to move to one end of the line for 'Yes' and the other end for 'No'. Then you can ask for their reasons for this view. You can progress to all sorts of topics and also use it for language conversation.

PSA *Celebrations: This is included in the communications section as these events celebrate the work done and confidence gained by all the pupils and share it with families and the school community.

Celebrations preparation

The most important feature is that everybody has a definite job. This can be done with up to 25 in the class.

Sample jobs

- Designing the invitations and sharing the template with all the group to decorate. The team keep a record of who has finished their invitation and brought it home and delivered it. *Team of four pupils.*
- Decorate the signing in book (a decorated copy for the day of the celebration). *Two pupils.*

- Two volunteers at each table display of the work, who are happy to talk about it and explain the significance. *Approximately 10–12 pupils.* If there are too many volunteers, have a draw or swap midway. They can do some interviews and write up some quotes if they'd like to.
- Room decorators to make paper decorations, hang them and put them away carefully afterwards. Making notices for the door and hall. *Approximately 4–6 pupils.*
- Materials managers who are issued with precious cellotape, blutack and coloured markers, and are responsible for return of these. *Four pupils.*

The absolutely most important thing is that everyone has a job that is real. You will be so grateful for the materials managers when the main piece of artwork sails to the floor for lack of blutack! Families of the children who never get to do anything will be delighted to see their child holding the door or speaking at a table of work. These celebrations are a form of review and can include posters of the class reviews of sections of the work. As it is a public event, keep all pupils' comments anonymous, although you type them exactly as they are. If pupils want to point out their hand on the ***helping hands poster**, that's fine – it is up to them. Keep it simple; it is the process of doing it themselves that is so important to the pupils and their families.

Practise with the pupils beforehand greeting people and explaining the work and the reason for the celebration. Also practise swapping out the favourite stall quickly and harmoniously!

The icing on the cake, literally, is if you can get some small refreshments and let the pupils serve them. Sometimes local shops will donate some small items. No hot drinks, just some squash and a few biscuits. This will be a popular stall and will probably need rotations.

Have everybody on stage or at front of the hall for a final bow. If you can, present certificates to all and have another staff member come to present them.

Section 5: Concentration

- **PSA *Listening to the gong**, bowl or bell: Everyone raises their hand. The teacher rings the gong or bell, and everyone listens as long as they can. When you can't hear it any more, you lower your hand. Time it and see

Activities

whether this changes. A Tibetan bowl with a gong stick makes a beautiful sound, but an ordinary bell that you shake works too.
- **PS *Tray away:** Put out a tray of everyday objects for a couple of minutes, then cover it and ask the pupils to list or draw the things on it. Do it first in groups of three or four, then individually.
- **PS *I spy** (by three types: colours, object, shapes):
  - I spy . . . something yellow.
  - I spy . . . something beginning with R (can be used for learning languages also).
  - I spy . . . a circle.
- **PS *Who has the ball?** A small ball or hacky sack is passed fast around the group who are seated in a circle. One person has their back turned and counts aloud to three and turns round. Whoever has the ball covers it and others fold their hands to pretend they have it. The outside person tries to guess who has it; if correct, they get one more turn of guessing – maximum of two rounds for the guesser. If the guesser is wrong, the holder of the ball is on next.
- **PSA *Count to 20** as a group. When the teacher sounds the gong, anyone can start by saying 'One'. Then someone else says 'Two'. If two speak together, begin again. The record is reaching 20 in three minutes 10 seconds!

 ## Section 6: Emotional integration approaches

These approaches take time to develop and depend on tuning in to distress or rage in the child and then working with them to regain balance (1).

It is essential to attune yourself to the child's emotional (right) brain and help them to regain balance before attempting logical left-brain approaches. If the reaction is trauma-based, it is vital to encourage them to be part of the plan to resolve the situation in a better way. This means boundaries of discipline and consequences are maintained but with some input from the child/person involved. '[W]hen a child is upset, logic often won't work until we have responded to the right brain's emotional needs' (1 p.33).

When the child has calmed down and feels heard and connected, the left brain can be involved in working out what happened and helping the child organise their feelings, integrating both sides of the brain's experience. Movement and exercises that swing the arms across the body help integration.

Modelling self-regulation by the educator

In the everyday situations, the educator can model and share the steps of becoming upset or angry, expressing it safely and returning to calm.

- I'm very upset that someone spilt paint on my desk and just left it to dry. My notebook is all spoilt.
- I feel annoyed and I feel let down. I am going to go to cosy corner and put a red ball of crossness on the feelometer.
- Now I'll take a couple of breaths – count two in and four out.
- I feel better – it was probably an accident. I will wipe the desk and put my notebook by the window to dry.
- Now, what are we doing next?

PSA *Bouquet of compliments

Primary-age children may need more help but even 5–6-year-olds love this.

The aim is to give a series of positive, truthful statements from each person in the group, to each individual in turn. Compliments on physical appearance are not relevant, and groups are reminded that it is possible to notice something small and positive about a fellow student without being friends.

The teacher starts by turning to the student on their right, 'John', and offering *one* positive compliment. Keep it small and simple. Examples:

- 'John, I like the way you help clear up breakfast'
- 'You have very neat writing'
- 'Your art is cool'
- 'You help other people with their work.'
- 'You are very fair-minded'
- 'I like your jokes'

The person to the right of 'John' continues, and it goes around the whole group with each person offering 'John' a compliment

Then 'John' turns to the person on his right, 'Mary', and begins the round of compliments for 'Mary'; it moves around the full circle again.

Ten is about the maximum number for this, so in a large group, split into two circles and have an assistant (who has done it before) lead the second group.

Activities

Some people find this awkward, so keep it moving and let repetitions pass (as long as it is not a chain of repetition). The same for personal comments about appearance or dress.

 ## Section 7: Movement

- **P *Walk on a line:** Paint or tape a circle or square line around the classroom. Pupils walk till the music stops and then either line up or go to their seats. A good transition exercise.
- **P *Marching on the spot:** Start marching in place, swinging the arms, then start to swing arms across the body to touch opposite knees.
- **PS Simon says:** One leader says, 'Simon says lift your hands' – you all do it. If the instruction is simply 'Lift your hands', you don't do it. Can be done sitting or walking on the line.
- **P *Musical chairs:** Play an inclusive version where you leave the chairs in place and the child without a chair gets to stop the music and dive on a chair next round.
- **P *Musical statues:** Play an inclusive version, varying the criteria: last to stop moving, first to stop moving, funniest statue, laughing the most. That person gets to stop the music next time.
- **PS *Build-up chasing:** Two people are on, and everyone they catch joins them in a line till everyone is caught.
- **PSA *Cornflakes for breakfast:** The group is in a circle with bases to stand on. Can be small mats, carpet tiles, chalk circles or marked with tape. The caller in the middle has no base. They call out something like 'Everyone who walked to school/had cornflakes this morning/likes chips/watches TV – change places.' Everyone who fits has to move more than one space. The caller jumps to a base and the next person is the caller in the centre. **Note:** Some groups can use this to bully or make inappropriate personal comments. Just talk over them with an ordinary suggestion, and if it continues, end the game. Anyone who pushes another is out for two rounds for the first offence, off completely for the second offence.
- **PSA *Colour boxes:** Use the lines and boxes in the hall or mark them yourself with tape or chalk. Allocate each one a colour, and then you call 'orange' and they all have to run and fit in the orange square. Depending on age, genders and comfort levels, the boxes can be big or small.

Energy exercises

- ***Wayne Cook posture** for concentration (2) calms and orders the mind. If participants are wearing skirts, you can do it standing up by crossing over feet and hands and taking four deep breaths each side, finishing off with steepling the hands between your eyes and then drawing your fingers from the centre hairline to around your head all the way back to your neck.
- **Zip-up** for keeping focused and maintaining balance. Draw your two hands close together up the front of your body to your chin three times – imagine you are zipping up and keeping yourself safe from upset. On the last zip-up, turn your hands and imagine locking the energy in. All these can be found on inner source, the website of Donna Eden: https://innersource.net

Section 8: Reflection

- **PSA *Plan–do–review** can be applied to tasks and issues in the classroom for all ages.
- PSA *Reflect in, on and with:
  - Reflect *in the moment* (also part of ***modelling self-regulation**). Pause a lesson or activity to check in with yourself and the group.
  - Reflect *on the session later*.
  - Reflect *on the session with the group*.
- **PSA *Group poster review** of work, group issues or process:
  - Primary pupils use visuals of questions with answers in emoji or *Yes, No, Maybe* card form.
  - Secondary or adult participants use posters with relevant questions – can be issue- or task-based.

  In groups of four, students go around each poster and add their views to the flipchart page poster. The small groups move around, a few minutes at each poster until everyone has been to each poster. (One poster per four students in your group).

  Sample questions – one per poster:
  - What do we need to do this task?
  - What is working well?

Activities

- ○ Were the changes an improvement?
- ○ Do we want to keep the new way or go back to the first method?
- **PSA *Buddy system** for support and ongoing review of the work. All ages of students can work in pairs/fours to encourage and support each other. Start with short task-focused activities that enable teamwork. The initial challenges can be fun quiz/memory-type tasks. This doesn't work for all students, so try it out in a few short forms to see what is effective or not.
- **SA** Developing ethical thinking and reflecting on decisions. **Spider's web** is a fun way to do this with teenagers and adults. You draw a web on a big page for a group exercise or A4 for individual exercise. You pose a question – in this example, 'Who would you give €50 back to when you saw them drop it?' Any relevant question on the theme will produce conversations: 'How do you know the person in the big car is rich? Maybe they lost their job, and it is €50 for their food that they dropped.' Participants colour in the sections, one colour for giving back and another for not giving it back.

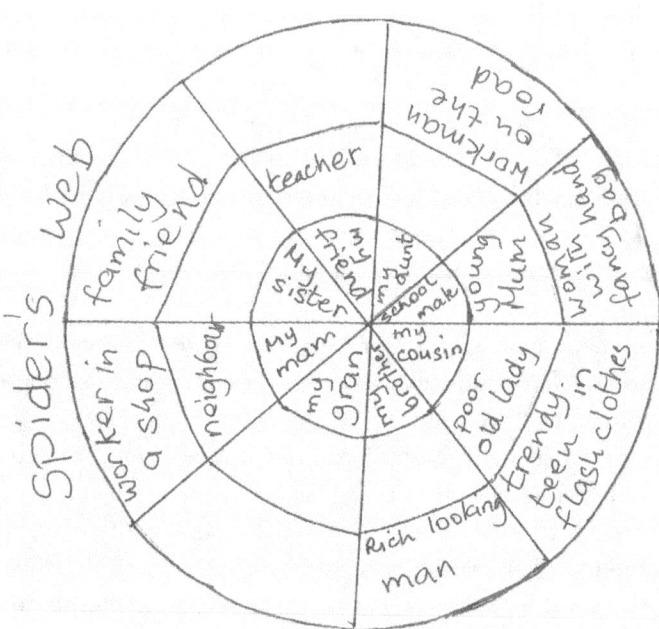

Figure 11.3 Spider's web diagram

Resilience

There are several principles that are important especially for traumatised children who have self-regulation difficulties. All the elements of resilience – seeing beyond the moment, good decision making and planning, building supportive relationships – require self-regulation in our relationships and tasks. See section on self-regulation in

Regaining emotional balance

- Share these understandings of the different sections of the brain with the pupils, which they can then discuss.
- Make a big poster of left brain and right brain and the river of integration. (1)
- Respond to the child's emotional (right-brain) feelings to attune yourself and help them to regain balance before attempting logical (left-brain) approaches to their upset.
- Use supports like the breathing exercises, cosy corner, colouring pages to help regain balance.
- Encourage them to be part of the plan to resolve the situation in a better way. This means boundaries of discipline and consequences are maintained but with input from the child/person involved.
- When the child feels heard and connected, the left brain (logical) can work out what happened and help the child organise their feeling, integrating both sides of the brain's experience.
- Review situations, both successful and not so much, making a coherent story:
  - 'So what happened then? You felt so angry? Then what happened? You thought about walking to the soft corner and marking it on the **feelometer**? Did that help? Was it a good choice?'
  - 'What would be different if you had pushed Jack over and grabbed your Lego? Was there an orange light, anything that you helped you?'

  You can use drawing, role play of assertiveness, the *feelometer or any other medium that helps understanding.
- **PSA** Aim for 100 per cent success in all activities until a sense of safety and enjoyment is established in the group/class, then gradually build up the challenge aspect.
- **PSA** Small group work is effective in building confidence to persist with tasks and challenges.

Section 9: Review

- **PSA** Simple *physical thumbs up or down after an activity.
- **PSA** *Rose or thorn review:** Students share one positive aspect of their day and one challenge – anyone can pass without comment if they choose.

PSA *Unfinished sentences

These review the event or process. Unfinished sentences are handed out individually to the group who answer in turn (always allow the option to pass in all activities). Laminate them and have a few different sets.

Younger pupils' version – simple and fun

- I liked it when we . . .
- I laughed when . . .
- I was surprised that . . .
- I was nervous when . . .
- I didn't know that . . .
- I found out that I can . . .
- It was funny when . . .
- I hope that we can do more . . .
- I learned that I . . .
- I loved the part when . . .
- I didn't understand why we . . .

An adult educator's review of a self-care programme

- I believe I have to . . .
- It's not possible to change it because . . .
- I always have to do it so . . .
- It's my responsibility to . . .
- I have learned how to care for myself by . . .
- I'd feel bad if I didn't do . . .
- It's down to me to do . . . Just the way it is.
- I get stressed because I . . .
- I want to respond like . . .

- I probably won't do these things because . . .
- I feel guilty so I continue to . . .
- I feel great when I . . .
- I want to change the way I . . .
- I could treat myself to . . .
- I want to commit to . . .

 ## Section 10: Self-care

(i) Self-care for your students

Some of the curriculum in schools is about well-being, so you can explore what works for your class and include it in your daily routine. A few minutes here and there is still worthwhile even if you have a busy timetable. There are many approaches using mindfulness, stretching and breathing that are effective, but every group is different. Be aware that meditative states can trigger flashbacks in trauma victims, so keep it short and simple, and keep your students grounded to your voice and instructions. Use the student feedback to inform your use of self-care for the group.

Remember that you are a barometer for your group. If you need to stop and stretch and take a breath, they probably do too.

(ii) Self-care for the educator

- **Awareness of your own feelings:** Learning where you feel it in your body when you are becoming stressed or overwhelmed. Have a phrase you say to yourself that calms you down. Silence the critical voice with something like 'I am doing my best and need to stop for a minute'.
- **Action to maintain balance:** Have a set of small actions that help you regain focus in the moment.
- **Activities for fun and joy in your life:** Commit to the things you love, ditch some of the things you don't! Noone cares if you never iron the duvet covers again or tidy the attic!
- ***Buddy system** to support and share – essential to stay in the flow of integration. Work with another person to maintain your commitment to yourself and process some of your work stress-related issues.

Activities

 # Section 11: Self-regulation

- **P *Soft space** in a corner of the room, with soft cushions, soft toys, fidgets, a weighted blanket, a curtain, toys to build with or shape.
- **PS *Modelling the steps of self-regulation** by the educator:
  - Identify a feeling/emotion or sensation (I'm feeling very let down. We can't go out today).
  - Mention its impact, location in body (I feel GRRRR . . . a bit like a cross cat/sad in my chest/wobbly in my tummy).
  - Share how you will release or express it (I think I am going to draw my cross cat and make some growling noises as I do it/breathe/move/take a break in the soft corner).
  - Reset – show how the storm has passed (Now that I feel relaxed again, let's think of a good game for the hall today). Group chooses something.
- **SA *Quiet chair:** A corner, a quiet corridor or a cubby hole can make a space for a quiet chair – obviously, this has to work with the school system. It could be located beside special needs assistant (SNA) room or similar.
- **SA *Free flow** offers a ten-minute exit pass for use by students to go out and calm themselves. Build up gradually to these privileges. Again, it has to work with the school system.
- **SA *Box breathing:** You imagine a box.
  - Start at the bottom left corner and go up to the top left corner – breathe in for a count of four.
  - Across the top to the top right corner – hold breath for four.
  - Down the right-hand side – breathe out for four.
  - Across the bottom of the box to the bottom left corner – hold empty breath for four.
  - Repeat.

  This demands concentration, so it is calming, but keep it short – maybe start with a count of two.
- **PSA *Breathing a longer outbreath** than inbreath is calming to the nervous system.
- **PSA *CHILL strategy** works best with older students. CHILL is an easy-to-use self-regulation method to reduce tension in a crisis and restore balance so the student can re-engage with the work and the class. C is for

267

Copyright material from Norah Sweetman (2026), *Trauma-Informed Practice in Education*, Routledge.

Calm down, H is for Hear yourself breathe, I is for Investigate your condition, L is for Let yourself know what you need, and the second L is for Let others know what you need. (See Section 1 in Chapter 4.)

Section 12: Supports that engage families and carers

*Parent/guardian and child club

This happens in school hours with an hour for parents/guardians to discuss their concerns informally in a group, followed by an hour where they can do simple craft and art with their child.

This programme is very effective and offers parents/carers a chance to chat with other adults about their issues and solutions they have found. The facilitator just guides the conversation and keeps it within agreed levels. Confidentiality is important and is always part of the framework, but I always discouraged intimate disclosures as people usually live in a closeknit community and may quickly regret over-sharing. The referrals I offered individually to local services, while 'clearing up' after group were often availed of.

You will need the help of support systems in the school to arrange the time off for the pupils, and some qualified supervision from a counsellor or family therapist to review your process with the group. In many educational institutions, there is a qualified career guidance counsellor or educational psychologist available. Use similar boundaries as with all participants and explain your reasons.

- Only speak for yourself.
- No naming of others.
- Confidentiality in the group.
- Speak and act with others with respect, even if you disagree.
- In the event of conflict (between the children), accept the decision of the facilitator.

Structure of the programme

- **Selecting families for the programme:** The purpose is to engage the child in school and encourage the parental involvement of hard-to-reach families.

It also offers the parent/guardian a special time to bond with their child and do something fun together.
- **Age range:** It works best if you keep to an age range of 3–4 years and include a maximum of six families. You can invite eight or nine to get six – if nine turn up, it is because they are all motivated.
- **Outreach:** You will need help from outreach staff (home–school liaison teacher, pastoral care team, family support worker, whoever can help) to make individual contact with the parents/guardians of the children and invite them.
- Make sure the children do the invitations themselves (as well as the one you send out) and bring them home. Tell the children two days and one day before to remind their carers about it. You need to remind teachers that certain children will be withdrawn for one hour.
- Two hours once a week for four weeks is long enough for the initial commitment as you are often working with a hard-to-reach group. If it is successful, you can run it again.
- Ask the receptionist to direct any attendees to you and put a few hand-drawn signs made by the children on the corridor and the door.
- It is very important to have some tasty snacks for the adults. One of my best attenders, who had never come to anything in the school before, said, 'I only come here for the sandwiches' For many who attended, it was the only time in the week they were handed teas and sandwiches.

First hour of group – the parents/guardians

- Your initial welcome is vital – relaxed, friendly, check how people like to be called, pour the tea and chat. Start within ten minutes of the agreed time; otherwise, the people who have come may feel that they are not enough and that you are waiting for more important people to arrive.
- Do some simple introductions in pairs (make a three if you have uneven numbers) where each person introduces their partner by name and one thing they hope for from the group. You start with the person beside you: 'Hi, this is Ann, and she hopes to meet some other mothers in this group.' Ann responds, 'Hi this is Norah, and she is hoping the group will be easy-going.'
- Explain that the group is a place to talk things over in a relaxed way, that other groups have found it very helpful to talk about stuff happening with their children.

Trauma-Informed Practice in Education

- Discuss the boundaries – confidentiality, discussions staying within the group and not going outside to the school or the community.
- Have some easy topics on the flipchart to start, such as homework, uniforms, pocket money – everyday issues that are not overly personal. Ask the group if they would like to add anything or remove anything from the list.
- Have some big sheets and markers for them to make illustrations of their ideas if they want.
- Keep the tea, coffee and snacks on the table so people can help themselves.

Ten minutes before the hour has passed, ask each parent/guardian to go and collect their child and bring them up to the group.

Second hour of group – parent/guardians with their child

- Have a snack for the children and let each parent briefly introduce their child by name and the child say one thing they like doing.
- Then each parent sits with their child at a small table, and they make a piece of art together. Set out the materials and have a prototype made to show how it was done. There may be some nervousness on day one, but as you go on, there will be plenty of ideas.
- Ten minutes before the end of the hour, gather up the materials and all tidy up together.
- Then ask each pair for a word to say what they thought of the work today. You could use the review words they gave you to make a wall frieze for the group next week and laminate it.
- Thank everyone for coming and say you really look forward to seeing them next week.

The artwork can be very simple – making name plates and colouring them, cutting and sticking a collage, drawing patterns using stencils, making paper chains at Christmas, cards for Easter, birthdays, etc. Clay is great if you can get some. When pieces of clay are dry, you can paint them with white/clear glue that acts like a varnish. There will be some in the school!

Include a short review each week so you keep informed as to what people like and ways they prefer to work with you. You can use unfinished sentences, posters, question game, suggestion boxes to review.

References

1. Siegel D, Bryson T. The Whole-Brain Child: 12 Revolutionary Strategies to Nurture Your Child's Developing Mind. New York: Delacorte Press; 2011.
2. Phillips C. The Daily Energy Routine Exercise 3: The Wayne Cook Posture. www.youtube.com/watch?v=LPT19Im8vnU2011.

Conclusion

I have been learning from my students, teachers in training and third-level tutors on a postgraduate programme while writing this book. The dedication and enthusiasm of educators and other professionals working in very difficult circumstances has inspired me at a time when the world looks rather dark.

The interviews with all those who work in the community have helped me understand what phrases like 'marginalised, underserved, traumatised' mean to people who live in this daily reality, and for those who work to alleviate distress and promote well-being and inclusion.

I have been encouraged by the increased focus in teacher training, and government policy, on understanding trauma and neglect, and how this affects development in all areas, including academic ability. At the same time, seeing the same problems that existed when I began teaching in 1988 is upsetting.

The aim of this book is to offer some background to the development and purpose of trauma-informed practice (TIP) in education, and to provide some approaches and activities that are easy to use and promote safety and integration in the classroom for all ages.

My expertise teaching in underserved communities, means that the activities suggested are designed with a social emotional learning (SEL) lens for mainstream groups. The extra awareness of the TIP approach makes these activities supportive and inclusive of those with high levels of trauma. Some ways to support students who become overwhelmed by emotion or have difficulty participating due to trauma are included.

I hope to encourage educators to take some steps towards a TIP approach in their class groups, and to expand their understanding of those already working in this way. Some educators have received extensive training and work in institutions where TIP is used across the board. Others are working in circumstances of relative isolation or where discipline is still based on exclusion and punishments. Many educators have said to me, 'Oh, yes, I always do that' or, 'That's an idea I could use; I never thought of it.'

My hope is that this book will be helpful in making small and large changes!

> ## Key points to remember
>
> - Start small and be guided by the response and feedback of your students.
> - Be consistent. Only promise what you can deliver.
> - Try things and review success and failure with your students.
> - Stay within the boundaries of your institution's structure.
> - Have a referral system for serious issues among students.
> - Take care of yourself – commit to it.
> - Have support for yourself – formal supervision or buddy system.
> - Enjoy the good days.

Many thanks to all the people who helped me and inspired me. I sometimes meet 'starfish' who benefited from work I did myself and in collaboration with others, and that makes it all worthwhile.

Index

accessible information 10
activities: art 247–9; communications 249–58; concentration 258–9; emotional integration 259–61; movement 261–2; parent/guardian and child club 268–70; reflection and resilience 262–4; review 265–6; selection of names for group tasks 246; self-care for students and educator 266; self-regulation 267–8; supplies for class 246–7; useful materials 245–6; welcoming environment 247
adolescence 61, 84; see also secondary school
adult education 66–8; actions to encourage respect and equity 178; empowering voice 153–5; reflection, resilience and relationships 134–5; relationship building 109–13; safe space 87–9
adverse childhood experiences (ACEs) 4; Covid-19 effects 19–20; effects on adolescence 84; effects on childhood and adult life 17; limitations of model 160, 166, 179; other impacts 17–18; research 16–17; and resilience 124–6; and underserved communities 18–19
Ainsworth MD 94
anger 46–7, 48
Anthony E 118, 119
anxiety 22, 66–7, 68, 87
apologies 187–8
Arao B 74
art activities 247–9; cartoons 248; draw to music 248; feelometer 248; make a magazine 248; name plates 247; tree of helping hands 248; visual charts 248–9; wall frieze 248
assertiveness programme: adult, use of 'bonio' 257; adult education 111, 178; happy head, aggro head and sad head 152–3, 254–6; secondary school 86, 108, 132, 133, 151
assessing support needs 166–7
assessment and exams, adult education 112
attachment 21, 22–3; secure 45, 93; see also child development and impacts of trauma
attitudes: beliefs and responses 127–9, 131–2, 134, 145–6; staff change in 237; see also modelling attitudes and behaviours
awareness: emotional and physical 234–5, 266; of injustice 172; wider community action and 241–3

Bailey S 95–6
Banks J 162
behaviours 24–5; see also classroom behaviours; modelling
body see entries beginning physical
boundaries 106, 183–4; apologies 187–8; information sharing and guiding frames 192–3; maintaining 37; physical, working with children with unsafe 190; physical touch 188–90; safeguarding 192; setting clear 97–8; staff training 190–1; task related information 185–7; to keep safe space 191–2; work and home 193–4; workload 193
Bourke N 23
Bowlby J 22
brain: development 23, 26; healing/plasticity 29, 55; and physical exercise 197; reptilian states 27, 44–5, 53, 107; right-left balance 259; see also neurological effects of trauma
'brave spaces' 74, 185

274

Index

breathing exercises 85, 104, 110, 267
Bronfenbrenner U 23
buddy system 224–6, 263, 266
Burke, N. 159
burnout 211–12

challenging behaviour (examples) 57–8, 59–60, 62
change at different levels 229–30; school 235–41; self 230–5; wider community action and awareness 241–3
child development and impacts of trauma 25–6, 53; abused, neglected child 26–7; interlinked 41–2; secure and abused child, compared 42–8
Children First Act 188
Children's Research Advisory Groups (CRAGs) 143
CHILL strategy 96, 267–8
choice principle 34, 49–50
Christian-Brandt AS 212
classroom behaviours 40–1; appearance of trauma effects 52–4; educator approach 55–6; emergence in age groups 56–68; example and perspective on parents 46–8; patterns 54–5; SAMHSA principles 68–70; TIP principles 48–51; trauma examples and effects 41; *see also* child development and impacts of trauma
Clemens K 74
clubs 127; expanding and developing school services 242; outings 75–6; parent/guardian and child 268–70
cognition: secure child 43; traumatised child 45–6
cognitive flexibility 233
collaboration: adult education 113; principle 34, 50; secondary school 86
Collaborative for Academic, Social, and Emotional Learning (CASEL) 32–4, 55–6, 94, 95, 106
collaborative research 148–9
communications: adult education 111; secondary school 86, 88; *see also* voice in classroom
communications activities (expressing ideas and experiences): adult assertiveness/use of 'bonio' 257; assertiveness programme/happy head, aggro head and sad head 254–6; celebrations 257–8; walking debate 257
communications activities (introductory): can't say no or yes 249; circle-time 249; dressing up and acting scenarios 249–50; hunting-hot or cold 249; matching emojis 250; paper ball throwing 250; story bags 249; swap game/what's changed 249
communications activities (sharing ideas and listening): question game with cards 250–4; story telling/a day in the life of 250
compassion fatigue 207, 210, 211
concentration activities 258–9; count to 20 as a group 259; I spy (colours, object, shapes) 259; listening to gong or bell 258–9; tray away 259; who has the ball 259
concentration and relationship building: adult education 110; primary school 103; secondary school 107
concentration and safe space, secondary school 85
concentration/focus difficulties (examples) 60–1, 65
confidentiality 32; buddy system 224; 'group confidentiality' 85; and mandatory reporting system 185, 192
conflict management: adult education 111; primary school 104–5; restorative justice approach 105, 109, 130, 168, 243; secondary school 109
conflicting responsibilities 5–6
cosy corner 77, 103, 108, 147, 247; boundaries around safeguarding 192
course workload management, adult education 112
Covid-19 effects 19–20, 206, 212
Crosby S 148, 150
cultural considerations: adult education 112; principle 35, 51–2; *see also* refugees/asylum seekers

delayed gratification 123–4
Delivering Equality of Opportunity in Schools (DEIS) initiative 169, 170, 171
developmental effects *see* child development and impacts of trauma
Diamond A 232
disability, medical model and social model of 161–2

275

Index

disciplines/professions 158–9; alternative views of trauma and recovery 158–63; TIP 164
discrimination and inclusion 171–2
domestic violence: example 165; research 2–4, 55
Durlak JA 33

early survival mode: secure child 43; traumatised child 44
Education Endowment Fund 34, 55–6
educator application of TIP 29–31; challenges in giving support 32; example 29–31
Eggleston K 63, 75, 170
Ellison J 73
emotional first aid 194–7; distressed pupil 198–9; or psychological first aid for groups 199–201; self-care 197–8
emotional integration approaches 259–61; bouquet of compliments 260–1; modelling by educator 260; right brain left brain balance 259
empowerment: adult education 153–5; principle 35, 50–1
environment: and approach 36–7, 69–70; welcoming 247; see also family/community; safe space
equity in school setting 164, 164–72; discrimination and inclusion 171–2; examples: unequal access 165–6; funding and resources 169–71; issues/challenges 167–8; methods of assessing support needs 166–7; social emotional learning (SEL) and TIP 168–9; strategies for educators 172–8
exceptionalism 123
executive function, elements of 232–3
exercise, physical see movement
'exercises of practical life' 82
experience and memory, integration of 122–3

FACES acronym 132, 215, 234
families: challenges in engaging with 32; see also entries beginning parent
family therapy service 242
family/community: effects 53–4; recovery and resilience 119–20
feedback see review and feedback, safe space

fight, flight, or freeze (FFF) mode 17, 53, 68, 81, 99
Figley C 210
Finley R 214
Fleming J, Ledogar RJ 118–19
Flynn P 108
focus see concentration
fostered young people and resilience 120
funding and resources 169–71

Gorard S 171
Gordon M 28
group poster review 262–3; adult education 88, 113, 134, 155; staff meetings 6
group work: boundaries 191; shared information 185–7
groups, psychological first aid for 199–201

Herman J 128
Houghton C 140, 143–4

inclusive education 161–2, 171–2
individual schedules/timetables 77
individual view of trauma and recovery 159–60
individuals, working with 174–5
information sharing: group work 185–7; and guiding frames 192–3
inhibitory function 232
Innovate Project, UK 164

leadership 106, 110
learning: foundations and attached relationships 21, 23; of past students 121–2; see also social emotional learning (SEL)
life and learning skills development 41–2
Loomis A 222
Lundy L 89, 140, 143

mandatory reporting system: confidentiality 185, 192; harm or threat of harm to a minor 188; negative aspects 189
'marshmallow test' 124
Maté G 47, 52, 213, 234
medical model and social model of disability 161–2

medical view of trauma 159
memory: and experience, integration of 122–3; short-term and working 232–3
Meredith C 212
Mindsight 122
Mischel W 124
modelling attitudes and behaviours: primary school 128, 130; secondary school 131
modelling behaviours and skills: adult education 110, 111; preschool and primary school 82; secondary school 106
movement: adult education 111; benefits for brain 197; physical factors in trauma 162, 163; and posture 197–8; preschool and primary school 82–3, 104; as stress relief 198
movement activities 261–2; build up chasing 261; colour boxes 261; cornflakes for breakfast 261; energy exercises: Wayne Cook and zip-up 262; march on the spot 261; musical chairs, musical statues 261; Simon says 261; walk on a line 261; Wayne Cook posture 262; zip-up 262

National Academies of Sciences, US 61
National Child Traumatic Stress Network and National Center for PTSD 200–1
National Education Association (NEA), US 207
National Education Psychology Service (NEPS), UK 28
neurological effects of trauma 52–3; adult education 67–8; primary school 60–1; secondary school 65
Nicholson J 29, 176
normal event, trauma as 27–8

Oberg G 206
Organisation for Economic Co-operation and Development (OECD) 164, 169
O'Toole C 160, 166

pain 162–3
parent engagement in research 144–5
parent issues 47–8
parent/guardian and child club 268–70

participation and safety, in secondary school 147–50
physical education, voice in 147
physical effects of trauma 52, 159, 162–3; adult education 66; primary school 57–8; secondary school 62
physical exercise *see* movement
physical touch and boundaries 188–90
Picardi A 93
plan-do-review 121, 133, 235, 262
poverty 161; example 166; *see also* equity in school setting; socioeconomic factors; underserved communities
power threat meaning (PTM) framework 163
preschool and primary school, safe space 81–4
pressure build-up on teachers, educators and support staff 208–10
primary school 57–61; actions to encourage respect and equity 177; enabling voice 145–7; and preschool, safe space 81–4; reflection, resilience and relationships 127–31; relationship building - aspects and activities 102–5
psychological analysis 163
psychological effects of trauma: adult education 66–7; primary school 58–9; secondary school 63
psychological first aid for groups 199–201
psychosocial effects of trauma 52; adult education 67; primary school 59–60; secondary school 63–4
PTSD: early trauma research 15–20; and secondary traumatic stress (STS) 210, 211, 212

question game: adult education 111, 155; primary school 146; secondary school 86, 108, 151; with cards 250–4

reasonable freedom from threat or harm 75–6
reflection, resilience and relationships: adult education 134–5; consultation and action 121–2; delayed gratification 123–4; exceptionalism 123; integration of memory and experience 122–3; personal story

Index

116–18; primary school 127–31; secondary school 131–3; self-care 214, 235; in trauma recovery 126; value of 126–7; *see also* reflection/reflective; relationship building; relationships; resilience

reflection activities 262–3; buddy system for mutual support and review 263; ethical thinking: spider's web 263; group poster review 262–3; plan-do-review 262; reflect in, on and with 262

reflective practice 120–1, 221

reflective supervision 222

refugees/asylum seekers 66, 68, 77, 80, 167; psychological first aid 199–200

relationship building: aspects and activities 102–13; difficulties 99–101; and trust 96–7; wider community 242

relationships: damage done by trauma 93–6; definition of 92; elements of 93; safe place and 32–4; skills and self-regulation 17–18; TIP training 235–6

resilience: in ACEs context 124–6; research 118–20; and support 23

resilience activities 264; 100% success in tasks 264; principles of 264; regain emotional balance 264; small group work 264

resistance and change 238–9

resources: and funding 169–71; sharing 237–8

respect and equity, actions to encourage 177–8

restorative justice approach 105, 109, 130, 168, 243

retraumatisation, preventing 76–7

review 68; *see also* group poster review; plan-do-review

review activities 265–6; rose or thorn 265; thumbs up or down 265; unfinished sentences 265–6

review and feedback, safe space: adult education 89; preschool and primary school 83–4; secondary school and education centre 87

Rose R 161

safe place and safe relationships 32–4

safe space 72–3; boundaries to keep 191–2; creating in classroom 81–9; definition of 73–4; knowing and needing 74–5; meanings for individuals 77–80; policies, practices, and safeguarding arrangements 77; preventing retraumatisation 76–7, 206–7; reasonable freedom from threat or harm 75–6

safeguarding: arrangements 77; boundaries 192

safety principle 34, 48–9

SAMHSA *see* Substance Abuse and Mental Health Services Administration, U.S.

saviour complex 187

schedules/timetables: individual 77; layout of work in stages 88–9

school setting, change in 235–41

Schore AN 23

secondary school 61–5; actions to encourage respect and equity 177–8; enabling voice 147–53; reflection, resilience and relationships 131–3; relationship building 105–9; safe space 84–7

secondary traumatic stress (STS) 210, 211, 212

secure and abused child development, compared 42–8

secure attachment 45, 93

self change 230–5

self-blame 128–9

self-care 197–8, 213–19; focusing on what makes you happy and relaxed 216–19; learning about your own needs, immediate and ongoing life choices 213–14; learning about your own stress responses 214–15

self-care for educators: actions that balance you in the moment 266; activities that bring joy 266; awareness of own feelings in body and thoughts 266; buddy system 266

self-care for students 266; awareness of trauma flashbacks with meditative state 266; ongoing student feedback on what works 266

self-regulation 17–18, 231–3; adult education 110–11; preschool and primary school 81–2, 103–4; secondary school 107–8; secure child 43; traumatised child 44–5

Index

self-regulation activities 267–8; box breathing 267; CHILL out 267–8; free flow pass for ten minutes to leave room 267; longer out breath than in breath 267; modelling steps by educator 267; soft space 267
Shapiro M 73
Shevrin Venet A 34, 104, 105–6, 128, 150, 166, 168, 175, 179, 187, 192–3, 239–40
Shonkoff JP 41–2
short-term and working memory 232–3
Siegel D 23, 122, 126, 132, 215, 234; Payne-Bryson T 130, 235; Sroufe A 45
Smyth E 171
social emotional learning (SEL): and ACEs research 237; CASEL 32–4, 55–6, 94, 95, 106; and TIP approaches 11–12, 29, 32–7, 55–6, 168–9
social emotional skills: secure child 43; traumatised child 45
social model and medical model of disability 161–2
Social Personal Health Education (SPHE) 33, 55
social workers 32, 120
socioeconomic factors 160–1
soft space 37, 239, 267
special needs assistants (SNAs) 238
Sroufe A, Siegel D 45
stability and flexibility 230–1
staff: change in attitude of 237; meetings 6; and school community 239–41; training and development 168, 179, 190–1, 243; understanding 178–9; working effectively with 180
Steele W 197, 204, 210–11; Malchiodi CA 55, 191–2
'strange situation' research 94
stress response: fight, flight, or freeze (FFF) mode 17, 53, 68, 81, 99; reptilian brain states 27, 44–5, 53, 107
stress in teachers 203; effects 204–10; types 210–13
students: change in 236–7; meeting needs of 241; need and educator well-being, balance between 8–9
Substance Abuse and Mental Health Services Administration (SAMHSA), U.S.: core competencies 95; principles 20, 34–5, 68–70, 95; safety 74, 82–3
superheroes 105
supervision: access for teachers and educators 224; and buddy system 224–6; importance of 219–22; resistance and change 238–9; of trainee and practicing teachers 222–4
supportive approach 175–7
Suzuki W 197

task completion 232
task related information and boundaries 185–7
technology, use of 123
therapists and tutors, difference between 9–10
third level *see* adult education
Tirrell-Corbin C 212
training: lack of TIP 206, 223; staff 168, 179, 190–1, 243
trauma: examples, effects and associated behaviours 24–5; and young people 27–32
trauma-informed practice (TIP): principles, research and application 7–8, 20–7
Treisman K 29, 81, 207
triggers, reducing and responding to 207–8
troublemakers label (example) 64
trust: enabling positive relationships 96–7; principle 34, 49
tutors: and teachers, trauma-informed practice for 5–6; and therapists, difference between 9–10, 184

underserved communities 18–19, 53–4, 143–4, 160–1, 173–4
unfinished sentences 113, 151, 155
Ungar M 119, 160
United Nations Convention on the Rights of the Child 142–3
University College Dublin (UCD) reflection programme 122
useful materials: development organisations 245–6; newspapers/magazines 245; travel agents 245

van der Kolk BA 15, 16, 162–3, 197–8
Venet A *see* Shevrin Venet A

Index

voice in classroom 138; communications and confidence 140–2; empowering in adult education 153–5; enabling in primary school 145–7; enabling in secondary school 147–53; experiences in community and education 139–40; hearing without imposing your values 144–5; meaning for young people 142–4; wider influence from research 140

walking debate 257; adult education 111, 155, 178; secondary school 86, 89, 151

Weiss EM, Weiss S 221, 222
welcoming environment: cosy corner 247; personal greeting 247; pictures 247; plants real or imagined 247; smile 247; time out space 247
wider community action and awareness 241–3
Winch G 197
window of tolerance 127–8
withdrawn behaviour (examples) 58–9, 63
work and home boundaries 193–4
working and short-term memory 232–3
workload: adult education 112; boundaries 193

For Product Safety Concerns and Information please contact our EU representative GPSR@taylorandfrancis.com
Taylor & Francis Verlag GmbH, Kaufingerstraße 24, 80331 München, Germany

www.ingramcontent.com/pod-product-compliance
Lightning Source LLC
Chambersburg PA
CBHW071814230426
43670CB00013B/2451